To James, Anna and Philip

Preface

- This book is written by a person with intimate knowledge of writing and marking all the componenents of GCSE Spanish papers. The author is also a Head of Modern Languages in a comprehensive school in Staffordshire.
- The book is designed as a revision guide for Spanish GCSE. All the boards have been catered for.
- There is a grammar section, a self-test section, a revision guide, a wealth of past papers to practise on, suggested answers to those papers, a cassette with GCSE recordings on and a complete GCSE paper with suggested answers for you to use at the end of your revision period.
- Grateful thanks to the following boards who have granted permission to reproduce questions which have appeared on their examination papers. The suggested answers or hints are solely the responsibility of the author.

    Midland Examining Group (*MEG*)
    Northern Examinations and Assessment Board (*NEAB*)
    Northern Ireland Council for the Curriculum Examinations and Assessment (*NICCEA*)
    Southern Examining Group (*SEG*)
    University of London Examinations and Assessment Council (*ULEAC*)
    Welsh Joint Education Committee (*WJEC*)
- Grateful thanks to Vernon Thomas for his help and suggestions.
- Photograph on page 114 reproduced by kind permission of Popper/Reuter.

Contents

Preface   iii

Starting points

Introduction   1
How to use this book   1

Analysis of examination syllabuses   2

The GCSE   3
Differentiation or differentiated assessment   3

Devising a revision programme   10
Organizing your revision   10
How to revise for Spanish   10

Examination Boards: addresses   12

Grammar

1   Grammar revision   13
1.1   Grammatical terms   13
1.2   Definite and indefinite articles   14
1.3   Nouns   15
1.4   Adjectives   16
1.5   Adverbs   17
1.6   Comparative and superlative of
       adjectives and adverbs   18
1.7   Numerals   19
1.8   Time   20
1.9   Negatives   21
1.10   Pronouns   21
1.11   Personal 'a'   23
1.12   Demonstrative adjectives
       and pronouns   23
1.13   Possessive adjectives   24
1.14   Possessive pronouns   25
1.15   Relative pronouns   25
1.16   Interrogatives   26
1.17   'Ser' and 'estar'   26
1.18   'Conocer' and 'saber'   27
1.19   'Deber' and 'tener que'   27
1.20   'Tener'   27
1.21   Prepositions   28
1.22   Verbs   28
1.23   Present tense   29
1.24   The present continuous   31
1.25   Perfect tense   32
1.26   Preterite tense   33
1.27   Imperfect tense   35
1.28   Pluperfect tense   35
1.29   Future tense   36
1.30   Conditional tense   37

2   Test yourself on grammar   38
2.1   Articles   38
2.2   Adjectives   38
2.3   Adverbs   39
2.4   Numbers   39
2.5   Time   39
2.6   Negatives   40
2.7   Pronouns   40
2.8   Personal 'a'   40
2.9   Demonstrative adjectives
       and pronouns   40
2.10   Possessive adjectives   40
2.11   Possessive pronouns   41
2.12   Relative pronouns   41
2.13   Interrogatives   41
2.14   'Ser' and 'estar'   41
2.15   'Conocer' and 'saber'   41
2.16   'Deber' and 'tener que'   42
2.17   'Tener'   42
2.18   Prepositions   42
2.19   Present tense   42
2.20   Perfect tense   43
2.21   Preterite tense   43
2.22   Imperfect tense   44
2.23   Pluperfect tense   44
2.24   Future tense   44
2.25   'Ir a' + infinitive   45
2.26   Conditional tense   45

3   Test yourself: suggested answers   46
3.1   Articles   46
3.2   Adjectives   46
3.3   Adverbs   47
3.4   Numbers   47
3.5   Time   47
3.6   Negatives   47
3.7   Pronouns   48
3.8   Personal 'a'   48
3.9   Demonstrative adjectives
       and pronouns   48
3.10   Possessive adjectives   48
3.11   Possessive pronouns   48
3.12   Relative pronouns   49
3.13   Interrogatives   49
3.14   'Ser' and 'estar'   49
3.15   'Conocer' and 'saber'   49
3.16   'Deber' and 'tener que'   49
3.17   'Tener'   49
3.18   Prepositions   50
3.19   Present tense   50
3.20   Perfect tense   51
3.21   Preterite tense   51
3.22   Imperfect tense   51
3.23   Pluperfect tense   52
3.24   Future tense   52
3.25   'Ir a' + infinitive   52
3.26   Conditional tense   52

GCSE
SPANISH

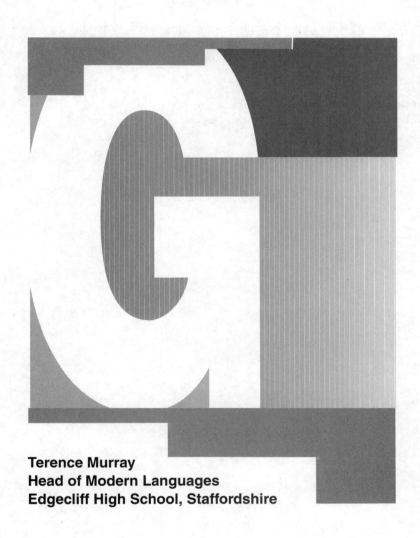

Terence Murray
Head of Modern Languages
Edgecliff High School, Staffordshire

EDUCATIONAL

Every effort has been made to trace copyright holders and to obtain their permission for the use of copyright material. The authors and publishers will gladly receive information enabling them to rectify any error or omission in subsequent editions.

First published 1995

Letts Educational
Aldine House
Aldine Place
London W12 8AW
0181 743 7514

Text: © Terence Murray
Design and illustrations: © BPP (Letts Educational) Ltd 1995

British Library Cataloguing in Publication Data
A CIP record for this book is available from the British Library.

ISBN 1 85758 330 2

Printed in Great Britain by W M Print Limited, Walsall, West Midlands, WS2 9NE

Letts Educational is the trading name of BPP (Letts Educational) Ltd

Vocabulary

4	Vocabulary topic areas, notions, functions	53
	Time	53
	Months and seasons	53
	Colours	54
	Myself	54
	Emotions	55
	Mental processes	55
	Work	55
	Animals	56
	The house	56
	In the country	57
	The town/city	58
	Directions	58
	School	59
	Free time and entertainment	60
	Sports	61
	Transport (car)	61
	Public transport	61
	Holidays	62
	Meeting people	63
	Shopping	64
	In the café/restaurant	66
	Weather	66
	Accommodation	67
	Work and future	67
	Emergencies	68
	Cleaning and repairing	68
	Post Office	69
	The Bank	69
	Lost property and robbery	69

Listening

5	Listening: Basic Level	70
5.1	Introduction	70
5.2	How to prepare for the Basic Listening test	70
5.3	During the exam	71
5.4	Examination questions	71
5.5	Examination practice questions	75
5.6	Transcripts	79
5.7	Suggested answers	83

6	Listening: Higher Level	86
6.1	Introduction	86
6.2	Higher Level skills	86
6.3	In the examination	87
6.4	Examination questions	87
6.5	Examination practice questions	90
6.6	Transcripts	93
6.7	Suggested answers	97

Speaking

7	Speaking: Basic Level	100
7.1	Introduction	100
7.2	Role-play situations	100
7.3	Examples of Basic role-plays	101
7.4	Suggested answers	105
7.5	Conversation	107
7.6	Example questions and answers	107

8	Speaking: Higher Level	109
8.1	Introduction	109
8.2	Higher Level role-play	109
8.3	The 'unprepared' questions	110
8.4	Examination role-play questions	110
8.5	Suggested answers	115
8.6	Higher Level conversation	117
8.7	Example questions and answers	117
8.8	MEG Narrator Higher Level Part 2	120
8.9	How to approach the Narrator exam	120
8.10	Example Narrator tasks and suggested answers	120

Reading

9	Reading: Basic Level	123
9.1	Introduction	123
9.2	How to prepare	123
9.3	During the exam	124
9.4	Examination questions	124
9.5	Examination practice questions	128
9.6	Suggested answers	144

10	Reading: Higher Level	148
10.1	Introduction	148
10.2	Higher Level skills	148
10.3	In the examination	149
10.4	Examination questions	149
10.5	Examination practice questions	151
10.6	Suggested answers	159

Writing

11	Writing: Basic Level	162
11.1	Introduction	162
11.2	The tasks you have to complete at Basic Level	162
11.3	Examination questions	167
11.4	Examination practice questions	169
11.5	Suggested answers	174

12	Writing: Higher Level	177
12.1	Introduction	177
12.2	Preparing for the examination	178
12.3	Survival kit	179
12.4	In the examination	180
12.5	Examination questions	180
12.6	Examination practice questions	182
12.7	Suggested answers	186

Exam practice

13	Complete GCSE paper	190
13.1	Introduction	190
13.2	The examination paper	190
13.3	Suggested answers	207

Index		213

Introduction

This book has been written to help you revise for the GCSE examination in Spanish. The key to success in these examinations lies in your ability to convince the examiner that you have mastered the four basic skills which all the Examining Groups test in one form or another. The skills are listening and reading comprehension, speaking and writing Spanish.

How to use this book

The first thing you need to find out before you plan your revision programme is exactly what will be expected of you in the examination itself. The analysis of the syllabuses of each of the Examining Groups on page 2 will help you do this. If you are a mature student it can be used to give you guidance on which Group's examination will suit you best. The analysis and summary of the Groups' requirements indicate the emphasis each Group gives to the different skills and how they are tested. You should concentrate on the types of question your Group sets and ensure that you are given the fullest possible information about the grammar, vocabulary and topic areas which your particular Group expects you to have studied. The syllabus content of each Examining Group is now defined under topic areas and settings – see the tables on pp4–8. If you cannot obtain this information from your teacher, you can always write to the Examining Group for your own copy. The addresses of the Examining Groups are listed on page 12.

Success at GCSE in Spanish means having a good knowledge of vocabulary and the grammar of the language. This is not a text book or a vocabulary book, but if you use it wisely as an aid to revision and in conjunction with your course books and specimen examination materials, there should not be any difficulty in achieving success in your Examining Group's tests. This book assumes that you have studied Spanish for at least two years. You should use it to help plan your revision programme over the last twelve months or so leading up to your examination. You should work systematically through the grammar sections and follow the advice and hints on how to tackle the tests which you will be expected to take in your examination. Finally you can practise the types of question which you will have to do.

Remember, there is a good deal of distilled experience and advice contained in the hints on examination technique. So if you know your vocabulary, you know your grammar and you follow the advice given and improve your examination technique you should find that the reward for your efforts will be the success you are anxious to achieve.

Enjoy your revision and good luck in your Spanish examinations.

Analysis of examination syllabuses

Examining Group	ULEAC		MEG			NEAB		SEG		NICCEA		SEB			WJEC	
Level	Basic	Higher	Basic	Higher I	Higher II	Basic	Higher	General	Extended	Basic	Higher	Foundation	General	Credit	Basic	Higher
Listening																
Questions	T/Sp	T/Sp	T/Sp	T/Sp	T/Sp	T/Sp	T/Sp	T/Sp/V	T/Sp/V	T/Sp	T/Sp	T/Sp	T/Sp	T/Sp	T/Sp/W	T/Sp/W
Answers	E	E	MCE or E	E	E	MCE or E	MCE or E	E	E	E	E	E	E	E	E/W	E/W
Time	30 mins	30 mins	20 mins	20 mins	20 mins	30 mins	30 mins	30 mins	35 mins	30 mins	30 mins	25 mins	25 mins	30 mins	30 mins	40 mins
Reading												††	††	††		
Questions	Sp/V	Sp/V	Sp/V	Sp/V	Sp/V	Sp/V	Sp/V	Sp/V	Sp	Sp/V	Sp/V	Sp	Sp	Sp	V/Sp/W	V/Sp/W
Answers	E	E	MCE or E	MCE or E	MCE or E	MCS or E	MCS or E	E	E	E	E	E	E	E	E/W	E/W
Time	30 mins	30 mins	25 mins	25 mins	25 mins	25 mins	40 mins	30 mins	40 mins	45 mins	40 mins	45 mins	45 mins	60 mins	30 mins	40 mins
Oral/ Speaking												★				
Role-play	2	3	2	3	3	2/V	4/V	2	2	2	2	5			2	4
Conversation	Gu	Gu+Gen	Gu	Gu	Gu+V	Gen	Gen	Gu	Gen	Gu	Gen				Gu	Gen
Time	10 mins	20 mins	10 mins	12 mins	15 mins	5–10 mins	10–15 mins	10 mins	12 mins	10 mins	15 mins	15 mins			10 mins	15 mins
Taped	T	T	T	T	T	T	T	T	T	T	T				T	T
Writing													††	††		
Forms & Lists	Op		●							●					●	
Postcards	Op		●			●				●					●	
Letters	●	Op		●		●	●	●	Op	●	●				●	●
Messages	Op		●			●		●		●			†●		●	
Visual/ Pictures		Op	●			●	●		Op		●					Op
Topic		Op		●			●		Op V	●	●			†●		Op
Time	45 mins	60 mins	25 mins	30 mins	35 mins	25 mins	50 mins	30 mins	60 mins	45 mins	50 mins		30 mins	45 mins	30 mins	70 mins

Key

E	English	**Op**	You have a choice	**†**	The writing element is an optional endorsement to General and Credit levels only
E/W	English and Welsh	**T**	Taped		
Sp	Material in Spanish with English questions	**V**	Visual material may be used in this test, e.g. pictures, diagrams, plans, etc.	**††**	Dictionaries are allowed in these SEB examinations
Gen	General				
Gu	Guided	**●**	Any or all of these may be included in this test	**★**	In Scotland the speaking skill will be assessed by on-going assessment during S4 as well as the final oral proficiency test.
MCE	Multiple choice English				
MCS	Multiple choice Spanish				

The GCSE

The General Certificate of Secondary Education replaced GCE O level and CSE in the summer of 1988. The examination is administered by five examining groups in England and Wales and monitored by the School Curriculum and Assessment Authority (SCAA).

At present there is a single eight-point scale: A★, A, B, C, D, E, F and G for GCSE. The system of grading for GCSE continues to be objective and criteria-related. Grades will continue to be awarded according to the extent to which candidates have demonstrated particular levels of attainment as defined in the published 'grade criteria'. In effect this means that candidates will be assessed positively on what they know, understand and can do.

Differentiation or differentiated assessment

One of the principles of ensuring that 90 per cent of all pupils can be positively assessed is contained in the statement on differentiated assessment which is part of the general national criteria for this examination.

'All examinations must be designed in such a way as to ensure proper discrimination, so that candidates across the ability range are given opportunities to demonstrate their knowledge, abilities and achievements – that is, to show what they know, understand and can do. Accordingly differentiated papers or differentiated questions within papers will be required in all subjects. In many subjects a mixture of common and differentiated elements will be appropriate.'

In modern languages differentiation is achieved by setting at least two papers at different levels in all four skill areas of listening, reading, speaking and writing. In most cases these different levels are described as 'basic' and 'higher' and the relationship between them and the awarding of grades needs explanation in detail and varies slightly from one Examining Group to another. It is essential to realize that the tasks set at 'Higher' level are more taxing and demanding than those at 'Basic' level.

ULEAC

The scheme of assessment for ULEAC Spanish examinations is as follows. All papers are numbered 1–8. Papers 1, 3, 5 and 7 represent the Basic Level in listening, reading, oral and writing. Papers 2, 4, 6 and 8 are the higher-level papers in each skill area. Each of the four areas has the same weighting of 25 per cent of the marks awarded.

List of papers	
Paper 1	Basic Listening Comprehension
Paper 2	Higher Listening Comprehension
Paper 3	Basic Reading Comprehension
Paper 4	Higher Reading Comprehension
Paper 5	Basic Oral
Paper 6	Higher Oral
Paper 7	Basic Writing
Paper 8	Higher Writing

The maximum GCSE grade which may be awarded for any particular combination of papers is as follows:

Combination of papers	Highest grade available
1, 3, 5	E
1, 3, 5 plus at least one paper from 2, 4, 6, 7	D
1, 3, 5, 7 plus at least one paper from 2, 4, 6, 8	C
1, 3, 5, 7, 8 plus one paper from 2, 4, 6	B
1, 3, 5, 7, 8 plus two papers from 2, 4, 6	
1, 3, 5, 7, 2, 4, 6, 8	A, A*

Topics

Personal Information and Social Interaction	Leisure Activities and Hobbies
Family and Other People	Health and Welfare
Daily Routine	School and Education
House, Home and Home Town	Work and Career
Shopping	Holidays, Festivals and Special Occasions
Food and Drink	Travel and Transport
Public Service	Environment and Current Issues

Settings

Home	Hospital, Chemist, Surgery
Shops, Markets	School, College, Place of Work
Restaurants, Cafés, Snack Bars	Hotel, Campsite, Youth Hostel
Public Services and Buildings	Public and Private Transport
Social Venue	Town, Country, Seaside
Places of Entertainment, Sport, Leisure, Interest	

MEG

The scheme of assessment for MEG is more complicated. There are three compulsory elements. These three common-core elements must be taken by all candidates. They are: Basic Listening, Speaking and Reading.

All other elements in this examination are optional additional elements. Please note that Higher Writing can only be offered if the candidate is also entered for Basic Writing. As can be seen from the analysis of syllabuses on page 2 there are four papers at Basic Level and each Higher Level is divided into two parts. The full scheme of assessment is therefore:

Listening	Reading	Speaking	Writing
Basic	Basic	Basic	Basic
Higher	Higher	Higher	Higher
Part 1	Part 1	Part 1	Part 1
Part 2	Part 2	Part 2	Part 2

The four skills of Listening, Reading, Speaking and Writing are equally weighted. All candidates must do Basic Listening, Speaking and Reading and will then choose additional elements according to their ability. Each higher-level element will be in two parts. Part 1 of any higher-level element must be attempted if entered for any higher-level examination. Part 2 is therefore an optional extra. Candidates will be able to decide on the day of the examination whether or not to attempt Part 2 although it is assumed in most cases that candidates and their teachers will have decided in the weeks prior to the examination whether Part 2 is to be attempted on the day. It will not be necessary to indicate on your entry form whether Parts 1 and 2 are both to be attempted.

The minimum number of elements which must be offered to qualify for the award of each of the Grades A★–G is summarized below. It is assumed that candidates will attempt as many elements of the examination as is consistent with their likelihood of success.

Summary

Grades	Papers to be attempted (minimum number of elements)
G, F, E	Basic Listening, Reading, Speaking
D	Basic Listening, Reading, Speaking *plus either* Basic Writing *or* Part 1 of any two higher-level elements *or* Parts 1 and 2 of any one higher-level element
C	Basic Listening, Reading, Speaking, Writing *plus* Part 1 of any two higher-level elements *or* Parts 1 and 2 of any one higher-level element
B	Basic Listening, Reading, Speaking, Writing *plus* higher-level Writing (Parts 1 and 2) *plus* one additional higher-level element (Parts 1 and 2)
A	Basic Listening, Reading, Speaking, Writing plus higher-level Writing (Parts 1 and 2) *plus* two additional higher-level elements (Parts 1 and 2)
A*	All papers must be attempted

Topics					
A	Personal Identification	G	Holidays	M	Work and Future
B	House and Home	H	Meeting People	N	Emergencies
C	Geographical Surroundings	I	Shopping	O	Services
D	School	J	Food and Drink	P	Lost Property
E	Free Time/Entertainment	K	Weather		
F	Travel	L	Accommodation		

Topics A –L are for both Basic and Higher
Topics M–P are for Higher only

Settings		
Town	Public Transport	Hotels, Campsites, etc
Home	Private Transport	Dentist, Doctor, Chemist
School	Tourist Office	Garage, Petrol Station
Work	Shops, Markets	Bank, Cambio
Places of Entertainment	Café, Restaurant	Lost Property, Police

NEAB

The NEAB scheme of assessment is similar to the ULEAC scheme. All candidates must be entered for what are called the common–core basic-level tests in Listening, Reading and Speaking. Candidates may be entered for any combination of additional tests considered appropriate by the centre. Please note higher-level Writing can only be entered if the candidate is also doing basic-level Writing.

The minimum entry requirements for the different grades can be summarized as follows:

Maximum grade	Minimum entry requirements
G, F, E	Basic Listening, Reading, Speaking
D	Basic Listening, Reading, Speaking *plus* any one other test
C	Basic Listening, Reading, Speaking, Writing *plus* any one other test
B	Basic Listening, Reading, Speaking, Writing, Higher Writing *plus* any one other test
A	Basic Listening, Reading, Speaking, Writing, Higher Writing *plus* any two other tests
A*	All papers must be attempted

It must be stressed that these are the *minimum* requirements to achieve the different grades and that in each case a very high level of competence in the stated number of tests will be required in order to achieve the maximum grade available. It is expected, therefore, that candidates aiming at a particular grade will normally attempt a wider range of tests than the minimum number on which the grade can be awarded. There will be equal weighting for each of the skill areas within any one level.

Topics	
Personal Identification	Social Relations
House and Home	Health and Welfare
Life at Home	Shopping
Education, Work, Future Prospects	Food and Drink
Free Time and Entertainment	Services
Travel	Language Problems
Holidays	Weather

Settings	
Home	Shops, Markets, Department Stores
Town	Public Buildings
Country	Places of Entertainment
Seaside	Sports Centre
Public Transport	Places of Interest
Private Transport	School, Place of Work
Accommodation	Social Venue
Restaurant, Café	Hospital, Chemist, Doctor's or Dentist's Surgery

SEG

SEG describes its assessment pattern in terms of general- and extended-level tests. There will be one of each in all four skill areas of Speaking, Listening, Reading and Writing. The minimum entry will be for the three tests of Speaking, Listening and Reading at General Level. These three are to be known as the common-core tests. The relationship between the award of grades and the level of tests entered is similar to the other Examining Groups and can be summarized as follows:

Maximum grade	Minimum entry requirements
G, F, E	Three common-core tests
D	Three common-core tests *plus* at least one Extended Level excluding Extended Writing or General Writing
C	Three common-core tests *plus* General Writing *plus* at least one extended-level test
B	Three common-core tests *plus* General Writing *plus* Extended Writing *plus* any one other extended-level test
A	Three common-core tests *plus* General Writing *plus* Extended Writing *plus* any two other extended-level tests
A*	All papers must be attempted

Equal weighting will be given to each of the skills attempted. Entry cannot be made to any extended-level test in any of the four skill areas unless it is also made at General Level in that skill. The only exception to this is Speaking, where candidates may enter for either General Level or Extended Level, since the extended-level test includes the general-level test.

Topics

Personal Details, Daily Routine, Home and Family	Money Matters
School/College/Work Routine and Future Plans	Public Services
Relationships with Other People	Health and Welfare
Free Time/Leisure Interests/Entertainments	Holidays/Accommodation
Local and Foreign Environment	Travel and Transport
Shopping	Weather
Food and Drink	

Settings

The Home, School or Place of Work	Bank, Post Office
Youth Club or Similar Social Venue	Information Office, Lost Property Office, Police Station
Places of Entertainment/Interest (cinema/ museum/theatre/galleries/historical buildings)	Pharmacy, Clinic, Surgery, Hospital
	Campsite, Youth Hostel, Hotel
Sports Centre/Swimming Pool/Beach	Public and Private Transport (railway station/bus
Town (street/square/park/public buildings)	stop/filling station/airport)
Shops or Market	Countryside, Mountains, National Parks
Café, Snack Bar, Restaurant	

WJEC

As with the other Examining Groups the Welsh Board has basic- and higher-level tests in each of the four skill areas. Basic Listening, Reading and Oral tests are known as the *compulsory core*, which all candidates must enter. All other tests are described as additional elements.

Maximum grade	Minimum entry requirements
E	Compulsory core
D	Compulsory core *plus* one additional element
C	Compulsory core *plus* Basic Writing *plus* one additional element
B	Compulsory core *plus* Basic and Higher Writing *plus* one additional higher element
A	Compulsory core *plus* Basic and HIgher Writing *plus* two additional higher elements
A*	All papers must be attempted

It should be noted that these are the minimum entry requirements and that to achieve the grades listed the overall level of competence required within the elements expected will be very high. Equal weighting will be given in assessment and grading to the various skill areas within each of the two levels.

Topics

Self, Family and Friends	Services
Home and Daily Routines	Language
Time, Weather, Dates and Numbers	Leisure
Finding the Way	Town and Region
Transport and Travel	School Routine and Education
Food and Drink	Communications and The Media
Accommodation	Emergencies
Shopping	Health and Welfare

Settings

Home, School

Public Buildings

Town, Country, Seaside

Post Office, Bank

Transport

Hospital, Doctor, Dentist

Café, Restaurant

Entertainment

Shop, Market

Hotel, Hostel, Campsite

Tourist Attractions

NICCEA

NICCEA describes its assessment objectives in a similar way to those of the Examining Groups in England and Wales. There are three common-core objectives: Basic Listening, Reading and Speaking. Additional assessment objectives are Basic Writing and Higher Listening, Reading, Speaking and Writing. Equal allocations of marks are given to the skill areas within each of the differentiated levels. In each of the skill areas the proportion of marks awarded to the basic- and higher-level components will be in the ratio of four to three. The relationship between assessment objectives and grades is summarized below:

Maximum grade	Minimum number of elements required
E	Three common-core elements
D	Three common-core elements *plus* one additional element
C	Three common-core elements *plus* Basic Writing *plus* any one higher-level additional element
B	Three common-core elements *plus* Basic Writing *plus* Higher Writing *plus* any one additional higher-level element
A	Three common-core elements *plus* Basic Writing *plus* Higher Writing *plus* any two additional higher-level elements
A*	All papers must be attempted

Topics

Identification of People	Travel
House and Home	Holidays
Life at Home	Health and Welfare
Environment	Shopping
Careers/Occupations	Food and Drink
Leisure	Services

Settings

Home	Bus and Train Stations, Airport, Port, Metro Station, Taxi Rank, Car Park
Town/Country/Seaside	
Spanish Family Home	Places of Interest, Public Buildings
School	Hotel/Apartment and such other Locations
Places of Work	Public Service Locations

Sports Centre and Other Leisure/
    Recreational Locations
	Shops, Markets, Department Store and such other
	    locations

Places of Entertainment, Social
    Venues
	Restaurant, Café, Snack Bar, Canteen and such
	    other locations

SEB

The SEB Standard examination became fully operational in 1990. However, SEB proposals are complex for the awarding of a Scottish Certificate of Education at Standard Grade. There are three levels described as Foundation, General and Credit. Grades are awarded on a seven-point scale: 1, 2, 3, 4, 5, 6 and 7. The terms 'Foundation', 'General' and 'Credit' relate only to particular ranges of grades: Foundation covering grades 7 to 5, General grades 5 to 2 and Credit covering grades 2 and 1. All candidates are assessed in the three elements of Reading, Listening and Speaking. Writing is an optional test. The assessment procedures for each skill area are as follows:

Reading: weighting 25 per cent
There will be three papers, Foundation, General and Credit. Candidates will be entered for one or two of the papers. The grade awarded will depend upon the highest grade at which the candidate shows competence on the papers entered. Candidates will be allowed to use a dictionary.

Listening: weighting 25 per cent
Three papers will be available. As with the assessment for reading, candidates can be entered for one or two papers only and the grade awarded will depend on the highest grade at which the candidate shows competence. This examination will be recorded on tape. The examination centre will be required to provide an estimated grade for Listening for each candidate.

Speaking: weighting 50 per cent
Speaking: on-going internal assessment
Schools will be required to monitor, for each candidate, a number of short speaking activities which will arise out of normal class work. For certification purposes this will be done over a period of one year during what is known as S4 in Scotland. A record in terms of grades will be kept by the teacher of individual performances and these grades will be used to form the basis of a final rating based on the grade-related criteria and giving evidence of the normal performance of each candidate in speaking activities. The whole process will be internally moderated within the school. The rating for the on-going internal assessment will have to be based on a wide variety of speaking activities and these activities should have a reasonable spread as far as the topic areas of the syllabus are concerned.

The examination centre will be required to provide an interim grade for Speaking, based on the on-going assessment, for each candidate.

Speaking: final proficiency test
This will take place in March of the S4 year and will comprise a formal oral test for each candidate. Up to five tasks will be set by the Board which all candidates will be expected to attempt. This final proficiency test in speaking will normally be carried out by the candidate's own teacher. A number of these oral tests will be observed by a moderator appointed by the Board who will agree levels of performance and award of appropriate grades with the teachers conducting the tests. Some of these tests will also need to be taped for future moderation exercises.

Optional endorsement in writing – General and Credit levels only
There will be two papers lasting 30 minutes for the General level and 45 minutes for the Credit level. At General level the candidate will be asked to write a number of short, simple messages in Spanish. These will be linked in English by context. At Credit level the stimulus will be a passage or passages requiring a personal response in Spanish from the candidate in some 200 words. The use of a dictionary is allowed in both writing examinations.

Examination centres will be required to provide an estimated grade for each candidate taking the written option.

Grade Related Criteria
GRC are defined at three levels of performance: Foundation, General and Credit.

Awards will be reported on six grades, two grades being distinguished at each level – Foundation: grades 6 and 5, General: grades 4 and 3, and Credit: grades 2 and 1. The grades at each level will be awarded in accordance with the stated criteria and on how each candidate meets these criteria. Grade 7 will be awarded to candidates who complete the course but fail to meet the criteria for any level.

Devising a revision programme

Organizing your revision

You cannot expect to remember all the grammar and vocabulary that you have learned over a period of three or four years unless you are prepared to revise. You need to be able to recall the vocabulary and rules of grammar from your memory during any part of the examination.

Organize your revision by making a timetable. Choose a time when you are at your most receptive. It might be best to revise in the early evening before you get too tired, or early in the morning after a good night's sleep. Having decided when to revise, put the times on to your revision timetable.

You also need a suitable place to revise. Find a quiet, or fairly quiet room away from distractions like TV or loud music. You need a table, a chair, adequate light (a table lamp will often help you to concentrate) and a comfortable temperature. It is better to revise when sitting at a table than when lying down. It is more effective to revise inside the house rather than basking in the sun.

How to revise for Spanish

When revising vocabulary do not just keep reading the words and their meanings through aimlessly. Try to learn the words in context. Remember you need to know the gender and the plural of all nouns.

Learn lists of words in short spells at a time and always give yourself a written test. In other words you must review the words you have learned. Without this review you will forget what you have learned very quickly.

When revising grammar points you should make notes on a postcard, which will then help you to do some light revision on the night before the exam. Look for the important key facts about Spanish grammar and make notes on them as you revise. Use the test yourself section of this book to test what you have revised. If you have not understood and are still getting it wrong then go back to the relevant grammar section and look at it again.

The reviewing of what you have revised is very important. You should try to carry out this testing and retesting of what you have learned during a revision session after 24 hours, then after a week and maybe again after a month. You should keep your summary notes for use just before the exam.

Plan all your revision in short bursts, depending on your span of concentration.

1. You learn most by studying for 20–40 minutes and then testing yourself to see how much you remember.
2. Take regular breaks. On your timetable you could split a two-hour session into four shorter periods, like this: revise for 25 minutes; break for 10 minutes; work another 25 minutes; then stop, have a longer break (20–30 minutes) and then work for another 35–40 minutes. Give yourself a reward at the end of the revision period, e.g. watch TV, read a book, listen to a record or the radio, or go and see a friend.
3. Have a definite start time and finish time. Learning efficiency tends to fall at the beginning of a revision session but rises towards the end.
4. Allow two hours each day for revision at the beginning of your programme and build up to three hours a day or more during the last three or so weeks of revision before the examinations start. Make sure Spanish has a weekly session in your revision programme.

Some other tips:

Don't waste revision time
(a) Recognize when your mind begins to wander.
(b) If you have things on your mind deal with them first; or make a list of the 'things you need to do' then go back to your revision.
(c) Get up and move about – do something different, make a cup of tea, etc.
(d) Think with your daydream – it will probably go away.
(e) Change your revision subject – move to another subject, then come back to Spanish revision.

Work in pairs
(a) Learning vocabulary is easy this way; you can test one another.
(b) Practise talking Spanish with a friend.
(c) Listen to Spanish radio broadcasts together.

Understand the work
Learning grammar 'parrot fashion' can lower recall. Remember: *work, test, rest, reward.*

Do not give up
You may feel irritable and depressed, but recognize that this is a common problem. Do not give up.

Here is the 'Ladder to Success' which can help you understand how to prepare properly not only for your Spanish examinations but other examinations as well.

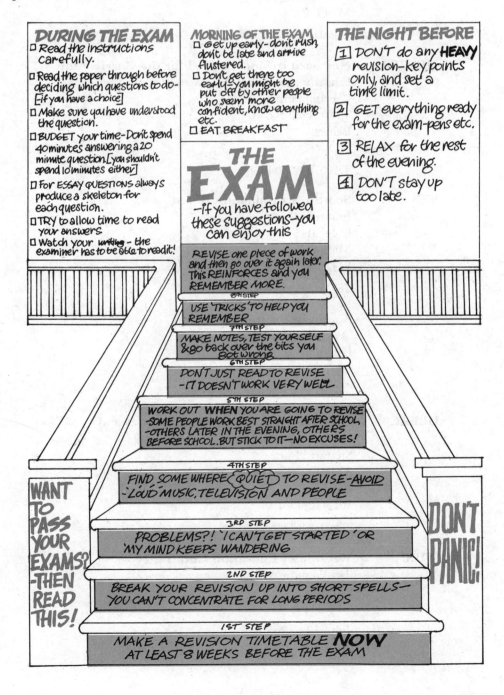

Examination Boards: addresses

To obtain syllabuses, past examination papers and further details, write to your Examining Group.

MEG   **Midland Examining Group**
1 Hills Road
Cambridge
CB1 2EU

Tel: 01223 553311

NEAB   **Northern Examinations and Assessment Board**
12 Harter Street
Manchester
M1 6HL

Tel: 0161 953 1180

NICCEA   **Northern Ireland Council for the Curriculum Examinations and Assessment**
Beechill House
42 Beechill Road
Belfast
BT8 4RS

Tel: 01232 704666

SEB   **Scottish Examination Board**
Ironmills Road
Dalkeith
Midlothian
EH22 1LE

Tel: 0131 663 6601

SEG   **Southern Examining Group**
Stag Hill House
Guildford
GU2 5XJ

Tel: 01483 506506

ULEAC   **University of London Examinations and Assessment Council**
Stewart House
32 Russell Square
London
WC1B 5DN

Tel: 0171 331 4000

WJEC   **Welsh Joint Education Committee**
245 Western Avenue
Cardiff
CF5 2YX

Tel: 01222 265000

Chapter 1
Grammar revision

This section provides a comprehensive guide to all the grammar required for the GCSE examinations for all the UK examination boards.

- If you are to communicate accurately in Spanish, an understanding of Spanish grammar is essential no matter how extensive your vocabulary may be.
- You will also find that as your knowledge of grammar increases, so will your confidence and this will improve your competence in all four skill areas.
- You need to plan your revision programme so that you have enough time to work through the following sections. Allow yourself a minimum of eight weeks before the exam.

1.1 Grammatical terms

Before you start your grammar revision, you need to familiarize yourself with some grammatical terms. Look at this sentence:

The boy eats a delicious dinner slowly in the kitchen.

The	definite article
boy	noun (subject)
eats	verb
a	indefinite article
delicious	adjective
dinner	noun (object)
slowly	adverb
in	preposition
the	definite article
kitchen.	noun

The *definite article* is the grammatical name given to the word 'the'.

The *indefinite article* is the name given to the word 'a' or 'an'.

A *noun* is a person, place, thing or animal.

A *verb* is a word that describes an action (e.g. eats).

An *adjective* is a word that describes a noun (e.g. delicious).

An *adverb* is a word that describes a verb. It tells you how an action is done (e.g. slowly). Many adverbs in English end in '-ly'.

A *preposition* is a word placed before a noun or a pronoun to indicate time, place or condition (e.g. *in* the kitchen).

A *conjunction* is a word that links two parts of a sentence e.g. he was eating *and* drinking. The most common conjunctions in English are 'and' and 'but'.

A *pronoun* is a word that stands in place of a noun. In the sentence above, we could replace the noun 'the boy' by the pronoun 'he'. Similarly, 'a dinner' could be replaced by 'it'.

A *negative* is a word like 'not' or 'never' that indicates an action is not being done.

Gender refers to whether a word is masculine or feminine.

The *subject* is the name given to the person or thing doing the action. In the sentence above, the subject is 'the boy'.

The *object* is the name given to the person or thing that has the action done to it. In the sentence above, 'a dinner' is the object.

1.2 Definite and indefinite articles

	Definite article (the)		Indefinite article (a, an, some)	
	masculine	*feminine*	*masculine*	*feminine*
singular	el	la	un	una
plural	los	las	unos	unas

(a) Note that   **de + el** becomes **del**

               a + el   becomes **al**

   e.g.   el libro **del** niño   *the boy's book*

               Fui **al** supermercado.   *I went to the supermarket.*

(b) el and **un** are used before feminine nouns that begin with a stressed **a-** or **ha-** (but not when separated by an adjective).

   e.g.   el agua   *the water*

               el arma   *the weapon*

               la vieja arma   *the old weapon*

   But   la alfombra   *the carpet* (the **a-** is not stressed)

However the noun stays feminine:

               El agua está fría.   *The water is cold.*

The plural is always **las** or **unas.**

   e.g.   las aguas   *the waters*

               las armas   *the weapons*

               unas armas   *some weapons*

(c) The definite article is used

1   when referring to nouns in a general sense:

               El vino es importante en España.   *Wine is important in Spain.*

2   with the name of a language except when it comes directly after **aprender, hablar** or **saber**:

               El español es fácil.   *Spanish is easy.*

               Hablo español.   *I speak Spanish.*

3   before titles:

               la reina Isabel   *Queen Elizabeth*

               el señor García   *Mr. García*

However, leave out the article when talking directly to the person:

               Buenos días, señor García.   *Good morning, Mr. García.*

4   when saying 'on Saturday', 'on Friday':

               el sábado   *on Saturday*

               el viernes   *on Friday*

5   in certain expressions when it is not used in English:

        en la cama   *in bed*   en el hospital   *in hospital*

        en la iglesia   *in church*   en la televisión   *on television*

        en la cárcel   *in prison*   en el colegio   *in school*

(d) The definite article is omitted with the numbers of monarchs:

               Felipe segundo   *Philip the Second*

(e) The indefinite article is omitted

1   before occupations and nationality:

               Ella es profesora.   *She is a teacher.*

               El es inglés.   *He is an Englishman.*

2   before **medio, mil, ¡qué … !, tal**:

               medio litro   *half a litre*

               mil pesetas   *a thousand pesetas*

               ¡qué día!   *what a day!*

               tal cosa   *such a thing*

1.3 Nouns

(a) All nouns are either masculine or feminine. When you learn a new noun, you must learn which it is.

(b) Usually nouns that end in **–o** are masculine and nouns that end in **–a** are feminine. Note the following words which end in **–a** but are *masculine*:

el crucigrama *crossword*	el problema *problem*
el futbolista *footballer*	el programa *programme*
el clima *climate*	el síntoma *symptom*
el día *day*	el sistema *system*
el idioma *language*	el telegrama *telegram*
el mapa *map*	el tema *theme*
el pijama *pyjamas*	el tranvía *tram*
el planeta *planet*	

The following words end in **–o** but are *feminine:*

la foto *photograph*	la moto *motorcycle*
la mano *hand*	la radio *radio*

(c) Compound nouns are masculine

e.g.
  el abrelatas *tin-opener*
  el sacacorchos *corkscrew*
  el parabrisas *windscreen*

(d) Countries that end in **–a** are feminine

e.g.
  (la) España *Spain*
  (la) Gran Bretaña *Great Britain*
  (la) Francia *France*

Otherwise they are masculine

e.g.
  (el) Perú *Peru*
  (el) Paraguay *Paraguay*

(e) Some words change their meaning according to their gender

e.g.

el capital *capital* (money)	la capital *capital* (city)
el coma *coma*	la coma *comma*
el cura *priest*	la cura *cure*
el frente *front* (e.g. military)	la frente *forehead*
el orden *order* (i.e. sequence)	la orden *order* (i.e. command)
el parte *report*	la parte *part*
el pendiente *earring*	la pendiente *slope*
el policía *policeman*	la policía *police*

(f) Fruits are often feminine and their fruit-trees masculine

e.g.

el cerezo *cherry tree*	la cereza *cherry*
el ciruelo *plum tree*	la ciruela *plum*
el manzano *apple tree*	la manzana *apple*
el naranjo *orange tree*	la naranja *orange*

(g) Words ending in **–eza, –ión, –dad, –tad, –umbre, –ie, –nza** are nearly always feminine

e.g.

la belleza *beauty*	la dirección *address, direction*
la verdad *truth*	la libertad *freedom*
la costumbre *custom*	la serie *series*
la enseñanza *education*	

(h) To form the plural of nouns add **–s** to an unstressed vowel and **–es** to a consonant

e.g.

el chico *the boy*	el dolor *pain*
los chicos *the boys*	los dolores *pains*
la silla *the chair*	la flor *flower*
las sillas *the chairs*	las flores *flowers*

However

Words ending in **–z** change the **–z** to **–ces** in the plural

e.g.

el lápiz *pencil*	la vez *time*
los lápices *pencils*	las veces *times*

Words ending in a stressed **–ión, –ón** or **–és** lose their accents in the plural

e.g.   la canción *song*   el francés *Frenchman*

              las canciones *songs*   los franceses *the French*

              el montón *pile*

              los montones *piles*

(i) Surnames are not normally made plural

e.g.   los García *the Garcías, the García family*

(j) Note that the following usually denote a mixture of sexes:

        los abuelos *grandparents*

        los hermanos *brothers and sisters*

        los hijos *children* (i.e. boys and girls)

1.4 Adjectives

Notice how the following adjectives agree in number and gender.

(a) Adjectives ending in **–o**:

	masculine	*feminine*
singular	blanco	blanca
plural	blancos	blancas

(b) Adjectives ending in **–e** or in a consonant do not change when feminine:

	masculine	*feminine*
singular	verde	verde
plural	verdes	verdes

	masculine	*feminine*
singular	azul	azul
plural	azules	azules

(c) Adjectives of nationality do not follow the above rule:

	masculine	*feminine*
singular	español	española
plural	españoles	españolas

(d) Adjectives that end in **–án** and **–or** like **holgazán** (lazy) and **hablador** (talkative) do not follow the rule (b):

	masculine	*feminine*
singular	holgazán	holgazana
plural	holgazanes	holgazanas

	masculine	*feminine*
singular	hablador	habladora
plural	habladores	habladoras

(e) Some adjectives (**bueno, malo, alguno, ninguno, primero, tercero**) drop the letter **–o** before a masculine singular noun, and **algún** and **ningún** require an accent:

        un buen/mal hombre *a good/bad man*

        algún/ningún dinero *some/no money*

        el primer/tercer ejemplo *the first/third example*

Also **santo** becomes **san** before the name of a saint:

        Felipe es un santo *Philip is a saint*

        San Felipe *Saint Philip*

However, **Santo Domingo** and **Santo Tomás** keep the **–to** to help pronunciation.

(f) **grande** becomes **gran** before a masculine singular and a feminine singular noun:

        un gran hombre *a great man*

        una gran mujer *a great woman*

(g) Some adjectives change their meaning according to their position:

        su **antiguo** amigo *his former friend*

        el edificio **antiguo** *the ancient building*

        el **pobre** chico *the poor boy* (i.e. unfortunate)

        el chico **pobre** *the poor boy* (i.e. without any money)

por **pura** curiosidad *from sheer curiosity*
el agua **pura** *pure water*
la **misma** cosa *the same thing*
el rey **mismo** *the king himself*

(h) cada (each) never changes:
cada niño *each boy*
cada niña *each girl*

(i) –ísimo, –ísima, –ísimos, –ísimas can be added to adjectives after the final vowel is removed to give the meaning 'extremely':
un chico guapo *a handsome boy*
un chico guapísimo *an extremely handsome boy*

1.5 Adverbs

In English most adverbs end in '–ly': slowly, quickly, carefully, briefly.

To form an adverb in Spanish, take the feminine form of the adjective and add **–mente**:

lento *slow*   cuidadoso *careful*
lentamente *slowly*   cuidadosamente *carefully*

rápido *fast*
rápidamente *quickly*

Notice how to make an adverb from an adjective that ends in **–e** or a consonant:

breve *brief*   normal *normal*
brevemente *briefly*   normalmente *normally*

If two adverbs come together, **–mente** is added to the second one only:

lenta y cuidadosamente *slowly and carefully*

Some adverbs do not end in **–mente**:

bien *well*
mal *badly*
despacio *slowly*

Some useful adverbs

abajo downstairs
La cocina está abajo. *The kitchen is downstairs.*
ahora now
Ahora son las seis. *It is six o'clock now.*
allí, allá there
¡El libro está allí! *The book is there!*
a menudo often
¿Vas a menudo al cine? *Do you often go to the cinema?*
apenas (si) scarcely
Apenas (si) pude verle. *I could scarcely see him.*
aquí here
¡Aquí está! *Here he is!*
arriba upstairs
Mi hermano está arriba. *My brother is upstairs.*
aún/todavía still
Duerme aún/todavía. *He is still asleep.*
bastante enough, quite
No tengo bastante dinero. *I haven't got enough money.*
Es bastante alto. *He is quite tall.*
casi almost
El equipo casi ganó. *The team almost won.*
de repente suddenly
El coche frenó de repente. *The car braked suddenly.*
desgraciadamente/por desgracia unfortunately
Desgraciadamente/por desgracia murió. *Unfortunately he died.*

17

immediately
until/even
then
so (therefore) -(2)
soon
perhaps
always
only (2)
also

en seguida immediately
Se fue en seguida. *He left immediately.*
hasta until, even
No vino hasta las seis. *He did not come till six.*
Hasta Pedro fue a la fiesta. *Even Pedro went to the party.*
luego then
Comió un bocadillo; luego salió. *He ate a sandwich, then went out.*
mucho a lot
La chica come mucho. *The girl eats a lot.*
por tanto/por consiguiente so (therefore)
Llovía y por tanto (por consiguiente) no salí. *It was raining and so I didn't go out.*
pronto soon
Pronto se va de vacaciones. *He is soon going on holidays.*
quizá perhaps
Quizá lo hizo. *Perhaps he did it.*
siempre always
Siempre llega tarde. *He always arrives late.*
sólo, solamente only
Sólo los franceses saben cocinar. *Only the French can cook.*
Tenemos solamente cinco. *We only have five.*
también also
Él fue y yo fui también. *He went and I went as well (too/also).*
ya now, already
Ya ha llegado. *He has already arrived.*
Ya es hora de irnos. *It is time for us to go now.*

1.6 Comparative and superlative of adjectives and adverbs

(a) Normally **más … que**, **menos … que** are used to form the comparative:
  Él es más rico que ella. *He is richer than she is.*
  Él es menos inteligente que ella. *He is less intelligent than she is.*
Notice these irregular forms:
  mejor *better*
  peor *worse*
  mayor *bigger/older*
  menor *smaller/younger*
más grande (bigger) and **más pequeño** (smaller) can also be used.
Notice also:
  la calle mayor *the main street*
  la plaza mayor *the main square*
(b) más is used to form the superlative:
  el libro **más** interesante que tengo *the most interesting book that I have*
  la chica **más** guapa *the prettiest girl*
Notice the following:
  el/la mejor, los/las mejores *the best*
  el/la peor, los/las peores *the worst*
  el/la mayor, los/las mayores *the biggest/the oldest*
  el/la menor, los menores/las menores *the smallest/the youngest*
When using a superlative, 'in' is translated by **de**:
  el mejor jugador del equipo *the best player in the team*
  las peores casas de la ciudad *the worst houses in the city*
(c) tan … como *as (so) … as*
  tanto como *as (so) much as*
  El chico es **tan** alto **como** la chica. *The boy is as tall as the girl.*
  La chica no es **tan** alta **como** el chico. *The girl is not as tall as the boy.*

Tengo **tanto** dinero **como** mi hermano. *I have as much money as my brother.*

No tengo **tantos** amigos **como** él. *I do not have as many friends as he does.*

(d) Adverbs also form the comparison with **más**:

Tú hablas **más** claramente que él. *You speak more clearly than he does.*

1.7 Numerals

Cardinal numbers

0	cero	31	treinta y uno
1	uno(un), una	32	treinta y dos
2	dos	40	cuarenta
3	tres	41	cuarenta y uno
4	cuatro	50	cincuenta
5	cinco	51	cincuenta y uno
6	seis	60	sesenta
7	siete	61	sesenta y uno
8	ocho	70	setenta
9	nueve	71	setenta y uno
10	diez	80	ochenta
11	once	81	ochenta y uno
12	doce	90	noventa
13	trece	91	noventa y uno
14	catorce	100	ciento (cien)
15	quince	101	ciento uno
16	dieciséis	102	ciento dos
17	diecisiete	200	doscientos/as
18	dieciocho	300	trescientos/as
19	diecinueve	400	cuatrocientos/as
20	veinte	500	quinientos/as
21	veintiuno	600	seiscientos/as
22	veintidós	700	setecientos/as
23	veintitrés	800	ochocientos/as
24	veinticuatro	900	novecientos/as
25	veinticinco	1000	mil
26	veintiséis	2000	dos mil
27	veintisiete	10,000	diez mil
28	veintiocho	100,000	cien mil
29	veintinueve	1,000,000	un millón
30	treinta	2,000,000	dos millones

(a) uno loses its **–o** when in front of a masculine singular noun:

Dáme uno. *Give me one.*

Dáme un caramelo. *Give me a sweet.*

(b) The hundreds have a separate feminine form:

doscientos libros *200 books*

doscientas pesetas *200 pesetas*

(c) cien is used for exactly 100:

Tengo cien libras. *I have £100.*

ciento is used for numbers 101–199:

ciento cuarenta *140*

(d) mil does not change and does not have **un** or **una** in front of it:

mil pesetas *a thousand pesetas*

dos mil pesetas *two thousand pesetas*

(e) un millón (plural **millones**) requires **de** before a noun:

un millón de pájaros *a million birds*

dos millones de pájaros *two million birds*

(f) **ciento** is not followed by **y**; **y** is only used between tens and units:

      ciento cuatro *104*

      ciento treinta y cinco *135*

(g) You cannot say 'nineteen hundred' in Spanish; **mil** must be used:

      mil novecientos *1900*

Ordinal numbers

primero	*first*	sexto	*sixth*
segundo	*second*	séptimo	*seventh*
tercero	*third*	octavo	*eighth*
cuarto	*fourth*	noveno	*ninth*
quinto	*fifth*	décimo	*tenth*

(a) Ordinal numbers agree like other adjectives ending in **–o**:

      la tercera calle *the third street*

(b) Do not confuse **cuatro** (four) with **cuarto** (fourth).

(c) **primero** and **tercero** lose their **–o** before a masculine single noun:

      el primer ejemplo *the first example*

      el tercer gol *the third goal*

(d) Although the ordinal numbers exist after **décimo,** they are rarely used. Use the cardinal number after the noun:

      el piso quince *the fifteenth floor*

      el siglo veinte *the twentieth century*

(e) With kings and queens, leave out 'the':

      Carlos quinto *Charles the Fifth*

1.8 Time

(a) ¿Qué hora es? *What time is it?*

¿A qué hora? *At what time?*

      Es la una. *It is 01.00.*

      Son las dos. *It is 02.00.*

      Son las tres. *It is 03.00.*

      Son las cuatro y cuarto. *It is 04.15.*

      Son las cinco y media. *It is 05.30.*

      Son las seis menos cuarto. *It is 05.45.*

      Son las siete y cinco. *It is 07.05.*

      Son las ocho menos diez. *It is 07.50.*

      Es (el) mediodía. *It is 12.00 noon.*

      Es (la) medianoche. *It is 12.00 midnight.*

      a las tres de la madrugada *at three in the (early) morning*

      a las siete de la mañana *at seven in the morning*

      a las dos de la tarde *at two in the afternoon*

      a las once de la noche *at eleven at night*

      a eso de las tres *at about three o'clock*

      a las cuatro en punto *at four o'clock exactly*

(b) Before dark, the Spaniards say **de la tarde**:

      a las cuatro de la tarde *at four in the afternoon*

After dark, use **de la noche**:

      a las siete de la noche *at seven in the evening*

(c) Use **por la mañana, por la tarde, por la noche** when no time is given:

      Fue de compras por la mañana. *He went shopping in the morning.*

      Fue de compras a las diez de la mañana. *He went shopping at ten in the morning.*

1.9 Negatives

(a)
nadie *nobody*
nada *nothing*
nunca/jamás *never*
ninguno,-a, *no*
ni … ni … *neither … nor …*
tampoco *(n)either*
No hay **nadie** en la calle. *There is nobody in the street.*
No hay **nada** en la calle. *There is nothing in the street.*
No voy **nunca**/no voy **jamás**. *I never go.*
No hay **ningún** trabajo allí. *There is no work there.*
Ni mi amigo **ni** yo lo vimos. *Neither my friend nor I saw it.*
No fui y ella no fue **tampoco.** *I did not go and she did not go either.*

(b) When the negative word comes after the verb, **no** must be placed before the verb:
Nunca voy a la iglesia. *I never go to church.*
No voy nunca al colegio. *I never go to school.*

(c) When **nadie** is the direct object it requires a personal **a**:
No veo **a** nadie. *I see nobody.*

(d) ninguno loses its **–o** before a masculine singular noun and requires an accent:
ningún trabajo *no work*

1.10 Pronouns

Subject pronouns

(a) A Spanish verb can be used with or without the subject pronoun:
yo miro *or* miro *I look*
tú miras *or* miras *you look* (sing. fam.)
él mira *or* mira *he looks*
ella mira *or* mira *she looks*
usted (abbreviated to 'Vd.') mira *or* mira *you look* (sing. polite)
nosotros/as miramos *or* miramos *we look*
vosotros miráis *or* miráis *you look* (pl. fam.)
ellos miran *or* miran *they look* (m.)
ellas miran *or* miran *they look* (f.)
ustedes (abbreviated to 'Vds.') miran *or* miran *you look* (pl. polite)

(b) It is normal to omit the subject pronoun except when its omission would cause confusion:
Él es de aquí pero **ella** es belga. *He is from here but she is Belgian.*

(c) Note that there are five subject pronouns meaning 'you'. **Tú** is used to address a friend, a relative or a child. **Vosotros** (fem. **vosotra**s) is used to address more than one of such people. **Usted** (**Vd.**) and **ustedes** (**Vds.**) are the singular and plural forms used to address people with whom you are not familiar.

(d) The use of **usted** and **ustedes** is becoming less and less frequent; however if in doubt you are always safe to use the polite form.

Direct object pronouns

(a)

me *me*	le, lo *you* (polite, sing. m.)
te *you* (fam. sing.)	la *you* (polite, sing. f.)
le, lo *him*	lo *it* (m.)
la *her*	la *it* (f.)

nos *us*	las *them* (f.)
os *you* (fam. pl.)	los, les *you* (polite, pl. m.)
les, los *them* (m.)	las *you* (polite, pl. f.)

él **me** ve *he sees me*	él **nos** ve *he sees us*
él **te** ve *he sees you*	él **os** ve *he sees you*
él **le/lo** ve *he sees him/it/you*	él **les/los** ve *he sees them/you*
él **la** ve *he sees her/it/you*	él **las** ve *he sees them/you*

(b) Pronouns normally come before the verb. When there are two parts to the verb, they normally come before the first part:

Me ha visto. *He has seen me.*

(c) Pronouns are attached to the end of the verb:

❶ when it is an infinitive (i.e. it ends in **–ar, –er** or **–ir**):

Voy a hacerlo. *I am going to do it.*

❷ when it is a present participle (i.e. it ends in **–ando** or **–iendo**):

Estoy haciéndolo. *I am doing it.* (notice the accent)

❸ when it is a positive command:

¡Escúchame! *Listen to me!*

but *not* with negative commands:

¡No le escuches! *Do not listen to him!*

(d) To avoid confusion with **lo**, **le**, **la**, **los**, **les**, **las**, the following words are often inserted after the verb:

a él, a ella, a Vd., a ellos, a ellas, a Vds.

Lo miro a él. *I am looking at him.*

Lo miro a Vd. *I am looking at you.*

Indirect object pronouns

(a)
me *to me*
te *to you* (fam. sing.)
le *to him, to her, to it, to you* (polite sing.)
nos *to us*
os *to you* (fam. pl.)
les *to them, to you* (polite pl.)
me da el dinero *he gives the money to me*
te da el dinero *he gives the money to you*
le da el dinero *he gives the money to him, to her, to you*
nos da el dinero *he gives the money to us*
os da el dinero *he gives the money to you*
les da el dinero *he gives the money to them, to you*

(b) When there is a direct and and an indirect object pronoun together, the indirect one always comes first:

Me lo ha vendido. *He has sold it to me.*

Dámelo. *Give it to me.*

(c) When two pronouns beginning with **l–** come together, the first one becomes **se**:

Se lo ha vendido. *He has sold it to him.*

Dáselo. *Give it to them.*

It is often necessary to add **a él, a ella, a Vd., a ellos, a ellas, a Vds.** to make the meaning clear as **se** can mean 'to him', 'to her', 'to you', 'to them':

Se lo ha vendido **a él**. *He has sold it to him.*

Se lo ha vendido **a ella**. *He has sold it to her.*

(d) When a pronoun is added to a present participle, the participle requires an accent:

dando *giving*

dándole *giving him*

(e) When two pronouns are added to an infinitive, the infinitive requires an accent:

No voy a dar el dinero al niño. *I am not going to give the money to the child.*

No voy a dárselo. *I am not going to give it to him.*

Prepositional pronouns

(a) These pronouns are used after a preposition:

mí *me*	nosotros, nosotras *us*
ti *you*	vosotros, vosotras *you*
él, sí *him, it*	ellos, sí *them*
ella, sí *her, it*	ellas, sí *them*
Vd., sí *you*	Vds., sí *you*

(b) El regalo es para mí. *The present is for me.*
Ella está detrás de ti. *She is behind you.*
¡Sus gafas están delante de Vd.! *Your glasses are in front of you!*

(c) Note that **sí** is used instead of **él**, **ella**, **Vd.**, **ellos**, **ellas**, **Vds.** when the person referred to after the preposition is the same as the subject of the sentence:
Lo quiere para sí. *He wants it for him* (i.e. himself).
Lo quiere para él. *He wants it for him* (i.e. for someone else).

(d) Note that **con mí** becomes **conmigo** *with me*
con ti becomes **contigo** *with you*
con sí becomes **consigo** *with him (her, you, it, them)*

(e) Prepositional pronouns are often used with the verb **gustar** to give emphasis:
¡A mí me gusta pero a ti no te gusta! *I like it but you do not!*

(f) Note that **mí** and **sí** have an accent but **ti** does not.

1.11 Personal 'a'

(a) When the direct object of a sentence is a person, **a** is placed before the person:
Visité **a** Juan. *I visited Juan.*
Visité la catedral. *I visited the cathedral.*

(b) It is sometimes used with regard to a pet when the speaker wishes to show affection for the animal:
¿Has visto **al** perro? *Have you seen the dog?*

(c) It is not used after **tener:**
Tengo un amigo. *I have a friend.*
But
Encontré a un amigo. *I met a friend.*

(d) It is not used when the person is not specified:
Busco un mecánico. *I am looking for a mechanic.*

1.12 Demonstrative adjectives and pronouns (this, that, these, those)

Demonstrative adjectives:

(a)

este chico *this boy*	aquel chico *that boy*
esta chica *this girl*	aquella chica *that girl*
estos chicos *these boys*	aquellos chicos *those boys*
estas chicas *these girls*	aquellas chicas *those girls*

ese chico *that boy*
esa chica *that girl*
esos chicos *those boys*
esas chicas *those girls*

(b) In the above examples, 'this', 'that', 'these' and 'those' are adjectives and they are immediately followed by a noun.

(c) Notice there are two ways of saying 'that' and 'those'. People or things which are referred to by **aquel** etc are further away than people or things referred to by **ese** etc:

> Me gusta ese libro pero no me gusta aquel libro.
> *I like that book but I don't like that book* (i.e. over there).

Demonstrative pronouns:

(d)

no me gusta éste *I don't like this one*
no me gusta ésta *I don't like this one*
no me gustan éstos *I don't like these*
no me gustan éstas *I don't like these*

no me gusta ése *I don't like that one*
no me gusta ésa *I don't like that one*
no me gustan ésos *I don't like those*
no me gustan ésas *I don't like those*

no me gusta aquél *I don't like that one*
no me gusta aquélla *I don't like that one*
no me gustan aquéllos *I don't like those*
no me gustan aquéllas *I don't like those*

(e) Notice that the above words **éste** etc are pronouns: they are not immediately followed by a noun.

(f) Opinions vary about whether an accent is required on the above pronouns. You are safer if you put the accent.

(g) **esto** (this); **eso** (that); **aquello** (that)

These three pronouns cannot refer to a particular verb. They refer to a whole idea or sentence.

> ¿Qué es esto? *What's this?*
> No tengo dinero y eso no me gusta.
> *I have no money and I don't like that.* (it is not the money that the speaker does not
> like but rather the idea of not having any money)

1.13 Possessive adjectives

(a)

mi libro *my book*
mis libros *my books*

tu libro *your book* (fam. sing.)
tus libros *your books* (fam. sing.)

su libro *his book*
su libro *her book*
sus libros *his/her books*
su libro *your book* (polite sing.)
sus libros *your books* (polite sing.)

nuestro hermano *our brother*
nuestra hermana *our sister*
nuestros hermanos *our brothers*
nuestras hermanas *our sisters*

vuestro hermano *your book* (fam. pl.)
vuestra hermana *your sister* (fam. pl.)
vuestros hermanos *your brothers* (fam. pl.)
vuestras hermanas *your sisters* (fam. pl.)

sus libros *their books*
su libro *your book* (polite pl.)
sus libros *your books* (polite pl.)

(b) **nuestro** and **vuestro** are the only possessive adjectives to have a feminine form.

(c) When saying 'your' in Spanish, first you must decide whether to use the familiar singular (**tu** or **tus**), the familiar plural (**vuestro, vuestra, vuestros, vuestras**), or the polite form (**su** or **sus**).

(d) Notice that these adjectives agree in number and gender with the noun that follows them and not with the possessor. For instance a common mistake is to think that **su** means 'his' or 'her' and that **'sus'** means 'their'. Both **su** and **sus** can mean 'his', 'her' or 'their'. The correct form depends on whether the thing possessed is singular (**su**) or plural (**sus**).

(e) **su** and **sus** can mean 'his', 'her', 'your' or 'their'. Confusion can be avoided as follows:

> su libro de él *his book*
> su libro de ella *her book*
> su libro de Vd. *your book*
> sus libros de ellos *their books*
> sus libros de ellas *their books* (feminine possessors)
> sus libros de Vds. *your books* (plural possessors)

(f) The definite article and not the possessive adjective is normally used with parts of the body and with clothing:

> Lo tengo en la mano. *I have it in my hand.*
> Voy a quitarme el abrigo. *I am going to take off my coat.*

1.14 Possessive pronouns

(a)

singular		*plural*		
masculine	*feminine*	*masculine*	*feminine*	
el mío	la mía	los míos	las mías	*mine*
el tuyo	la tuya	los tuyos	las tuyas	*yours* (sing. fam.)
el suyo	la suya	los suyos	las suyas	*his, hers, yours* (sing. polite)
el nuestro	la nuestra	los nuestros	las nuestras	*ours*
el vuestro	la vuestra	los vuestros	las vuestras	*yours* (pl. fam.)
el suyo	la suya	los suyos	las suyas	*theirs, yours* (pl. polite)

(b) Here are some examples of the above:

> Tengo mi libro y **el tuyo**. *I have my book and yours.*
> Tienes tu libro y **el mío**. *You have your book and mine.*
> He vendido mi coche y **el vuestro**. *I have sold my car and yours.*

(c) When the verb **ser** is used, omit the article:

> Éste es mío y ése es tuyo. *This one is mine and that one is yours.*

(d) Notice the following:

> Es amigo mío. *He is a friend of mine.*
> Son amigos nuestros. *They are friends of ours.*

(e) As **suyo** can mean 'his', 'hers', 'yours' or 'theirs', confusion is often avoided as follows:

> es de él *it's his*   es de ellos *it's theirs* (m.)
> es de ella *it's hers*   es de ellas *it's theirs* (f.)
> es de Vd. *it's yours* (sing. polite)   es de Vds. *it's yours* (pl. polite)

1.15 Relative pronouns

(a) In English the relative pronouns are 'who', 'whom', 'which' and 'that'.

(b) In the following sentences, it is correct to use **que** when referring to people or things, whether subject or object:

> el hombre que está esperando *the man who is waiting*
> el hombre que vi *the man that I saw*
> (*or* el hombre a quien vi)
> la casa que me gusta *the house that I like*
> la casa que vendí *the house that I sold*

(c) Notice that in English the relative pronoun is often omitted but it must always be inserted in Spanish:

> el libro que leí anoche *the book I read last night*

(d) After prepositions, use **el que**, **la que**, **los que** or **las que**. **Quien** (plural **quienes**) may be
used for people:

> la playa por la que anduvo *the beach that he walked along*
> la chica con la que/con quien salí *the girl with whom I went out/the girl I went out with*
> el pueblo cerca del que vivo *the town near which I live*

(e) Instead of **el que**, **la que**, **los que** or **las que**, **el cual**, **la cual**, **los cuales**, **las cuales** may be
used. However, **el que** etc is far more common.

(f) **lo que** means 'what' in the sense of 'that which' when no question is being asked:

> Describe lo que vas a hacer. *Describe what you are going to do.*
> Dime lo que hiciste. *Tell me what you did.*

(g) **todo lo que** means 'everything that':

> Todo lo que hace sale bien. *Everything that he does turns out well.*

(h) **cuyo, cuya, cuyos, cuyas** mean 'whose' or 'of which':

> Notice that **cuyo** etc agrees with the noun that follows it and not with the possessor:
> el hombre cuya hija es actriz *the man whose daughter is an actress*
> la casas cuyas ventanas estaban rotas *the house, the windows of which were broken*

1.16 Interrogatives

(a)

¿adónde? *where to?*	¿cuánto tiempo? *how long?*
¿a qué hora? *what time?*	¿desde cuándo? *since when?*
¿cómo? *how?*	¿dónde? *where?*
¿cuándo? *when?*	¿para qué? *what for?*
¿cuál? (pl. ¿cuáles?) *which?*	¿por qué? *why?*
¿cuánto? (f. ¿cuánta?) *how much?*	¿qué? *what?*
¿cuántos? (f. ¿cuántas?) *how many?*	¿quién? (pl. ¿quiénes?) *who?*

(b) Note that all interrogatives have an accent. An accent is still required when the question is
indirect:

> No sé d**ó**nde está. *I don't know where he is.*
> Le pregunté qui**é**n era. *I asked him who he was.*

(c) **qué** can be used in exclamations:

> ¡Qué día! *What a day!*
> ¡Qué desastre! *What a disaster!*

If an adjective is used, **más** or **tan** is inserted:

> ¡Qué día más hermoso! *What a beautiful day!*
> ¡Qué desastre tan horroroso! *What a horrible disaster!*

(d) **cuál** is used to differentiate between a choice of two or more:

> ¿Cuál es su hermano? *Which one is his brother?*

(e)

> ¿Cómo está? *How is he?*

But
> ¿Cómo es? *What is he like?*

1.17 'Ser' and 'estar'

Both these verbs mean 'to be'. To work out which to use, the following formula is useful:

(a) In a 'who' situation, use **ser**:

> ¿Quién es? Es nuestro profesor. *Who is he? He is our teacher.*
> Él es francés y ella es belga. *He is French and she is Belgian.*

(b) In a 'what' situation, use **ser**:

> ¿Qué es eso? Es una mesa. *What is that? It's a table.*

(c) In a 'when' situation, use **ser**:

> ¿Qué hora es? Son las dos. *What time is it? It is two o'clock.*
> ¿Qué fecha es? Es el dos de mayo. *What's the date? It's the second of May.*
> Es verano. *It's summer.*

(d) In a 'where' situation, use **estar**:

¿Dónde está la estación? Está allí. *Where is the station? It's there.*

(e) In a 'what like' situation, you must work out whether the description refers to a temporary characterisic or a permanent characteristic. If the characteristic is temporary use **estar**; if permanent use **ser**:

El cielo está azul. *The sky is blue* (but it may well change colour soon).

La puerta es azul. *The door is blue* (although it may be repainted, the colour is a fairly permanent feature of the door).

Note also that with continuous tenses, **estar** is used:

Estoy corriendo. *I am running.*

Estaba lloviendo. *It was raining.*

Estaremos trabajando. *We will be working.*

1.18 'Conocer' and 'saber'

Both of these verbs mean 'to know'. **Conocer** is to know a person or a place, and **saber** is to know a fact or how to do something:

Conozco Madrid muy bien. *I know Madrid very well.*

¿No conoces a María? *Don't you know María?*

Sé la hora pero no sé la fecha. *I know the time but not the date.*

Ella sabe nadar y él sabe cocinar. *She can swim and he can cook.*

1.19 'Deber' and 'tener que'

Both of these verbs mean 'to have to'. **Deber** implies a moral responsibility whereas **tener que** implies a physical necessity:

Debo visitar a mi abuela esta semana. *I must visit my grandmother this week.*

Tengo que tomar el autobús. No tengo coche. *I have to get the bus. I have no car.*

1.20 'Tener'

Note these expressions which use **tener**:

tengo quince años *I am fifteen*

tengo calor *I am hot*

tengo éxito *I am successful*

tengo frío *I am cold*

tengo ganas de ir al cine *I want to go to the cinema*

tengo hambre *I am hungry*

el partido tiene lugar mañana *the match takes place tomorrow*

tengo miedo *I am frightened*

tengo prisa *I am in a hurry*

tengo que ir *I have to go*

tengo razón *I am right*

tengo sed *I am thirsty*

tengo sueño *I am sleepy*

tengo suerte *I am lucky*

With these expressions, to say 'very' use **mucho** or **mucha**:

tengo mucho calor *I am vey hot*

tengo mucha prisa *I am in a great hurry*

tengo mucho miedo *I am very frightened*

1.21 Prepositions

Prepositions are words that come before a noun and link the noun with the rest of the sentence.

a, en to, into (**a** does *not* mean 'at' which is usually **en**).

	Fui al campo. *I went to the countryside.*
	Estoy en el campo. *I am in the countryside.*
a lo largo de/por along	Anduvimos a lo largo de/por la playa. *We walked along the beach.*
a pesar de in spite of	Salimos a pesar del tiempo. *We went out in spite of the weather.*
al lado de beside	Vive al lado de la iglesia. *He lives beside the church.*
alrededor de around	Corrió alrededor de la mesa. *He ran round the table.*
antes de before	Llegué antes de las seis. *I arrived before six.*
	Antes de salir, me duché. *Before going out, I had a shower.*
cerca de near	La ciudad está cerca del mar. *The city is near the sea.*
con with	Le vi con su hermana. *I saw him with his sister.*
contra against	Jugó contra un equipo francés. *He played against a French team.*
debajo de/bajo under	El banco está debajo del/bajo el árbol. *The bench is under the tree.*
delante de in front of	Se paró delante de la casa. *He stopped in front of the house.*
desde from	Desde la casa, se ve la calle. *From the house, you can see the street.*
después de after	Después de llegar, se acostó. *After arriving, he went to bed.*
detrás de behind	Se escondió detrás de la puerta. *He hid behind the door.*
durante during	Durante el viaje, durmió. *He slept during the journey*
en in	Está en casa. *He is in the house.*
en vez de instead of	Yo fui en vez de él. *I went instead of him.*
encima de above	La luz está encima de la mesa. *The light is above the table.*
enfrente de opposite	Se encontraron enfrente del cine. *They met opposite the cinema.*
entre between, among	Está entre los dos puntos. *It is between the two points.*
	Los distribuyó entre sus amigos. *He gave it out among his friends.*
hacia towards	Viajó hacia el norte. *He travelled towards the north.*
hasta until, as far as, up to	Trabajó hasta las seis. *He worked up to six o'clock.*
lejos de far from	Vive lejos de aquí. *He lives far from here.*
más que, más de (with a number) more than	Tengo más que él. *I have more than he has.*
	Tengo más de tres. *I have more than three.*
salvo except	Todos fuimos salvo ella. *We all went except her.*
según according to	Según el periódico, está muerto. *According to the paper, he is dead.*
sin without	Sin perder un momento, se fue. *Without wasting a moment, he went.*
sobre on, about (with time), concerning	Está sobre la mesa. *It is on the table.*
	Vino sobre las seis. *He came about six.*
	Hablamos sobre el tiempo. *We spoke about the weather.*

1.22 Verbs

Verbs are the most important part of any sentence and your command or otherwise of verbs will be one of the major factors that influence the grade you get. In English we have few changes in the ending of our verbs:

> I eat, you eat, he eats, we eat, you eat, they eat.

The verb-ending changes once for the 'he' part of the present tense. In Spanish there are six different endings to be learnt for the verb **comer** in the present tense.

Also the meaning of a verb often changes depending on where the stress lies:

> llego *I arrive*   llegó *he arrived*

so accents are very important.

You will be expected to know the following tenses: the *present*, the *imperfect*, the *perfect*, the *preterite*, the *pluperfect*, the *future* and the *conditional*. Your board's syllabus mentions the subjunctive but the board will not expect you to *produce* a subjunctive: in the exam there may be a verb in the subjunctive that you have to recognize. You will not have to recognize that the verb is in the subjunctive: you will just have to recognize what the verb means. So the subjunctive need not concern you overmuch until you start A level! The one exception to the above is the use of the subjunctive as a command. But there are ways of making a command in Spanish without a detailed knowledge of the subjunctive. So make sure you know all the other tenses before you start worrying about the subjunctive.

Another peculiarity of Spanish verbs is the radical-changing verb. It is worth remembering that there are no radical changes in the imperfect, the perfect, the pluperfect, the future or the conditional. There are no radical changes in **-ar** and **-er** verbs in the preterite. So you need only be concerned with radical changes in the present tense and some **-ir** verbs in the preterite.

When you read a verb table, you will usually see a Spanish verb in a list of six.

e.g.	miro	miramos
	miras	miráis
	mira	miran

It is important to know the significance of each of these six.

The first is for 'I' so **miro** means 'I look'.

The second is for 'you' (singular familiar), so **miras** means 'you look'.

The third is for 'he', 'she', 'it' or 'you' (polite singular), so **mira** means either 'he looks' or 'she looks' or 'it looks' or 'you look'.

The fourth is for 'we' so **miramos** means 'we look'.

The fifth is for 'you' (familiar plural) so **miráis** means 'you look'.

The sixth is for 'they' or 'you' (polite plural) so **miran** means either 'they look' or 'you look'.

1.23 Present tense

The infinitives of all verbs end in either **-ar, -er** or **-ir**.

Regular verbs

-ar verbs	**-er verbs**	**-ir verbs**
miro *I look*	como *I eat*	vivo *I live*
miras *you look*	comes *you eat*	vives *you live*
mira *he, she looks, you look*	come *he, she eats, you eat*	vive *he, she lives, you live*
miramos *we look*	comemos *we eat*	vivimos *we live*
miráis *you look*	coméis *you eat*	vivís *you live*
miran *they look, you look*	comen *they eat, you eat*	viven *they live, you live*

Radical-changing verbs

Radical-changing means that the stem of the verb changes in numbers 1, 2, 3 and 6.

If there are two vowels in the stem of the infinitive e.g. **entender, preferir,** it is the last vowel of the stem that changes:

entiendo *I understand*
prefiero *I prefer*

There are three groups:

Group 1
Verbs that change **-e** to **-ie**; **-ar** verbs, **-er** verbs and **-ir** verbs fall into this group.
Examples of Group 1 **-ar** verbs:

cerrar *to close*	cierro *I close*
despertar *to awaken*	cierras *you close*
empezar *to begin*	cierra *he, she closes, you close*
pensar *to think*	cerramos *we close*
sentarse *to sit down*	cerráis *you close*
nevar *to snow*	cierran *they close, you close*

Examples of Group 1 **-er** verbs:

encender *to light*
entender *to understand*
perder *to lose*
querer *to want, to like, to love*

p**ie**rdo *I lose*	perdemos *we lose*
p**ie**rdes *you lose*	perdéis *you lose*
p**ie**rde *he, she loses, you lose*	p**ie**rden *they lose, you lose*

Examples of Group 1 **-ir** verbs:

divertirse *to amuse oneself*
preferir *to prefer*
sentir *to feel*

pref**ie**ro *I prefer*	preferimos *we prefer*
pref**ie**res *you prefer*	preferís *you prefer*
pref**ie**re *he, she prefers, you prefer*	pref**ie**ren *they prefer, you prefer*

Group 2

Verbs that change **-o** or **-u** to **-ue**; these can be either **-ar, -er** or **-ir** verbs.

Examples of Group 2 **-ar** verbs:

acordarse *to remember*
contar *to tell*
costar *to cost*
encontrar *to find*
jugar *to play*
volar *to fly*

enc**ue**ntro *I meet*	encontramos *we meet*
enc**ue**ntras *you meet*	encontráis *you meet*
enc**ue**ntra *he, she meets, you meet*	enc**ue**ntran *they meet, you meet*

Examples of Group 2 **-er** verbs:

doler *to hurt*
poder *to be able*
llover *to rain*
volver *to return*

v**ue**lvo *I return*	volvemos *we return*
v**ue**lves *you return*	volvéis *you return*
v**ue**lve *he, she returns, you return*	v**ue**lven *they return, you return*

Examples of Group 2 **-ir** verbs:

dormir *to sleep*
morir *to die*

d**ue**rmo *I sleep*	dormimos *we sleep*
d**ue**rmes *you sleep*	dormís *you sleep*
d**ue**rme *he, she sleeps, you sleep*	d**ue**rmen *they sleep, you sleep*

Group 3

Examples of verbs that change **-e** to **-i**:

despedirse de *to say goodbye to*
pedir *to ask for*
reir *to laugh*
repetir *to repeat*
seguir *to follow*
vestirse *to dress oneself*

p**i**do *I ask*	pedimos *we ask*
p**i**des *you ask*	pedís *you ask*
p**i**de *he, she asks, you ask*	p**i**den *they ask, you ask*

Verbs that are irregular in the present tense

Many verbs that are irregular in the present tense are only irregular in the first person singular. After that they are regular:

hacer	**hago** *I do, make*
	haces *you do, make*
	hace *he does, makes, you do*
	hacemos *we make*
	hacéis *you make*
	hacen *they make, you make*

Other verbs that are irregular in the first person only are:

caber *to be room for*	**quepo,** cabes etc
caer *to fall*	**caigo,** caes etc
conducir *to drive*	**conduzco,** conduces etc
conocer *to know*	**conozco,** conoces etc
dar *to give*	**doy,** das etc
ofrecer *to offer*	**ofrezco,** ofreces etc
poner *to put*	**pongo,** pones etc
saber *to know*	**sé,** sabes etc
salir *to go out*	**salgo,** sales etc
traer *to bring*	**traigo,** traes etc
ver *to see*	**veo,** ves etc

Other irregular verbs

decir *to say*	**huir** *to flee*	**ser** *to be*
digo	huyo	soy
dices	huyes	eres
dice	huye	es
decimos	huimos	somos
decís	huís	sois
dicen	huyen	son
estar *to be*	**ir** *to go*	**tener** *to have*
estoy	voy	tengo
estás	vas	tienes
está	va	tiene
estamos	vamos	tenemos
estáis	vais	tenéis
están	van	tienen
haber *to have*	**oír** *to hear*	**venir** *to come*
he	oigo	vengo
has	oyes	vienes
ha	oye	viene
hemos	oímos	venimos
habéis	oís	venís
han	oyen	vienen

1.24 The present continuous

To form the present continuous, you need to know how to form the present participle.

To form the present participle of an **–ar** verb, remove the **–ar** and add **–ando.**

e.g. habl**ar** *to speak*, habl**ando** *speaking*

To form the present participle of an **–er** verb, remove the **–er** and add **–iendo.**

e.g. com**er** *to eat*, com**iendo** *eating*

To form the present participle of an **–ir** verb, remove the **–ir** and add **–iendo.**

e.g. viv**ir** *to live*, viv**iendo** *living*

To form the present continuous, take the present tense of **estar** and add the present participle. Here are examples of regular verbs in the present continuous tense:

hablar
estoy hablando *I am talking*
estás hablando *you are talking*
está hablando *he, she is talking, you are talking*
estamos hablando *we are talking*
estáis hablando *you are talking*
están hablando *they, you are talking*

comer
estoy comiendo *I am eating*
estás comiendo *you are eating*
está comiendo *he, she is eating, you are eating*
estamos comiendo *we are eating*
estáis comiendo *you are eating*
están comiendo *they, you are eating*

vivir
estoy viviendo *I am living*
estás viviendo *you are living*
está viviendo *he, she is living, you are living*
estamos viviendo *we are living*
estáis viviendo *you are living*
están viviendo *they, you are living*

1.25 Perfect tense

The perfect tense in English always has 'has' or 'have' in it.
e.g.   I have gone, they have run, he has seen
    The perfect tense in Spanish is formed by taking the present tense of **haber** and adding the past particple. So you need to know about **haber** and you need to know about past participles.

Present tense of haber

he *I have*   hemos *we have*
has *you have*   habéis *you have*
ha *he has, she has, you have*   han *they have, you have*

Past participles

To find a past participle of a verb in English, just imagine that the words 'I have' are in front of it. So in English if you want to find the past participle of the verb 'to write', put 'I have' in front of it. We would say 'I have written' so 'written' is the past participle of 'to write'. In the same way, 'gone' is the past participle of 'to go' and so on.
    In Spanish, to form the past participle of an **-ar** verb, take off the **-ar** and add **-ado**.
So the past participle of **hablar** is **hablado**.
    To form the past participle of an **-er** verb or an **-ir** verb, take off the **-er** or **-ir** and add **-ido**.
So the past participle of **comer** is **comido** and the past participle of **vivir** is **vivido**.
    Here is the perfect tense of three regular verbs:

hablar
he hablado *I have spoken*
has hablado *you have spoken*
ha hablado *he, she has spoken, you have spoken*
hemos hablado *we have spoken*
habéis hablado *you have spoken*
han hablado *they have, you have spoken*

comer
he comido *I have eaten*
has comido *you have eaten*
ha comido *he, she has eaten, you have eaten*
hemos comido *we have eaten*
habéis comido *you have eaten*
han comido *they have, you have eaten*

vivir
he vivido *I have lived*
has vivido *you have lived*
ha vivido *he, she has lived, you have lived*
hemos vivido *we have lived*
habéis vivido *you have lived*
han vivido *they have, you have lived*

Irregular past participles

Some past participles do not obey the rules and must be learnt separately:

abrir *to open*	he **abierto** *I have opened*
cubrir *to cover*	he **cubierto** *I have covered*
decir *to say*	he **dicho** *I have said*
descubrir *to discover*	he **descubierto** *I have discovered*
escribir *to write*	he **escrito** *I have written*
hacer *to do, to make*	he **hecho** *I have done/made*
morir *to die*	ha **muerto** *he has died*
poner *to put*	he **puesto** *I have put*
romper *to break*	he **roto** *I have broken*
ver *to see*	he **visto** *I have seen*
volver *to return*	he **vuelto** *I have returned*

1.26 Preterite tense

The preterite is sometimes known as the simple past. It is used to tell about events in the past – e.g. I went, you ran, they bought.

Here is the preterite of three regular verbs. Note that there are two sets of endings, one for **–ar** verbs and one for **–er** and **–ir** verbs.

hablar
hablé *I spoke*
hablaste *you spoke*
habló *he, she, you spoke*
hablamos *we spoke*
hablasteis *you spoke*
hablaron *they, you spoke*

comer
comí *I ate*
comiste *you ate*
comió *he, she, you ate*
comimos *we ate*
comisteis *you ate*
comieron *they, you ate*

vivir
viví *I lived*
viviste *you lived*
vivió *he, she, you lived*
vivimos *we lived*
vivisteis *you lived*
vivieron *they, you lived*

Note the role played in English by 'did' in the negative and question forms of the preterite:
hablé *I spoke*
no hablé *I did not speak*
¿hablé? *did I speak?*

Radical–changing verbs in the preterite

There are no **-ar** or **-er** radical-changing verbs in the preterite.

Some **-ir** verbs change to an **i** in numbers 3 and 6, i.e. in the third persons singular and plural. Some such verbs are:

pedir *to ask for*	preferir *to prefer*	reir *to laugh*
seguir *to follow*	sentir *to feel*	servir *to serve*
sonreir *to smile*	vestirse *to get dressed*	

pedir	pedí	pedimos
	pediste	pedisteis
	pidió	pidieron

Note what happens to the first person singular of verbs that end in **-zar, -gar** and **-car**.

empezar *to start*	empe**cé** *I started*
jugar *to play*	ju**gué** *I played*
buscar *to look for*	bus**qué** *I looked for*

Note the preterite of **caer** and the spelling changes that take place in the third persons singular and plural:

caí	caímos
caíste	caísteis
cayó	cayeron

Irregular preterites

dar *to give*	di	dimos
	diste	disteis
	dio	dieron

ser (to be) and **ir** (to go) have the same preterite:

fui	fuimos
fuiste	fuisteis
fue	fueron

Preteritos graves

These are irregular and are called **grave** because the stress in the first and third persons singular does not fall as it usually does on the last syllable but on the second to last.

andar *to walk*	**haber** *to have*	**querer** *to want*	**traer** *to bring*
anduve	hube	quise	traje
anduviste	hubiste	quisiste	trajiste
anduvo	hubo	quiso	trajo
anduvimos	hubimos	quisimos	trajimos
anduvisteis	hubisteis	quisisteis	trajisteis
anduvieron	hubieron	quisieron	trajeron (note there is no **i** here)

decir *to say*	**hacer** *to do, make*	**saber** *to know*	**venir** *to come*
dije	hice	supe	vine
dijiste	hiciste	supiste	viniste
dijo	hizo	supo	vino
dijimos	hicimos	supimos	vinimos
dijisteis	hicisteis	supisteis	vinisteis
dijeron (note there is no **i** here)	hicieron	supieron	vinieron

estar *to be*	**poder** *to be able*	**tener** *to have*
estuve	pude	tuve
estuviste	pudiste	tuviste
estuvo	pudo	tuvo
estuvimos	pudimos	tuvimos
estuvisteis	pudisteis	tuvisteis
estuvieron	pudieron	tuvieron

1.27 Imperfect tense

The imperfect tense is used for things that 'used to happen' or 'were happening' – e.g. I used to play football, I was going to the cinema etc. It is often used to describe situations in the past – e.g. it was raining, she was wearing a coat.

To form the imperfect, add one of two sets of endings to the stem of the verb as follows (the **–aba** endings are for **–ar** verbs and the **–ía** endings are for **–er** and **–ir** verbs):

hablar	hablaba *I was speaking, I used to speak*
	hablabas *you were speaking, you used to speak*
	hablaba *he, she, was speaking, you were speaking, he, she, you used to speak*
	hablábamos *we were speaking, we used to speak*
	hablabais *you were speaking, you used to speak*
	hablaban *they, you were speaking, they, you used to speak*
comer	comía *I was eating, I used to eat*
	comías *you were eating, you used to eat*
	comía *he, she, was eating, you were eating, he, she, you used to eat*
	comíamos *we were eating, we used to eat*
	comíais *you were eating, you used to eat*
	comían *they, you were eating, they, you used to eat*
vivir	vivía *I was living, I used to live*
	vivías *you were living, you used to live*
	vivía *he, she was living, you were living, he, she, you used to live*
	vivíamos *we were living, we used to live*
	vivíais *you were living, you used to live*
	vivían *they, you were living, they, you used to live*

Irregular imperfects

ir *to go*	**ser** *to be*	**ver** *to see*
iba	era	veía
ibas	eras	veías
iba	era	veía
íbamos	éramos	veíamos
ibais	erais	veíais
iban	eran	veían

1.28 Pluperfect tense

The pluperfect is used for things that had happened. This tense is identified in English by the word 'had' – e.g. he had seen, they had gone.

To form the pluperfect in Spanish, take the imperfect of **haber** and add the past participle:

hablar	había hablado *I had spoken*
	habías hablado *you had spoken*
	había hablado *he, she, you had spoken*
	habíamos hablado *we had spoken*
	habíais hablado *you had spoken*
	habían hablado *they had spoken, you had spoken*
comer	había comido *I had eaten*
	habías comido *you had eaten*
	había comido *he, she, you had eaten*
	habíamos comido *we had eaten*
	habíais comido *you had eaten*
	habían comido *they had eaten, you had eaten*

vivir

había vivido *I had lived*
habías vivido *you had lived*
había vivido *he, she, you had lived*
habíamos vivido *we had lived*
habíais vivido *you had lived*
habían vivido *they had lived, you had lived*

1.29 Future tense

The future tense is used to describe future events and in English the words 'will' and 'shall' are used to convey the future tense – e.g. I shall see, they will go.

To form the future tense in Spanish, you add endings to the infinitive. There is only one set of endings for the future:

–é, –ás, –á, –emos, –éis, –án

hablar	**comer**	**vivir**
hablaré *I will speak*	comeré *I will eat*	viviré *I will live*
hablarás *you will speak*	comerás *you will eat*	vivirás *you will live*
hablará *he, she, you will speak*	comerá *he, she, you will eat*	vivirá *he, she, you will live*
hablaremos *we will speak*	comeremos *we will eat*	viviremos *we will live*
hablaréis *you will speak*	comeréis *you will eat*	viviréis *you will live*
hablarán *they, you will speak*	comerán *they, you will eat*	vivirán *they, you will live*

Irregular futures

Note that all have the same ending.

decir *to say*	**hacer** *to do, make*	**poner** *to put*	**saber** *to know*	**tener** *to have*
diré	haré	pondré	sabré	tendré
dirás	harás	pondrás	sabrás	tendrás
dirá	hará	pondrá	sabrá	tendrá
diremos	haremos	pondremos	sabremos	tendremos
diréis	haréis	pondréis	sabréis	tendréis
dirán	harán	pondrán	sabrán	tendrán

haber *to have*	**poder** *to be able*	**querer** *to want*	**salir** *to go out*	**venir** *to come*
habré	podré	querré	saldré	vendré
habrás	podrás	querrás	saldrás	vendrás
habrá	podrá	querrá	saldrá	vendrá
habremos	podremos	querremos	saldremos	vendremos
habréis	podréis	querréis	saldréis	vendréis
habrán	podrán	querrán	saldrán	vendrán

'Ir a' + infinitive

Another way of expressing the future is to say that you are 'going to do something'. This is done in Spanish by **ir a** + the infinitive:

voy a comer *I am going to eat*
vas a trabajar *you are going to work*

1.30 Conditional tense

This is recognized in English by the use of the word 'would' or sometimes 'should' – e.g. I would go, I should like etc.

In Spanish you form the conditional by adding the endings used for the imperfect of **–er** and **–ir** verbs to the infinitive.

hablar	**comer**	**vivir**
hablaría *I would speak*	comería *I would eat*	viviría *I would live*
hablarías *you would speak*	comerías *you would eat*	vivirías *you would live*
hablaría *he, she, you would speak*	comería *he, she, you would eat*	viviría *he, she, you would live*
hablaríamos *we would speak*	comeríamos *we would eat*	viviríamos *we would live*
hablaríais *you would speak*	comeríais *you would eat*	viviríais *you would live*
hablarían *they, you would speak*	comerían *they, you would eat*	vivirían *they, you would live*

Irregular conditionals

The same verbs that are irregular in the future are irregular in the conditional. The irregular conditionals use the same stems as the irregular futures.

decir *to say*	**hacer** *to do, make*	**poner** *to put*	**saber** *to know*	**tener** *to have*
diría	haría	pondría	sabría	tendría
dirías	harías	pondrías	sabrías	tendrías
diría	haría	pondría	sabría	tendría
diríamos	haríamos	pondríamos	sabríamos	tendríamos
diríais	haríais	pondríais	sabríais	tendríais
dirían	harían	pondrían	sabrían	tendrían

haber *to have*	**poder** *to be able*	**querer** *to want*	**salir** *to go out*	**venir** *to come*
habría	podría	querría	saldría	vendría
habrías	podrías	querrías	saldrías	vendrías
habría	podría	querría	saldría	vendría
habríamos	podríamos	querríamos	saldríamos	vendríamos
habríais	podríais	querríais	saldríais	vendríais
habrían	podrían	querrían	saldrían	vendrían

Chapter 2
Test yourself on grammar

2.1 Articles

Revise the Grammar section and then before you look at the answers give the Spanish for:

1 The teacher's chair.
2 I went to the market.
3 The new carpet.
4 The dirty water.
5 The water is dirty.
6 I like cats.
7 English is easy.
8 I learn English.
9 I speak English.
10 I know English.
11 King Charles.
12 Good evening, Mr. Gómez.
13 I know Mr. Gómez
14 I went there on Saturday.
15 King Charles the Third.
16 He is a lawyer and his wife is a Spaniard.
17 The crossword, the climate, the map, the problem, the programme, the tram.
18 The photo, the hand, the radio, the corkscrew, the windscreen.
19 The priest found a cure.
20 The captain gave an order.
21 He found an earring.
22 The apples on the appletree.
23 The address, the series, the customs.
24 He lost his pencils twice.
25 The French like the songs.
26 I like the Suárez family.

2.2 Adjectives

Revise the Grammar section and then before you look at the answers give the Spanish for:

1 The white chair and the green table.
2 Spanish cooking, talkative people.
3 We have had a good day.
4 The first book, the third table.
5 Saint Thomas was a great man.

6 His former job was in an ancient building.
7 The poor man asked for money.
8 The teacher himself made the same error.
9 Each book is extremely expensive.

2.3 Adverbs

Revise the Grammar section and then before you look at the answers give the Spanish for:

1 Carefully, simply, quietly.
2 Carefully and quietly.
3 He did it slowly and badly.
4 I am upstairs, he is downstairs.
5 I am here, he is there.
6 I often go there when I have enough money.
7 He did not come till seven, then he ate a lot and also drank a lot.
8 He has already arrived.
9 He is taller than him and a better player.
10 The main square is the most interesting place in the town.
11 She is as tall as her mother.
12 I do not have as much money as my brother.
13 Speak more slowly.

2.4 Numbers

Revise the Grammar section and then before you look at the answers write the Spanish words for:

1 16
2 23
3 34
4 101
5 506
6 702
7 950
8 200 books
9 190
10 100,000
11 1000 pounds
12 a million pounds
13 He was born in 1946.
14 The four people stayed on the fourth floor.

2.5 Time

Revise the Grammar section and then before you look at the answers give the Spanish for:

1 It is four in the morning.
2 It is eleven at night.
3 It is ten to seven in the morning.
4 It is a quarter past six in the evening.
5 At a quarter to four in the afternoon.

2.6 Negatives

Revise the Grammar section and then before you look at the answers give the Spanish for:

1 Nobody visits him.
2 He never goes to church.
3 He has no money.
4 Neither his brother nor his sister helped him.
5 I did not go and he did not go either.

2.7 Pronouns

Revise the Grammar section and then before you look at the answers give the Spanish for:

1 I saw him but he did not see me.
2 We saw her but she did not see us.
3 I visited them, they visited you, he visited us.
4 I am watching you. I am going to visit you.
5 Give it to me.
6 Do not give it to them.
7 I sent it to him.
8 I sent them to them.
9 The present is for him.
10 He wants it for himself.
11 She is with me.

2.8 Personal 'a'

Revise the Grammar section and then before you look at the answers give the Spanish for:

1 I saw my mother.
2 I saw the match.
3 I have a friend.
4 I am looking for a doctor.
5 I saw the dog in the kitchen.

2.9 Demonstrative adjectives and pronouns

Revise the Grammar section and then before you look at the answers give the Spanish for:

1 I saw this book in this room.
2 I saw that book in that room.
3 I saw these books in these rooms.
4 I saw those books in those rooms.

2.10 Possessive adjectives

Revise the Grammar section and then before you look at the answers give the Spanish for:

My chair, my chairs, your sister, your sisters, his dog, her dog, his dogs, her dogs, our house, our friends, your book, your books, their friend, their friends.

2.11 Possessive pronouns

Revise the Grammar section and then before you look at the answers give the Spanish for:
Your friend and mine, my friend and yours, your friend and ours, my friend and theirs.

2.12 Relative pronouns

1 The book that I bought.
2 The town near which I live.
3 Tell me what is happening.
4 I want to know everything that is happening.
5 The man whose wife works here.

2.13 Interrogatives

Revise the Grammar section and then before you look at the answers give the Spanish for:
1 Where are you going?
2 What time will you be back?
3 When will he arrive?
4 How many friends has he?
5 Why did he do it?
6 Who is with him?
7 Which is your favourite?

2.14 'Ser' and 'estar'

Revise the Grammar section and then before you look at the answers give the Spanish for:
1 He is a teacher.
2 It is a chair.
3 It is late.
4 It is near here.
5 The traffic lights are red.
6 The car is red.
7 I am listening.

2.15 'Conocer' and 'saber'

Revise the Grammar section and then before you look at the answers give the Spanish for:
1 I know London.
2 I know his friend.
3 I know the time.
4 I can ride a bicycle.

2.16 'Deber' and 'tener que'

Revise the Grammar section and then before you look at the answers give the Spanish for:

1 I must not keep him waiting.
2 I must work in order to live.

2.17 'Tener'

Revise the Grammar section and then before you look at the answers give the Spanish for:

1 I am hot.
2 I am cold.
3 I am hungry.
4 I am thirsty.
5 I am successful.
6 I want to go out.
7 The match takes place on Sunday.
8 I am in a great hurry.

2.18 Prepositions

Revise the Grammar section and then before you look at the answers give the Spanish for:

1 I walked along the river in spite of the weather.
2 The apple-tree is beside the house. The flowers are around the house.
3 Before arriving, I stopped near his house.
4 It is under the window against the wall.
5 From the house, you can see it in front of you.
6 After arriving, he put his coat behind the door.
7 During the exam he smoked instead of writing.
8 The flat is opposite the cinema, between two shops and is over a Post Office.
9 He is travelling towards Valencia and will not arrive until eight.
10 He earns more than me: he earns more than two thousand pounds a month. He is far from being poor.
11 According to his friends, he left without his money … everything except his credit card.
12 We arrived at about six and talked about the weather.

2.19 Present tense

Revise the Grammar section and then before you look at the answers give the Spanish for:

1 I eat fish.
2 I watch the film while he looks for his book.
3 They live in a city but I live in the country.
4 I close the door.
5 He awakens me at six.
6 They begin to study at seven.
7 We think that it is silly.
8 They sit down to eat.

9 It never snows in Spain.
10 I light the candle at nine.
11 We understand what he says.
12 They lose every game.
13 I want to go home.
14 I always have a good time in Spain.
15 He prefers France.
16 I feel tired.
17 Do you remember that day?
18 I tell the story to the child.
19 We find things under his bed.
20 They play tennis on Saturdays.
21 I fly to Spain tomorrow.
22 My arm hurts.
23 I can do it.
24 It rains in the winter.
25 We return tomorrow.
26 Do you sleep till six?
27 I am dying of hunger.
28 He says goodbye to his friends.
29 You ask for the bill.
30 They laugh when he repeats the question.
31 I continue to get dressed.
32 I do, I fall, I drive, I know, I give, I offer, I put, I know, I go out, I bring, I see.
33 I say that I am in the dining room.
34 She flees the danger.
35 We go when we hear the noise.
36 I am a member and I have a card.
37 They come from Barcelona.
38 I am eating the meal while she is talking.

2.20 Perfect tense

Revise the Grammar section and then before you look at the answers give the Spanish for:
1 I have spoken, he has eaten, they have lived.
2 I have opened the box.
3 We have covered the food.
4 They have said what they think.
5 You have discovered the truth.
6 She has written a letter.
7 I have done the same.
8 He has died.
9 I have put it on the table.
10 He has broken the chair.
11 We have seen the beach.
12 I have returned.

2.21 Preterite tense

Revise the Grammar section and then before you look at the answers give the Spanish for:
1 I spoke, he ate, she spoke, we lived, they lived, you ate (sing. fam.), you ate (pl. fam.).
2 He asked for wine though he preferred beer.
3 She laughed and followed him.
4 They felt cold as he opened the door.

5 He served the meal.
6 She smiled as she dressed.
7 I started, I played, I looked for an opportunity.
8 When he fell, they fell.
9 I gave her a kiss.
10 I went to the party. It was marvellous.
11 I walked towards him.
12 I said 'hello'.
13 He was there.
14 There was an accident.
15 I did it.
16 He could not do it.
17 We did not want to go.
18 They knew what to do.
19 I had to do it.
20 He brought me a beer.
21 He came at six.

2.22 Imperfect tense

Revise the Grammar section and then before you look at the answers give the Spanish for:

1 I was looking through the window.
2 She was eating paella.
3 We were living in Valencia.
4 I was going to visit Spain.
5 He was my friend.
6 From the balcony, one could see the city.

2.23 Pluperfect tense

Revise the Grammar section and then before you look at the answers give the Spanish for:

1 Someone had stolen my bicycle!
2 I had visited her already.
3 She had never eaten paella.
4 They had never seen Valencia.

2.24 Future tense

Revise the Grammar section and then before you look at the answers give the Spanish for:

1 I will find the book.
2 He will eat in a restaurant.
3 They will not see the film.
4 She will not say who did it.
5 There will be an accident.
6 I will do it.
7 I will be able to go.
8 He will put it on the table.
9 We will not want to go.

10 He will know the address.
11 We will go out this evening.
12 The match will not take place.
13 They will come at six.

2.25 'Ir a' + infinitive

Revise the Grammar section and then before you look at the answers give the Spanish for:
1 I am going to study this evening.
2 We are going to eat at six.
3 They are going to visit his friends.

2.26 Conditional tense

Revise the Grammar section and then before you look at the answers give the Spanish for:
1 He said that he would speak to her.
2 He said that he would not eat it.
3 He said that he would live there all his life.
4 He said that he would tell the truth.
5 He said that there would be an accident.
6 He said that he would do his homework.
7 He said that he would not be able to do it.
8 He said that he would put the book on the table.
9 He said that he would like to see me.
10 He said that he would know the result.
11 He said that he would go out with her.
12 He said that he would have to go.
13 He said that he would come to the party.

Chapter 3
Test yourself: suggested answers

Here are suggested answers to the *Test yourself* section. It should be noted that these suggestions are not the only way to translate the sentences. If in doubt you should ask your teacher.

3.1 Articles

1 La silla del profesor.
2 Fui al mercado.
3 La alfombra nueva.
4 El agua sucia.
5 El agua es sucia.
6 Me gustan los gatos.
7 El inglés es fácil.
8 Aprendo inglés.
9 Hablo inglés.
10 Sé inglés.
11 El rey Carlos.
12 Buenas tardes, señor Gómez.
13 Conozco al señor Gómez.
14 Fui allí el sábado.
15 El rey Carlos tercero.
16 Él es abogado y su esposa es española.
17 El crucigrama, el clima, el mapa, el problema, el programa, el tranvía.
18 La foto, la mano, la radio, el sacacorchos, el parabrisas.
19 El cura encontró una cura.
20 El capitán dio una órden.
21 Encontró un pendiente.
22 Las manzanas en el manzano.
23 La dirección, la serie, la aduana.
24 Perdió sus lápices dos veces.
25 A los franceses les gustan las canciones.
26 Me gusta la familia Suárez.

3.2 Adjectives

1 La silla blanca y la mesa verde.
2 La cocina española, la gente habladora.
3 Hemos tenido un buen día.
4 El primer libro, la tercera mesa.
5 Santo Tomás era un gran hombre.
6 Su antiguo puesto estaba en un edificio antiguo.

7 El hombre pobre pidió dinero.
8 El profesor mismo hizo el mismo error.
9 Cada uno de los libros es carísimo.

3.3 Adverbs

1 Cuidadosamente, sencillamente, silenciosamente.
2 Cuidadosa y silenciosamente.
3 Lo hizo lentamente y mal.
4 Estoy arriba, él está abajo.
5 Estoy aquí, él está allí.
6 Voy allí a menudo cuando tengo bastante dinero.
7 No vino hasta las siete; luego comió mucho y también bebió mucho.
8 Ya ha llegado.
9 Él es más alto que él y un mejor jugador.
10 La plaza mayor es el sitio más interesante del pueblo.
11 Ella es tan alta como su madre.
12 No tengo tanto dinero como mi hermano.
13 Habla más despacio.

3.4 Numbers

1 dieciséis
2 veintitrés
3 treinta y cuatro
4 ciento uno
5 quinientos seis
6 setecientos dos
7 novecientos cincuenta
8 doscientos libros
9 ciento noventa
10 cien mil
11 mil libras
12 un millón de libras
13 Nació en mil novecientos cuarenta y seis.
14 Las cuatro personas se quedaron en el cuarto piso.

3.5 Time

1 Son las cuatro de la madrugada.
2 Son las once de la noche.
3 Son las siete menos diez de la mañana.
4 Son las seis y cuarto de la tarde.
5 A las cuatro menos cuarto de la tarde.

3.6 Negatives

1 Nadie le visita.
2 Nunca va a la iglesia.

   3 No tiene ningún dinero.
   4 Ni su hermano ni su hermana le ayudaron.
   5 No fui y él no fue tampoco.

3.7 Pronouns

   1 Le vi pero él no me vio.
   2 La vimos pero ella no nos vio.
   3 Les visité, te visitaron, nos visitó.
   4 Estoy mirándote. Voy a visitarte.
   5 Dámelo.
   6 No se lo dé.
   7 Se lo mandé.
   8 Se los mandé.
   9 El regalo es para él.
 10 Lo quiere para sí.
 11 Está conmigo.

3.8 Personal 'a'

   1 Vi a mi madre.
   2 Vi el partido.
   3 Tengo un amigo.
   4 Busco un médico.
   5 Vi al perro en la cocina.

3.9 Demonstrative adjectives and pronouns

   1 Vi este libro en esta sala.
   2 Vi ese libro en esa sala.
   3 Vi estos libros en estas salas.
   4 Vi esos libros en esas salas.

3.10 Possessive adjectives

Mi silla, mis sillas, tu hermana, tus hermanas, su perro, su perro, sus perros, sus perros, nuestra casa, nuestros amigos, vuestro libro, vuestros libros, su amigo, sus amigos.

3.11 Possessive pronouns

Tu amigo y el mío, mi amigo y el tuyo, vuestro amigo y el nuestro, mi amigo y el suyo.

3.12 Relative pronouns

1 El libro que compré.
2 El pueblo cerca del que vivo.
3 Dime lo que pasa.
4 Quiero saber todo lo que pasa.
5 El hombre cuya esposa trabaja aquí.

3.13 Interrogatives

1 ¿Adónde vas?
2 ¿A qué hora vuelves?
3 ¿Cuándo llegará?
4 ¿Cuántos amigos tiene?
5 ¿Por qué lo hizo?
6 ¿Quién está con él?
7 ¿Cuál es tu favorito?

3.14 'Ser' and 'estar'

1 Él es profesor.
2 Es una silla.
3 Es tarde.
4 Está cerca de aquí.
5 Los semáforos están rojos.
6 El coche es rojo.
7 Estoy escuchando.

3.15 'Conocer' and 'saber'

1 Conozco Londres.
2 Conozco a su amigo.
3 Sé la hora.
4 Sé montar a bicicleta.

3.16 'Deber' and 'tener que'

1 No debo hacerle esperar.
2 Tengo que trabajar para vivir.

3.17 'Tener'

1 Tengo calor.
2 Tengo frío.

3 Tengo hambre.
4 Tengo sed.
5 Tengo éxito.
6 Tengo ganas de salir.
7 El partido tiene lugar el domingo.
8 Tengo mucha prisa.

3.18 Prepositions

1 Fui de pie a lo largo del río a pesar del tiempo.
2 El manzano está al lado de la casa. Las flores están alrededor de la casa.
3 Antes de llegar, me paré cerca de su casa.
4 Está debajo de la ventana contra la pared.
5 Desde la casa, puedes verlo delante de ti.
6 Después de llegar, puso el abrigo detrás de la puerta.
7 Durante el examen fumó en vez de escribir.
8 El piso está enfrente del cine, entre dos tiendas y está encima de una oficina de correos.
9 Viaja hacia Valencia y no llegará hasta las ocho.
10 Gana más que yo: gana más de dos mil libras al mes. Está lejos de ser pobre.
11 Según sus amigos, se fue sin su dinero … todo salvo su tarjeta de crédito.
12 Llegamos sobre las seis y hablamos sobre el tiempo.

3.19 Present tense

1 Como pescado.
2 Miro la película mientras él busca su libro.
3 Viven en la ciudad pero yo vivo en el campo.
4 Cierro la puerta.
5 Me despierta a las seis.
6 Empiezan a estudiar a las siete.
7 Pensamos que es tonto.
8 Se sientan para comer.
9 Nunca nieva en España.
10 Enciendo la vela a las nueve.
11 Entendemos lo que dice.
12 Pierden todos los partidos.
13 Quiero ir a casa.
14 Siempre me divierto en España.
15 Prefiere Francia.
16 Me siento cansado.
17 ¿Te acuerdas de aquel día?
18 Cuento la historia al niño.
19 Encontramos cosas debajo de su cama.
20 Juegan al tenis los sábados.
21 Vuelo a España mañana.
22 Me duele el brazo.
23 Sé hacerlo.
24 Llueve en invierno.
25 Volvemos mañana.
26 ¿Duermes hasta las seis?
27 Me muero de hambre.
28 Se despide de sus amigos.
29 Pides la cuenta.
30 Se ríen cuando repite la pregunta.
31 Sigo vistiéndome.

32 Hago, me caigo, conduzco, sé, doy, ofrezco, pongo, conozco, salgo, traigo, veo.
33 Digo que estoy en el comedor.
34 Huye del peligro.
35 Nos vamos cuando oímos el ruido.
36 Soy miembro y tengo una tarjeta.
37 Vienen de Barcelona.
38 Estoy comiendo la comida mientras ella está hablando.

3.20 Perfect tense

1 He hablado, él ha comido, han vivido.
2 He abierto la caja.
3 Hemos cubierto la comida.
4 Han dicho lo que piensan.
5 Has descubierto la verdad.
6 Ella ha escrito una carta.
7 He hecho igual.
8 Se ha muerto.
9 Lo he puesto en la mesa.
10 Ha roto la silla.
11 Hemos visto la playa.
12 He vuelto.

3.21 Preterite tense

1 Hablé, comió, habló, vivimos, vivieron, comiste, comisteis.
2 Pidió vino aunque prefiría cerveza.
3 Se rió y le siguió.
4 Se sintieron fríos cuando abrió la puerta.
5 Sirvió la comida.
6 Sonrió mientras se vistió.
7 Empecé, jugué, busqué una oportunidad.
8 Cuando se cayó él, se cayeron ellos.
9 Le di un beso.
10 Fui a la fiesta. Fue maravillosa.
11 Anduve hacia él.
12 Dije 'hola'.
13 Estuvo allí.
14 Hubo un accidente.
15 Lo hice.
16 No pudo hacerlo.
17 No quisimos marcharnos.
18 Supieron qué hacer.
19 Tuve que hacerlo.
20 Me trajo una cerveza.
21 Vino a las seis.

3.22 Imperfect tense

1 Miraba por la ventana.
2 Comía paella.
3 Vivíamos en Valencia.

4   Iba a visitar España.
5   Era mi amigo.
6   Desde el balcón, se veía la ciudad.

3.23 Pluperfect tense

1   Alguien había robado mi bicicleta.
2   Ya la había visitado.
3   Nunca había comido paella.
4   Nunca habían visto Valencia.

3.24 Future tense

1   Encontraré el libro.
2   Comerá en un restaurante.
3   No verán la película.
4   No dirá quién lo hizo.
5   Habrá un accidente.
6   Lo haré.
7   Podré ir.
8   Lo pondrá en la mesa.
9   No querremos ir.
10 Sabrá la dirección.
11 Saldremos esta tarde.
12 El partido no tendrá lugar.
13 Vendrán a las seis.

3.25 'Ir a' + infinitive

1   Voy a estudiar esta tarde.
2   Vamos a comer a las seis.
3   Van a visitar a sus amigos.

3.26 Conditional tense

1   Dijo que hablaría con ella.
2   Dijo que no lo comería.
3   Dijo que viviría allí toda su vida.
4   Dijo que diría la verdad.
5   Dijo que habría un accidente.
6   Dijo que haría sus deberes.
7   Dijo que no podría hacerlo.
8   Dijo que pondría el libro en la mesa.
9   Dijo que querría verme.
10 Dijo que sabría el resultado.
11 Dijo que saldría con ella.
12 Dijo que tendría que ir.
13 Dijo que vendría a la fiesta.

Chapter 4
Vocabulary topic areas, notions, functions

The syllabus for your examination board will list the following:

❶ A series of *Notions*. A *Notion* is something like presence, absence, location, duration, dimension and difference.

❷ A series of *Functions*. A *Function* is what we do with language, e.g. we can use language to assert, question, command, persuade, apologize.

❸ A list of vocabulary which the person who sets the exams uses. He or she cannot test you on a word that is not on this list.

The following lists are all you need to cover the Notions, Functions and Vocabulary requirements.

TIME

lunes Monday
martes Tuesday
miércoles Wednesday
jueves Thursday
viernes Friday
sábado Saturday
domingo Sunday

el lunes on Monday
los lunes on Mondays
por la mañana in the morning
por la tarde in the afternoon
por la noche at night
todos los días every day
todas las tardes every afternoon
todas las noches every night

a menudo often
a veces sometimes
anoche last night
anteayer the day before yesterday
ayer yesterday
de vez en cuando sometimes
el año próximo next year
el año que viene next year
el fin de semana the weekend
el viernes pasado last Friday
el viernes que viene next Friday
este año this year
hace una semana a week ago
hoy today
la semana que viene next week
mañana tomorrow
pasado mañana the day after tomorrow
en el siglo veinte in the twentieth century

el día de Año Nuevo New Year's Day
el día de Navidad Christmas Day
el día de Reyes Twelfth Night
la Nochebuena Christmas Eve
la Nochevieja New Year's Eve
la Semana Santa Holy Week
el Viernes Santo Good Friday

MONTHS AND SEASONS

la estación season
el mes month

enero January
febrero February
marzo March
abril April
mayo May
junio June
julio July
agosto August
se(p)tiembre September
octubre October
noviembre November
diciembre December

¿qué fecha es? what date is it?
es el dos de mayo it is the second of May
¿a cuántos estamos hoy? what date is it?
estamos a dos de mayo it is the second of May
¿qué día es? what day is it?
es lunes it's Monday

la primavera spring
el verano summer
el otoño autumn
el invierno winter
la estación season

a principios de marzo at the beginning of March

a mediados de abril in the middle of April

a fines de mayo at the end of May

COLOURS

amarillo yellow
azul blue
blanco white
color naranja orange
gris grey
marrón brown
moreno/oscuro dark
negro black
rojo red
rubio blond
verde green
¿de qué color es? what colour is it?
es azul it is blue

MYSELF

el apellido surname
el nombre first name
el nombre de pila first name
me llamo … my name is …

la avenida avenue
la casa house
la calle street
la ciudad city
la dirección, las señas, el domicilio address
el número number
el país country
la plaza square
el pueblo town

vivir to live
¿cuál es tu número de teléfono? what is your telephone number?

Age

el adulto adult
el año year
el bebé baby
el cumpleaños birthday
la edad age
la fecha de nacimiento date of birth
el lugar place
mayor older
menor younger
el mes month
el santo saint's day

morir to die
nacer to be born
nací en Madrid I was born in Madrid
tengo dieciséis años I am 16

Nationality

soy alemán I am German
soy británico I am British
soy español I am Spanish
soy escocés I am Scottish
soy francés I am French

soy galés I am Welsh
soy inglés I am English
soy irlandés I am Irish

soy de Alemania I am from Germany

España	Spain
Escocia	Scotland
Francia	France
Gales	Wales
Inglaterra	England
Irlanda	Ireland

Family

el/la abuelo/a grandfather/grandmother
los abuelos grandparents
el/la cuñado/a brother-in-law/sister-in-law
el esposo, el marido husband
la esposa, la mujer wife
el hermano brother
la hermana sister
la hija daughter
el hijo son
el hijo único only child
la madre mother
el/la nieto/a grandson/daughter
el/la novio/a boy/girlfriend, fiancé(e), bridegroom/bride
el padre father
el/la pariente relative
el/la primo/a cousin
el/la sobrino/a nephew/niece
el/la suegro/a father-in-law/mother-in-law
el/la tío/a uncle/aunt

Status

casado married
divorciado divorced
prometido engaged
separado separated
soltero single
viudo widower

Descriptions

¿cómo es? what is he/she like?
soy alto I am tall
soy bajo I am small
soy mediano I am medium-size
soy joven I am young
soy viejo I am old
soy delgado I am thin
soy gordo I am fat
soy guapo I am handsome
soy feo I am ugly
soy fuerte I am strong

algo guapo rather handsome
bastante feo rather ugly
demasiado alto too tall

llevo gafas I wear glasses
mido un metro setenta I am one metre 70 tall
soy calvo I am bald
soy moreno I am dark
soy pálido I am pale
soy pelirrojo I am red-headed
soy rubio I am blond

tengo barba I have a beard
tengo bigote I have a moustache
tengo el pelo corto I have short hair
tengo el pelo largo I have long hair
tengo los ojos azules I have blue eyes

envejecer to get old
parecerse a to look like

activo active
alegre happy
amable nice
antipático nasty
callado quiet
cortés polite
cruel cruel
divertido amusing
encantador enchanting
estúpido stupid
feliz happy
hablador talkative
imbécil stupid
infeliz unhappy
inteligente intelligent
listo clever
loco mad
perezoso lazy
reservado shy
simpático nice
tímido shy
tonto silly
trabajador hard-working
triste sad
vivo lively

EMOTIONS

aburrirse to be bored
estar contento to be happy
gozar de to enjoy
inquietarse por to be worried about
llorar to cry
odiar to hate
preocuparse por to worry about
pasarlo bien to have a good time
pasarlo bomba to have a great time
querer to love
reírse de to laugh at
sonreír to smile
tener miedo to be frightened

aburrido bored
alegre happy
de buen humor in a good mood
de mal humor in a bad mood
preocupado worried
triste sad

el amor love
la lágrima tear
el miedo fear
el odio hatred
la risa laughter
la sonrisa smile

MENTAL PROCESSES

acordarse de to remember
aprender to learn

comprender to understand
conocer to get to know
creer to believe
darse cuenta de to realize
dudar to hesitate
estar seguro to be sure
olvidar to forget
pensar to think
preguntarse to wonder
querer to want
recordar to remember
suponer to suppose

WORK

el abogado lawyer
el actor actor
la actriz actress
el ama de casa (f) housewife
el arquitecto architect
el/la artista artist
la azafata air-hostess
el bombero fireman
el/la cajero/a cashier
el camarero waiter
el/la cantante singer
el carnicero butcher
el carpintero carpenter
el cartero postman
el/la científico/a scientist
el/la cocinero/a cook
el/la conductor/a driver
el cura priest
el dentista dentist
el dependiente shop assistant
el/la deportista sportsperson
el director headmaster
el dueño owner
el electricista electrician
el/la empleado/a employee
el/la enfermero/a nurse
el/la escritor/a writer
el/la estudiante student
el fontanero plumber
el/la fotógrafo/a photographer
el/la funcionario/a civil servant
el/la gerente manager
el/la granjero/a farmer
el hombre de negocios businessman
el/la ingeniero engineer
el/la jardinero gardener
el/la jefe boss
el/la juez judge
el/la maestro/a primary-school teacher
el marinero sailor
el/la mecanógrafo/a typist
el/la médico/a doctor
el/la músico/a musician
el obrero workman
el/la panadero/a baker
el/la peluquero/a hairdresser
el/la periodista journalist
el pescador fisherman
el/la piloto pilot

el/la **policía** policeman/woman
el **portero** doorman
el/la **profesor/a** teacher
el/la **propietario/a** owner
el/la **recepcionista** receptionist
el/la **representante** rep
el/la **secretario/a** secretary
el **soldado** soldier
el/la **taquimecanógrafo/a** shorthand typist
el/la **tendero/a** shopkeeper
el/la **vendedor/a** salesperson
el/la **verdulero/a** greengrocer

estar al paro to be unemployed
ganarse la vida to earn your living

ANIMALS

el **burro** donkey
el **caballo** horse
la **cabra** goat
el **cerdo** pig
el **conejo** rabbit
la **gallina** hen
el **gato** cat
la **oveja** sheep
el **pájaro** bird
el **perro** dog
el **pez** fish
el **pez rojo** goldfish
el **pollo** chicken
la **rata** rat
el **ratón** mouse
la **tortuga** tortoise
la **vaca** cow

THE HOUSE

el **ascensor** lift
el **balcón** balcony
la **bombilla** bulb
la **calefacción central** central heating
la **cerradura** lock
el **cristal** pane of glass
la **chimenea** chimney
el **edificio** building
la **electricidad** electricity
la **entrada** entrance
la **escalera** stairs
el **garaje** garage
el **gas** gas
la **habitación** room
el **humo** smoke
el **interruptor** switch
la **luz** light
la **llave** key
el **muro** wall
la **pared** wall
la **persiana** shutter
la **planta baja** ground floor
el **primer piso** first floor
el **rincón** corner
el **sótano** basement
el **suelo** floor
el **techo** ceiling

el **tejado** roof
la **terraza** terrace
la **ventana** window
el **vestíbulo** hall
el **vidrio** glass

abajo downstairs
amueblado furnished
arriba upstairs
cómodo comfortable
espacioso spacious
lujoso luxurious
moderno modern
pintado painted

alquilar to rent, to hire
apagar to switch off
arreglar to tidy
cerrar con llave to lock
encender to switch on
funcionar to work properly
hacer los quehaceres to do the household
   chores
limpiar to clean
llamar a la puerta to knock at the door
mudarse to move house
pasar la aspiradora to vacuum-clean
tocar el timbre to ring the bell

almorzar to have lunch
cenar to have your evening meal
comer to eat, to have lunch
desayunar to have breakfast
merendar to have a snack

el **almuerzo** lunch
la **cena** evening meal
la **comida** lunch
el **desayuno** breakfast
la **merienda** snack, picnic

acostarse to go to bed
despertarse to wake up
dormir to sleep
dormir la siesta to have a snooze
dormirse to fall asleep
levantarse to get up
madrugar to wake up early
soñar to dream

bañarse to have a bath
ducharse to have a shower
peinarse to comb your hair
ponerse to put on (clothes)
vestirse to get dressed

barrer to sweep up
limpiar la casa to clean the house
quitar el polvo to do the dusting

The garden

el **árbol** tree
el **banco** bench
el **césped** lawn
el **columpio** swing
la **flor** flower
la **fuente** fountain
las **malas hierbas** weeds

el manzano apple tree
el peral pear tree
la planta plant

cortar la hierba to cut the grass
regar las plantas to water the plants

The kitchen
la aspiradora vacuum cleaner
la bandeja tray
la basura rubbish
la cacerola saucepan
la cafetera coffee pot
la cocina de gas gas cooker
la cocina eléctrica electric cooker
el congelador freezer
el estante shelf
la lavadora washing machine
el lavaplatos dishwasher
la nevera fridge
la plancha iron
el platillo saucer
el plato plate
la sartén frying pan
el taburete stool
la taza cup

barrer to sweep
calentar to heat up
cocinar to cook
congelar to freeze
cortar to cut
fregar to scrub
freír to fry
hervir to boil
lavar los platos to wash the dishes
planchar la ropa to do the ironing

The dining room
el aparador sideboard
la cuchara spoon
el cuchillo knife
el mantel tablecloth
la mesa table
la servilleta serviette
la silla chair
el tenedor fork
el vaso glass

beber to drink
cenar to have the evening meal
comer to eat
merendar to have an afternoon snack
desayunar to have breakfast
poner la mesa to lay the table
quitar la mesa to clear the table

The living room
la alfombra carpet
la butaca armchair
la chimenea fireplace
la cortina curtain
el cuadro picture
el disco record
el estéreo stereo
el florero vase

la fotografía photograph
la radio radio
el reloj clock
el sillón armchair
el sofá settee
el televisor TV set
el tocadiscos record player
el vídeo video recorder

descansar to rest

The bathroom
el aseo toilet
el baño bath
el cepillo de dientes toothbrush
el champú shampoo
el espejo mirror
la esponja sponge
el grifo tap
el jabón soap
el lavabo sink
la pasta de dientes toothpaste
la toalla towel

abrir el grifo to turn on the tap
afeitarse to shave
arreglarse to tidy oneself up
cerrar el grifo to turn off the tap
ducharse to shower
lavarse to wash
peinarse to comb your hair

The bedroom
la almohada pillow
el armario cupboard
la cama de matrimonio double bed
la cama individual single bed
la cómoda chest of drawers
el despertador alarm clock
la guardarropa wardrobe
la manta blanket
la sábana sheet
el tocador dressing table

despertarse to wake up
dormir to sleep
dormirse to fall asleep
hacer la cama to make the bed
levantarse to get up
vestirse to get dressed

IN THE COUNTRY
las afueras outskirts
el/la aldeano/a villager
los alrededores outskirts
el ambiente atmosphere
el animal animal
el árbol tree
el bosque wood
el/la campesino/a country person
el campo field
el castillo castle
la colina hill
la finca farm
la flor flower

la granja farm
el mar sea
la montaña mountain
el paisaje countryside
el prado meadow
la provincia province
el pueblecito small town
la región region
la sierra mountain range

THE TOWN/CITY

la acera pavement
el almacén store
el aparcamiento car park
la arquitectura architecture
el autobús bus
el autocar coach
la autopista motorway
la avenida avenue
el ayuntamiento town hall
el baile dance
el barrio district
la biblioteca library
la bocacalle side-street
el buzón post box
la cabina telefónica phone box
la calle mayor main street
la capital capital
la carretera road
el cartel poster
la catedral cathedral
el centro centre
la ciudad city
el/la ciudadano/a citizen
el club para jóvenes youth club
la comisaría police station
el concurso competition
correos post office
el cruce crossroads
la discoteca disco
la distancia distance
el edificio building
el embotellamiento traffic jam
el escaparate shop window
la esquina outside corner
el estadio stadium
el estanco shop that sells tobacco and stamps
la estatua statue
la feria fair
la industria industry
el jardín zoológico zoo
el lago lake
el letrero sign
el lugar place
el mercado market
el metro underground railway
el monumento monument
la muchedumbre crowd
la mudanza house move
el muro wall
el museo museum
el país country
el parque park

el paseo stroll
el paso de peatones pedestrian crossing
la plaza mayor main square
la plaza de toros bullring
el pueblo town
el puente bridge
el puerto port
RENFE Spanish Railways
el río river
los semáforos traffic lights
el sitio place
la tienda shop
la torre tower
el tráfico traffic
el transporte público public transport
la vecindad neighbourhood
el/la vecino/a neighbour

acercarse to approach
alejarse to move away
andar to walk
aparcar to park
aproximarse to approach
atravesar to cross
cruzar to cross
dar un paseo to go for a walk
dirigirse to head for
doblar la esquina to turn the corner
encontrar to meet, to find
mostrar to show
pasearse to go for a walk
perderse to get lost
quedarse to stay
torcer a la derecha to turn right
vivir to live

ancho wide
antiguo ancient
atractivo attractive
cercano nearby
clásico classic
estrecho narrow
largo long
limpio clean
moderno modern
municipal municipal
peligroso dangerous
recto straight
ruidoso noisy
sano healthy
sucio dirty
tranquilo quiet

DIRECTIONS

alrededor de around
a la derecha to the right
a la izquierda to the left
al final de at the end of
al fondo at the bottom
al lado de beside
allá there
allí there
a lo largo de along
a mano derecha on the right-hand side

a mano izquierda on the left-hand side
antes de before
aquí here
cerca de near
debajo de under
delante de in front of
detrás de behind
dentro de inside
después de after
encima de above
enfrente opposite
entre between
frente a opposite
fuera de outside
lejos de far from
todo derecho straight on
todo recto straight on
todo seguido straight on

el este east
el norte north
el oeste west
el sur south

SCHOOL

el bolígrafo ball-point pen
el colegio school
la escuela primary school
el instituto school
la universidad university

el aula (f) classroom
la biblioteca library
el campo de deportes sports field
la cantina canteen
la clase class
el computador computer
el despacho office
la goma rubber
el gimnasio gym
el laboratorio laboratory
el lápiz pencil
el libro book
la oficina office
el ordenador computer
el papel paper
la pared wall
el patio playground
la piscina swimming pool
la pizarra blackboard
la pluma pen
la regla ruler
la sala de profesores staff room

el/la alumno/a pupil
el/la estudiante student
el/la interno/a boarder
el/la externo/a non-boarder
el/la maestro/a primary teacher
el/la profesor/a teacher
el/la director/a headteacher

mixto mixed
moderno modern
viejo old

amable nice
antipático nasty
estricto strict
exigente demanding
hablador talkative
inteligente intelligent
listo clever
perezoso lazy
severo strict
simpático nice
tonto stupid
torpe clumsy
trabajador hard-working

encontrarse to be found
estar situado to be found
hallarse to be found

Subjects

el alemán German
el arte art
la biología biology
las ciencias sciences
la cocina cookery
el comercio commerce, business studies
el dibujo drawing, art
la educación física PE
el español Spanish
la física physics
el francés French
la geografía geography
la gimnasia gymnastics
la historia history
los idiomas languages
la informática IT (information technology)
el inglés English
el latín Latin
las lenguas languages
las matemáticas maths
la mecanografía typing
la música music
la química chemistry
la religión religion
la taquigrafía shorthand
los trabajos manuales craft

aburrido boring
difícil difficult
fácil easy
interesante interesting
pesado boring
práctico practical
útil useful

Daily routine

ir al colegio to go to school
en autobús by bus
en bicicleta by bicycle
en coche by car
a pie on foot
andando on foot

empezar to begin
llegar to arrive
terminar to finish

venir to come
volver to return

la hora de comer lunchtime
el horario timetable
el recreo break

aprender to learn
aprobar un examen to pass an exam
contestar to answer
enseñar to teach
escoger to choose
escribir to write
escuchar to listen
estudiar to study
fracasar los exámenes to fail exams
hacer deberes to do homework
hacer un examen to take an exam
leer to read
mirar to look at
odiar to hate
pasar lista to call the register
practicar to practise
preguntar to ask
repetir to repeat
responder to answer
sacar buenas notas to get good marks
sacar malas notas to get bad marks
seguir un curso to follow a course
suspender to fail someone (in an exam)
tener éxito to be successful
trabajar to work
traducir to translate

Discipline
castigar to punish
copiar to copy
corregir to correct
charlar to chat
desobedecer to disobey
prohibir to forbid

Activities
el ajedrez chess
el atletismo athletics
el baloncesto basketball
la fotografía photography
la natación swimming

encantar (me encanta el arte) to please
 (I love art)
interesar to interest
organizar to organize
pertenecer to belong
ser miembro/socio to be a member
tener lugar to take place
tomar parte en to take part in

School uniform
el abrigo overcoat
la blusa blouse
los calcetines socks
la camisa shirt
la corbata tie
la chaqueta jacket

la falda skirt
el impermeable raincoat
las medias stockings
el pantalón trousers
el vestido dress
los zapatos shoes

estar vestido de to be dressed in
llevar to wear
ponerse to put on
quitarse to take off
vestirse to put on

FREE TIME AND ENTERTAINMENT
el baile dance
la cámara camera
la caña de pescar fishing rod
el cine cinema
la colección collection
el computador computer
el concierto concert
el concurso competition
el conjunto pop group
los dibujos animados cartoons
el disco record
la discoteca disco
la entrada ticket
el equipo team
el estadio stadium
la exposición exhibition
la guitarra guitar
el instrumento instrument
el interés interest
la lectura reading
el libro book
la localidad ticket (e.g. for concert)
la lotería lottery
la música pop pop music
la música rock rock music
la novela novel
la novela policíaca detective novel
la novela de ciencia-ficción science-fiction
 novel
la orquesta orchestra
el parque park
el parque de atracciones theme park
el partido game (e.g. football)
el pasatiempo hobby
el paseo stroll
la película film
la película de miedo horror film
la película de ciencia-ficción science
 fiction film
la radio radio
la sala de billar billiard hall
la sala de fiestas dance hall
la sesión showing (of a film)
la taquilla ticket office
el/la taquillero/a ticket seller
el teatro theatre

bailar to dance
coleccionar to collect
cantar to sing

citarse to arrange to meet
conocer to know, to get to know
coser to sew
dar una vuelta/un paseo to go for a walk
dibujar to draw
divertirse to have a good time
empatar to draw (a game)
entrenarse to train
escuchar música to listen to music
estrenar to give the premiere
ganar to win
hacer cola to queue
interesarse en/por to be interested in
invitar to invite
ir en bicicleta to go cycling
leer to read
mirar to watch
montar a caballo to go horse-riding
pasarlo bien to have a good time
pasarlo bomba to have a great time
pasearse to go for a walk
patinar to skate
perder to lose
pescar to fish
pintar to paint
reunirse to meet up
sacar fotos to take photos
ser aficionado a to be keen on
tocar un instrumento to play an instrument
vencer to win

SPORTS

el atletismo athletics
el baloncesto basketball
la balonred netball
el billar billiards
la carrera race
el ciclismo cycling
la corrida de toros bullfight
la equitación horse-riding
el esquí skiing
el footing jogging
el fútbol football
la gimnasia gymnastics
la natación swimming
el patinaje skating
la pesca fishing
la plancha de vela windsurfing
el tenis tennis
la vela sailing
el voleibol volleyball

TRANSPORT (CAR)

el aceite oil
el agua (f) water
el aparcamiento car park
la autopista motorway
el/la autostopista hitchhiker
la avería breakdown
la batería battery
la bombilla light bulb
el carnet de conducir driving licence
la carretera road

el coche car
el/la conductor/a driver
el faro headlamp
el freno brake
la gasolina petrol
la gasolina sin plomo lead-free petrol
la gasolina súper four-star petrol
el maletero boot (of car)
el mapa map
la matrícula car registration
el motor engine
el neumático tyre
las obras roadworks
el paso de peatones pedestrian crossing
el parabrisas windscreen
el pinchazo puncture
la rueda wheel
la rueda de repuesto spare wheel
el seguro insurance
los semáforos traffic lights
el tubo de escape exhaust pipe
la velocidad speed
el volante steering wheel

adelantar to overtake
aparcar to park
averiarse to break down
comprobar to check
conducir to drive
hacer autostop to hitchhike
frenar to brake
llenar el depósito to fill up
quedarse sin gasolina to run out of petrol
reparar to repair

averiado broken down

PUBLIC TRANSPORT

el aeropuerto airport
el aterrizaje landing
el avión plane
la azafata air-hostess
el cinturón de seguridad seatbelt
el despegue take-off
el vuelo flight

abrochar to fasten (seatbelt)
aterrizar to land
despegar to take off
volar to fly

el barco ship
el buque ship
la costa coast
la isla island
el mar sea
el/la pasajero/a passenger

desembarcarse to disembark
embarcarse to embark
ir a bordo to go on board
ir a tierra to land
marearse to get sea-sick

agitado rough (sea)
tranquilo smooth

el andén platform
el aviso notice
el billete ticket
el billete de ida single ticket
el billete de ida y vuelta return ticket
el billete de primera clase first-class ticket
el billete de segunda clase second-class
    ticket
la cantina buffet
el coche coach
el coche-cama sleeping car
el coche-restorán dining car
la consigna left luggage
el departamento compartment
el despacho de billetes ticket office
el destino destination
el equipaje luggage
la estación station
el ferrocarril railway
el horario timetable
el jefe de la estación station master
la llegada arrival
la maleta suitcase
la máquina engine
el mozo porter
el paso subterráneo subway
el precio price
el rápido express train
RENFE Spanish Railways
la reserva reservation
el retraso delay
el revisor ticket inspector
la sala de espera waiting room
la salida exit
la señal de alarma alarm signal
el Talgo luxury train
la taquilla ticket office
el/la taquillero/a ticket seller
la ventanilla window
la vía track
el viaje journey
el/la viajero/a traveller

asomarse to lean out of the window
bajar to get off
cambiar to change
coger to catch (e.g. the train)
durar to last
hacer transbordo to change (train)
llegar to arrive
perder to lose
sacar un billete to buy a ticket
salir to depart
subir to board
viajar to travel

HOLIDAYS

Alemania (f) Germany
América (f) del Sur South America
Argentina (f) Argentina
Austria (f) Austria
Bélgica (f) Belgium
Colombia (f) Colombia
Cuba (f) Cuba

Dinamarca (f) Denmark
Escocia (f) Scotland
España (f) Spain
Los Estados Unidos USA
Francia (f) France
Grecia (f) Greece
Inglaterra (f) England
Irlanda (f) Ireland
Italia (f) Italy
Méjico (m) Mexico
País (m) de Gales Wales
Portugal (m) Portugal
el Reino Unido UK
Rusia (f) Russia
Suiza (f) Switzerland

alemán German
americano American
argentino Argentinian
austriaco Austrian
belga Belgian
colombiano Colombian
cubano Cuban
danés Danish
escocés Scottish
español Spanish
francés French
galés Welsh
griego Greek
inglés English
irlandés Irish
italiano Italian
mejicano Mexican
portugués Portuguese
ruso Russian
sudamericano South American
suizo Swiss

estar de vacaciones to be on holiday
ir de vacaciones to go on holidays
sacar fotos to take photos
pasar las vacaciones to spend the holidays
valer la pena to be worth while

las vacaciones de Navidad Christmas
    holidays
las vacaciones de Semana Santa Easter
    holidays
las vacaciones de verano Summer holidays

la aduana customs
la frontera border
el pasaporte passport
el/la turista tourist

algo que declarar something to declare
nada que declarar nothing to declare

abrir la maleta to open your suitcase
esconder to hide
mostrar to show
pasar por la aduana to go through customs

el hotel de lujo luxury hotel
el hotel de dos estrellas two-star hotel
la pensión boarding house

la caravana caravan
la linterna torch

el saco de dormir sleeping bag
la tienda (de compaña) tent

acampar to camp
alquilar to hire
bajar una tienda to take down a tent
hacer camping to camp
ir de camping to camp
montar una tienda to put up a tent

el albergue juvenil youth hostel
la arena sand
el bañador swimming costume
el bikini bikini
la costa coast
el cubo bucket
las gafas de sol sun glasses
la insolación sun stroke
la loción bronceadora sun lotion
el mar sea
la mochila rucksack
la montaña mountain
la playa beach
la ola wave
la silla plegable deckchair
el sol sun
la sombra shade
la toalla towel
el traje de baño bathing costume

alojarse to stay
bañarse to bathe
broncearse to sunbathe
cazar to hunt
dar un paseo en barco de vela to go for a sail
descansar to rest
esquiar to ski
hacer el esquí acuático to go water-skiing
nadar to swim
ponerse moreno to go brown
tenderse al sol to sunbathe
tomar el sol to sunbathe
tostarse to sunbathe
zambullirse to dive

MEETING PEOPLE

buenos días good day
buenas tardes good afternoon
buenas noches good night
hola hello

encantado pleased to meet you
mucho gusto pleased to meet you

bienvenido welcome
¡buen viaje! have a good trip!
¡enhorabuena! congratulations!
¡felices pascuas! happy Christmas!
¡felicitaciones! congratulations!
¡suerte! good luck!

¿cómo estás? how are you?
¿qué tal? how are you?
¿cómo vas? how are you?
¿qué pasa? what's the matter?
te presento a mi amigo I'll introduce you
   to my friend
así así so so

bien, gracias fine thank you
adiós goodbye
hasta luego goodbye
hasta el lunes see you on Monday
hasta la vista goodbye

el abrazo hug
el beso kiss
el cariño affection

abrazar to hug
besar to kiss
saludar to greet

estoy bien I'm fine
me siento bien I feel fine
gracias thank you
de nada don't mention it
¿qué hay? what's new?
¡regular! things are OK
¡tirando! I'm OK

el/la amigo/a friend
la amistad friendship
el/la compañero/a friend
el/la correspondiente penfriend
el/la chico/a boy/girl
la gente people
el/la muchacho/a youngster
la persona person

¡caramba! gosh!
¡dios mío! good heavens!
¡ni hablar! no way!
¡qué asco! how disgusting!
¡qué bien! how nice!
¡qué horror! how horrible!

¡qué lástima! what a pity!
¡qué suerte! how lucky!
¡qué susto! what a fright!
¡qué pena! what a pity!

¿de veras? really?
¡salud! cheers!
¡que aproveche! enjoy your meal!

¡claro! of course!
¡desde luego! of course!
lo siento I'm sorry
no entiendo I don't understand
¡vale! OK!

tutearse to use 'tú' (not 'Usted')

la cita date, meeting
la fiesta party
el guateque party
la invitación invitation

aceptar to accept
dar las gracias to thank
invitar to invite
llamar por teléfono to phone someone

el auricular receiver
la cabina kiosk
la guía telefónica phone book
la llamada phone call
la moneda coin
el recado message

¡al aparato! speaking!
¿de parte de quién? who is speaking?
¡diga! hello (when answering)
¡está comunicando! it's engaged!
¿quién habla? who is speaking?
¡oiga! hello (when you are phoning)
póngame con... please may I speak to ...?
soy Toni it's me, it's Tony

colgar to hang up
introducir monedas to put in coins
llamar to call
mandar to send
marcar to dial

SHOPPING

la carnicería butcher's
la confitería sweet shop
la droguería hardware store
el estanco shop for tobacco and stamps
la frutería fruit shop
los grandes almacenes store
la lechería dairy
la librería bookshop
el mercado market
la panadería bakery
la papelería stationer's
la pastelería cake shop
la pescadería fishmonger's
el supermercado supermarket
la tienda de comestibles grocer's
la tienda de ultramarinos grocer's
la verdulería greengrocer's
la zapatería shoe shop

el/la carnicero/a butcher
el/la confitero/a sweetshop owner
el/la frutero/a fruit seller
el/la panadero/a baker
el/la papelero/a stationer
el/la pastelero/a cake shop owner
el/la pescadero/a fishmonger
el/la verdulero/a greengrocer
el/la zapatero/a cobbler

el biftec/bistec steak
la carne meat
la carne de vaca beef
la carne picada minced beef
el cerdo pork
el cocido stew
el conejo rabbit
el cordero lamb
el chorizo garlic sausage
la chuleta chop
el filete fillet steak
la hamburguesa hamburger
el hígado liver
el jamón ham
el lomo loin
el pato duck
el pollo chicken
la salchicha sausage
el solomillo sirloin
la ternera veal

el bacalao cod
los boquerones anchovies
los calamares squid
la langosta lobster
el lenguado sole
las gambas prawns
los mariscos sea-food
los mejillones mussels
la merluza hake
el pescado fish
el pulpo octopus
las sardinas sardines
la trucha trout

la aceituna olive
el albaricoque apricot
la cereza cherry
la ciruela plum
la frambuesa raspberry
la fresa strawberry
la fruta fruit
el higo fig
el limón lemon
la manzana apple
el melocotón peach
el melón melon
la naranja orange
la pera pear
la piña pineapple
el plátano banana
la sandía watermelon
la uva grape

el arroz rice
el ajo garlic
la cebolla onion
la col de Bruselas sprouts
la coliflor cauliflower
los champiñones mushrooms
la ensalada salad
las espinacas spinach
los guisantes peas
las judías beans
la lechuga lettuce
las legumbres vegetables
las patatas potatoes
el pimiento pepper
el repollo cabbage
los tomates tomatoes
las verduras vegetables
la zanahoria carrot

el aceite cooking oil
el azúcar sugar
el chocolate chocolate
la sal salt
la salsa sauce
el vinagre vinegar

los alimentos congelados frozen food
el bocadillo sandwich
el bollo bun
el caramelo sweet
el churro churro, doughnut
los entremeses starters
el flan crème caramel
el gazpacho cold soup
el helado ice cream
el huevo egg
la mantequilla butter

la mayonesa mayonnaise
la mermelada jam
la nata cream
la paella paella
el pan bread
el panecillo roll
el pastel cake
el postre dessert
el queso cheese
la sopa soup
el suizo bun
la tapa bar snack
la tarta cake
la tortilla omelette
la tostada slice of toast
el yogur yoghurt
el agua (f) **mineral con gas** mineral water (fizzy)
el agua (f) **mineral sin gas** mineral water (still)
el café con leche white coffee
el café solo black coffee
la cerveza beer
el coñac brandy
el jerez sherry
la leche milk
la limonada lemonade
la naranjada orangeade
el refresco soft drink
el ron rum
el té tea
el vino blanco white wine
el vino rosado rosé wine
el vino tinto red wine
el zumo de fruta juice

la barra de pan a loaf of bread
la bolsa bag
la botella bottle
la caja box
la cucharada spoonful
la docena dozen
el gramo gramme
el kilo kilo
la lata tin
la libra pound
el paquete packet
el pedazo piece
la taza cup
el trozo piece
la ración portion
el vaso glass

el abrigo overcoat
la bata dressing gown
la blusa blouse
las botas boots
la bufanda scarf
los calcetines socks
la camisa shirt
la camiseta tee shirt
el cinturón belt
la corbata tie
la chaqueta jacket
la falda skirt
los guantes gloves
el impermeable raincoat
el jersey jersey

las medias stockings
la moda fashion
el número size
el pantalón trousers
el pantalón corto shorts
un par de pair of
el pijama pyjamas
el probador changing cubicle
la ropa clothes
la ropa interior underclothes
el sombrero hat
la talla size
el traje suit
el traje de baño bathing costume
los vaqueros jeans
el vestido dress
los vestidos clothes
los zapatos shoes

el algodón cotton
el cuero leather
la lana wool
el nilón nylon
la piel leather
la seda silk

ancho wide, loose
barato cheap
caro expensive
corto short
de moda in fashion
estrecho tight
grande big
largo long
demasiado pequeño small
pasado de moda out of fashion

cambiar to change
costar to cost
devolver to give back
envolver to wrap up
escoger to choose
hacer las compras to do the shopping
ir de compras to go shopping
ir de escaparates to window-shop
mostrar to show
probarse to try on
valer to be worth, to cost

los artículos de tocador toiletries
el cepillo de dientes toothbrush
el champú shampoo
el desodorante deodorant
el jabón soap
el pañuelo handkerchief
la pasta de dientes toothpaste
el peine comb
el talco talc
los tisús tissues
los artículos de cuero leather goods
la cerámica pottery
las cerillas matches
los cigarillos cigarettes
el disco record
la guitarra guitar
el juguete toy
el mechero cigarette lighter

la **muñeca** doll
el **perfume** perfume
el **periódico** newspaper
la **pila** battery
la **porcelana** porcelain
la **postal** postcard
el **recuerdo** souvenir
el **regalo** present
la **revista** magazine
el **sello** stamp

el **autoservicio** selfservice
el/la **cliente** customer
el **cheque** cheque
el/la **dependiente/a** shop assistant
el **escaparate** shop window
la **liquidación** sale
el **mostrador** counter
la **moneda** coin
el **precio** price
la **rebaja** reduction
las **rebajas** sale
la **tarjeta de crédito** credit card
el/la **tendero/a** shopkeeper
el/la **vendedor/a** shop assistant
la **vuelta** change

IN THE CAFÉ/RESTAURANT

el **aceite** oil
el **cenicero** ashtray
la **cuchara** spoon
el **cuchillo** knife
el **mantel** tablecloth
la **mostaza** mustard
la **pimienta** pepper
el **platillo** saucer
el **plato** plate
la **sal** salt
la **taza** cup
el **tenedor** fork
el **vaso** glass
el **vinagre** vinegar

el **camarero** waiter
el **menú** menu
el **menú del día** menu of the day
el **postre** dessert
el **primer plato** first course
la **señor(it)a** waitress
los **servicios** toilets
el **teléfono** telephone
la **terraza** open-air area

bien hecho well done
medio hecho medium
poco hecho rare

la **cuenta** bill
el/la **dueño/a** owner
el **error** mistake
la **propina** tip
el **servicio** service

escoger to choose
limpiar to clean
oler to smell

pedir to order
reservar to book
tener hambre to be hungry
tener sed to be thirsty

¿el servicio está incluido? is service included?
¿puede traerme...? can you bring me...?
¡que aproveche! enjoy your meal!
¡quédese con la vuelta! keep the change!
¿qué hay en el menú? what is on the menu?
una mesa para tres a table for three

For items of food, see the section on Shopping

WEATHER

el **aire** air
la **brisa** breeze
la **borrasca** storm
el **calor** heat
el **cielo** sky
el **clima** climate
la **escarcha** frost
el **frío** cold
el **grado** degree
el **granizo** hail
el **hielo** ice
la **lluvia** rain
la **neblina** mist
la **niebla** fog
la **nieve** snow
la **nube** cloud
el **pronóstico** forecast
el **relámpago** lightning
el **rayo** flash of lightning
el **rocío** dew
el **sol** sun
la **sombra** shade
la **temperatura** temperature
el **tiempo** weather
la **tormenta** storm
el **trueno** thunder
el **viento** wind

agradable pleasant
caliente hot
fresco cool
frío cold
tibio mild

brillar to shine
helar to freeze
llover to rain
nevar to snow
soplar to blow
tronar to thunder

está lloviendo it is raining
está lloviendo a cántaros it is pouring
está nevando it is snowing
está nublado it is cloudy
estoy mojado hasta los huesos I am soaked to the skin
hace calor it is hot
hace fresco it is cool
hace frío it is cold

hace mal tiempo it is bad weather
hace sol it is sunny
hace viento it is windy
hay escarcha it is frosty
hay neblina it is misty
hay niebla it is foggy

ACCOMMODATION

el albergue inn
el albergue juvenil youth hostel
la casa de huéspedes guest house
el camping campsite
el hotel hotel
el parador state-run luxury hotel
la pensión boarding house

Hotel

el agua (f) **caliente** hot water
el agua (f) **fría** cold water
el aparcamiento car park
el ascensor lift
el balcón balcony
el baño bath
la cama bed
las camas gemelas twin beds
la cama individual single bed
la cama de matrimonio double bed
la cuenta bill
la ducha shower
el equipaje luggage
la ficha registration form
el grifo tap
la habitación room
la habitación doble double room
la habitación individual single room
la llave key
la media pensión half board
el papel higiénico toilet paper
el pasillo corridor
la pensión completa full board
la piscina swimming pool
el portero porter (in hotel)
la recepción reception
el/la recepcionista receptionist
el restaurante restaurant
el ruido noise
la toalla towel

aparcar to park
llenar una ficha to fill in a form
marcharse to leave
quedarse to stay
quejarse to complain
rellenar una ficha to fill in a form
reservar to book

Youth hostel

la almohada pillow
el cubo de basura dustbin
la cocina kitchen
el comedor dining room
el dormitorio dormitory

la manta blanket
la mochila rucksack
los objetos de valor valuables
la sábana sheet
el saco de dormir sleeping bag
la sala de juegos games room

alquilar to hire
cocinar to cook
planchar to iron

At the campsite

la caravana caravan
las duchas showers
la sombra shade
la tienda shop
la tienda (de campaña) tent

hacer camping to camp
bajar la tienda to take down the tent
montar la tienda to put up the tent

WORK AND FUTURE

la compañía company
la compañía de seguros insurance company
la empresa firm
la fábrica factory
la oficina office
la universidad university

los ahorros savings
la ambición ambition
el empleo job
los estudios studies
la formación training
el/la jefe/a boss
el oficio job
el patrón/la patrona boss
el porvenir future
el salario salary
el sindicato trade union
la solicitud job application
el sueldo salary

aprobar to pass (an exam)
cobrar to earn
conseguir to obtain, to acheive
continuar to continue
estudiar to study
ganar to earn
ganarse la vida to earn one's living
seguir to continue
solicitar un puesto to apply for a job
suspender to fail (a candidate)
trabajar to work

aburrido boring
agotador exhausting
cansador tiring
científico scientific
difícil difficult
entretenido amusing
fácil easy
interesante interesting

EMERGENCIES

la **boca** mouth
el **brazo** arm
la **cara** face
el **codo** elbow
el **corazón** heart
el **cuello** neck
el **cuerpo** body
el **dedo** finger
el **diente** tooth (front)
el **estómago** stomach
la **espalda** back
la **espina** spine
la **frente** forehead
la **garganta** throat
el **hombro** shoulder
el **hueso** bone
el **labio** lip
la **lengua** tongue
la **mejilla** cheek
la **muela** tooth (back)
la **muñeca** wrist
la **nariz** nose
el **oído** ear
el **ojo** eye
la **oreja** ear
el **pecho** breast, chest
el **pie** foot
la **piel** skin
la **pierna** leg
la **rodilla** knee
el **rostro** face
el **tobillo** ankle
la **uña** nail
el **vientre** stomach

el **catarro** cold
el **dolor** pain
el **empaste** filling
la **enfermedad** illness
la **fiebre** temperature
la **gripe** flu
la **herida** injury
la **insolación** sunstroke
la **picadura** sting
la **quemadura** burn
el **resfriado** cold
la **salud** health
la **sed** thirst
el **síntoma** symptom
la **tos** cough

atropellar to knock over (in a car)
caerse to fall
cortarse to cut oneself
desmayarse to faint
doler to hurt
empastar to fill (a tooth)
hacerse daño to hurt oneself
hincharse to swell
herirse to get injured
llamar a un médico to call a doctor
llamar una ambulancia to call an ambulance
mejorar to improve

morir to die
no poder andar to be unable to walk
no poder dormir to be unable to sleep
no poder mover el pie to be unable to move your foot
no tener apetito to be off your food
patinar to skate
picar to sting
quemarse to get burnt
romperse to break
sentirse to feel
temblar to shiver
torcerse to sprain
toser to cough
vomitar to vomit

bien fine
constipado having a cold
enfermo ill
grave serious
herido injured
infectado infected
mareado feeling sick
mejor better
muerto dead
peor worse
roto broken
sano healthy
sin sentido unconscious

la **ambulancia** ambulance
la **aspirina** aspirin
la **cama** bed
el **centro de urgencia** first aid post
el **empaste** filling
el/la **enfermo/a** nurse
la **farmacia** chemist's
el **hospital** hospital
el **medicamento** medicine
el/la **médico/a** doctor
la **pastilla** tablet
la **receta** prescription
la **tirita** plaster
la **venda** bandage

cuidar to look after
descansar to rest
empastar to fill (tooth)
guardar cama to stay in bed
sacar to take out (tooth)

CLEANING AND REPAIRING

limpio clean
roto broken
sucio dirty
usado worn, worn-out

arreglar to fix, mend
funcionar to work
lavar to wash
limpiar to clean
manchar to stain
necesitar to need
rasgar to tear
reparar to repair

la **aguja** needle
el **agujero** hole
el **alfiler** needle
el **hilo** thread
la **suela** sole
el **tacón** heel

POST OFFICE

el **buzón** post box
la **cabina** kiosk
la **carta** letter
el **cartero** postman
el **código** postcode
Correos post office
la **dirección** address
la **lista de correos** post restante
el **paquete** packet
el **peso** weight
la **postal** postcard
el **recado** message
el **sello** stamp
el **sobre** envelope

echar to post
enviar to send
mandar to send

THE BANK

el **banco** bank
el **billete** banknote
la **caja** till
el/la **cajero/a** cashier
el **cambio** change
el **cheque** cheque
el **dinero** money
las **divisas** currency
el **duro** 5–peseta coin
el **empleado/la empleada** clerk
la **identificación** proof of identity
la **libra esterlina** pound sterling
la **moneda** coin
el **pasaporte** passport
la **ventanilla** counter

cambiar to change
cobrar un cheque to cash a cheque
firmar to sign
pagar to pay
rellenar to fill in
valer to be worth

LOST PROPERTY AND ROBBERY

el **anillo** ring
el **billete de banco** banknote
la **bolsa** bag
la **cárcel** gaol
la **cartera** wallet
el **collar** necklace
la **comisaría** police station
la **descripción** description
el **dinero** money
el **gamberro** thug
la **joya** jewel
el **ladrón** thief
la **maleta** suitcase
la **máquina fotográfica** camera
la **oficina de objetos perdidos** lost property office
el **oro** gold
la **plata** silver
la **policía** police
el/la **policía** police officer
la **pulsera** bracelet
la **recompensa** reward
el **reloj** watch
el **robo** theft
la **sorpresa** surprise
el/la **testigo/a** witness
la **víctima** victim

atracar to mug/hold up
buscar to look for
contener to contain
dejar to leave behind
denunciar to report
describir to describe
descubrir to discover
devolver to give back
encontrar to find
hallar to find
pegar to hit
perder to lose
pertenecer to belong to
robar to steal
tener miedo to be frightened
valer to be worth

Chapter 5
Listening: Basic Level

5.1 Introduction

This is what you need to know about the listening test at Basic Level:
- All the UK exam boards insist that you take this test as part of your GCSE exam.
- You will have to listen to a cassette recorded by native Spanish speakers.
- The scenarios for the listening situations will be taken from the list of topic areas and settings as set out by your exam board in its defined content.
- All questions are in English; you are expected to answer in English (or in Welsh if you are taking WJEC and prefer to answer in Welsh).
- Sometimes the questions are box-ticking types or grid-filling types.
- The situations will be authentic such as:
  conversations, discussions, interviews
  spoken instructions
  recorded telephone messages
  news items, weather forecasts, traffic reports
  announcements (e.g. at a supermarket)
- There will probably be background noises on the cassette.
- Each recorded item is heard twice; the recordings will be relatively short.
- At Basic Level you will be expected to understand specific details (at Higher Level you will have to draw conclusions).
- You are not expected to understand every single word.

5.2 How to prepare for the Basic Listening test

- You must get a cassette with Spanish GCSE practice material.
- You must have the transcript to what is on the cassette so that you can look up words when you get stuck.
- This book is accompanied by a cassette of GCSE questions and a transcript.
- Your teacher will be able to get you cassettes, or you can get cassettes from your local library.
- You can record Spanish-language programmes from the TV.
- After you have equipped yourself with a suitable cassette or walkman, you must spend time listening to it. Listen to each item many times over. Then check the transcript, make a list of the words you don't know and learn them.
- If you go to school by car, have a Spanish cassette in the car; or if you go by coach, listen to a walkman on the way.
- Get a friend to read out the transcript in Spanish; then do the same for him/her.

- There is certain vocabulary which is always going to be needed because this test is looking for specific items:

    jobs and professions
    relatives
    physical descriptions
    items of clothing
    numbers (If a price is asked for, remember that as there are about 190 pesetas to the pound, the number of pesetas may be very high and involve hundreds and thousands. Be ready for -**cientos** and **mil**.)
    days of the week, months of the year, seasons
    weather
    places in a town
    shops
    landmarks in the country
    directions (e.g. left, straight on)
    time expressions (e.g. last week, yesterday)
    school subjects

5.3 During the exam

- Fill in the front of your booklet quickly (have your candidate number and centre number ready) so that you can spend as much time as possible reading through the questions before the cassette starts.
- There is very often a clue to the question in the introduction or setting to the question. Read the setting carefully.
- On the exam paper it will tell you how many marks are being awarded for that question. This mark allocation will give you a clue to what the examiner is looking for.
- You may find it useful to underline the key words in the question to help you remember what you are listening for. For example, if the question is:

    What did Pedro do after he went out?

    you might like to underline it like this:

    What did Pedro do after he went out?

- You may find it helps to write things down in Spanish on your paper to give you time to work them out in English. For example, if you know the answer is a number, then when you hear **mil cuatrocientos** write it down in *Spanish* and then take your time working out that it is 1,400.
- Remember that you do not have to answer in a full sentence – a brief note will do. Often a one-word answer is enough. However do not omit information that is asked for. If you give the right answer but add other information which is wrong then you may lose the mark. The key is to read the question carefully and make sure you have understood what you are being asked for.
- If you are really stuck, guess! Don't leave the question space blank.

5.4 Examination questions

- The following items are on the cassette available with this book. They are a mixture of all the types of questions that you can expect from any of the exam boards.
- Recordings 1–20 are Basic Level, Recordings 21–36 are Higher Level and Recordings 37–48 are for the complete GCSE paper in Chapter 13.
- All the text of what is said is written out for you in full in the transcript.
- The questions are all past GCSE questions but they have not been repeated as they will be in your actual GCSE test. Suggested answers are provided at the end of this chapter.
- **Do not be confused if you hear a different number question on the cassette to the one you were expecting.** The numbering of the questions as they were in the actual GCSE has been kept on the cassette and in this book.

● For the first five recordings, student's answers with examiner's comments are provided. Do not look at the student's answers till you have attempted the questions.

Recording 1

Read the setting and questions below. Then listen to the recording. The transcript is on page 79. Do not look at the transcript until you have attempted the questions.

Questions

You and your family have just arrived at La Siesta campsite in Spain. You are at the reception.

1   The receptionists, Christina and Manuel, tell you that they cannot find your reservation. What does Cristina ask you?   (1)

2   What does Cristina want to know? Mention three things.   (3)

3   Manuel describes where you can put your tent. What three things will you find near your tent?(3)

4   Cristina interrupts.
    (a)   What does she ask you to give her?   (1)
    (b)   When can you have it back?   (1)

5   You ask Manuel the way to the pitch where you will put up your tent.
    (a)   What does he tell you? Mention one thing.   (1)
    (b)   What is the number of your pitch?   (1)

NEAB 1994

Student's answers

1   She asks me to give her my name.

2   **(i)**   How many people are there.
    (ii)   How many nights have we stayed.
    (iii) She wants to know if we have a tent.

3   **(i)**   Pool.
    (ii)   Showers.
    (iii) Services.

4   **(a)**   Passport.
    (b)

5   **(a)**   Our pitch is in front of the phones.
    (b)   50.

Examiner's Comments

1   Correct but a shorter answer would have got the mark. You do not need the first six words of your answer.

2   **(i)**   Do you mean 'How many people are on the campsite?' You must make your answers clear. 'How many people are there in our group' is a far better answer.
    (ii)   No. You have only just arrived. You have not read the setting properly. No mark.
    (iii) Good answer but you could have omitted the first four words of your answer.

3   **(i)** and **(ii)** are good answers but in **(iii)** **servicios** means 'toilets'.

4   **(a)** is a good answer but the student has left the next space blank! He/she should have guessed! Any answer is better than none!

5   **(a)**   A very common error. 'In front of' is **delante de**. **Enfrente** means 'opposite'.
    (b)   Correct.

Recording 2

Read the setting and questions below. Then listen to the recording. The transcript is on page 79. Do not look at the transcript until you have attempted the questions.

Questions

1   You are in Spain on an exchange and you have been asked by your teacher to collect details of shopping habits in Spain for use in a project. Your partner's mother has just been out shopping so you ask her what she has bought, where she bought it from and how much it cost.

    Fill in the blank spaces in the form below in English. Some of the spaces have already been filled in.

SHOP	ARTICLE	PRICE
1	stamp	2
3	4	250
5	6	2000
supermarket	7	8
9	10	500

(10)

MEG 1991

Student's answers

1 Post office.

2 40.

3 Paper shop

4

5 Clothes shop.

6 Present.

7 Tooth paste.

8 20.

9 Library.

10 Map.

Examiner's comments

1 Correct.

2 Correct.

3 Not a good answer. A paper shop is where you sell newspapers. You should have written 'Stationer's'.

4 A difficult question but you should at least have guessed.

5 Correct.

6 'A present' is not really an article. You have homed in on the wrong part of the recording.

7 Correct.

8 No. You did not understand **ciento.** Many candidates find it easier to write down the numbers in Spanish and then carefully work out what the number is from your notes.

9 No. A library is **biblioteca.**

10 Not enough information given. You should have said 'road map'.

Recording 3

Read the setting and questions below. Then listen to the recording. The transcript is on page 79. Do not look at the transcript until you have attempted the questions.

Questions

You arrive in Spain by air for a holiday and travel with a friend to a city-centre hotel by taxi. The taxi-driver gives a commentary on the features of the city as you drive along.

Answer the questions in *English*.

1 You pass a tower. What part of the tower does the taxi-driver suggest you visit? (1)

2 What two things can be seen from the tower? (2)

3 According to the taxi-driver, in which century was the church built? (1)

4 What advice does the taxi-driver give about visiting the church? (1)

5 Your taxi is in a traffic jam. According to the driver, what is the cause of the traffic jam problems? (1)

6 According to the driver, what is needed to solve the traffic problems? (1)

7 Later you pass a park. According to the driver:
   (a) What is the park famous for?
   (b) Why should you be careful in the park? (1)

8 Your taxi-driver points out a restaurant. What does he like to eat there? (1)

MEG 1992

Student's answers

1 The lift.

2 **(a)** The city.
   (b) Rio.

3 Third.

4 Go tomorrow.

5 Traffic lights.

6 A motorway.

7 **(a)** Its trees.
   (b) Robbers.

8 Sea-food.

Examiner's comments

1 You have homed in on the wrong part of the text. The correct answer is 'the balcony'.

2 **(a)** Correct.
   (b) No. The correct answer is 'the river'.

3 Your common sense should have told you that it is unlikely to find a church from the third century.

4 If **mañana** is preceded by **por la** then it means 'in the morning', not 'tomorrow'.

5 Correct.

6 Not a good answer because you have not given all the information. 'A motorway that crosses the city' gives all the relevant information.

7 **(a)** Again, not enough information given. You should have answered 'foreign trees'.

8 Your answer is not precise enough. 'Fish' is the correct answer.

Recording 4

Read the setting and questions below. Then listen to the recording. The transcript is on page 80. Do not look at the transcript until you have attempted the questions.

Questions

1 In a street in Spain you hear a van with a loudspeaker make the following announcement.
   (a) How does the Continente supermarket claim to be special? (1)
   (b) What is said about its prices? (1)
   (c) What is said about car parking? (1)
   (d) When is Continente open? (2)

WJEC 1993

Student's answers

1 **(a)** It's big.
   (b) They are cheap.
   (c) It's free.
   (d) From 10 till 10 in the evening.

Examiner's comments

1 **(a)** Not enough information given. **El ... más grande** means 'the biggest'.
   (b) Again you have not given enough information. **Los precios más bajos** means 'the cheapest prices'.
   (c) Correct.
   (d) You have made a serious error here even though you have interpreted the 24-hour clock accurately. You have not detected the (2) on the question paper which indicates that a longer answer is required. You should have mentioned the supermarket was open from Monday till Saturday.

Recording 5

Read the setting and questions below. Then listen to the recording. The transcript is on page 80. Do not look at the transcript until you have attempted the questions.

Questions

A woman walks into the travel agency.

13 What does she want?	(1)
14 What *two* things is she asking for?	(2)
15 (a) Josefina can't help. Where does she send the woman to?	(1)
(b) What directions does Josefina give her?	(1)
16 The woman leaves. What does Josefina say about her?	(1)
17 You tell Josefina that you want to go to El Arenal. When must you pay for the holiday?	(1)
18 (a) How does she suggest you might pay for the holiday?	(1)
(b) If you decide to pay this way what else will you need?	(1)

NEAB 1993

Student's answers

13 She wants to interrupt.

14 (i) Brochures.
(ii) Posters.

15 (a) To the tourist office.
(b) Go right to the end of the street then turn left.

16 She said thank you.

17 On Wednesday.

18 (a) Traveller's cheque.
(b) To bring my passport.

Examiner's Comments

13 No. You have not understood the relevant part of the recording. She wants to ask a question.

14 (i) Correct.
(ii) Correct.

15 (a) Correct.
(b) No. You have confused **todo derecho** (straight on) with **a la derecha** (to the right).

16 You should have given more information. The lady said 'thank you' two or three times and was courteous.

17 No. The travel agent says **antes de miércoles** i.e. before Wednesday.

18 (a) Correct.
(b) Correct.

5.5 Examination practice questions

Here are fifteen more GCSE questions for you to practise on.

For each of the following recordings read the setting and questions, then listen to the recording. The transcripts are on pp 80–3. Do not look at the transcripts until you have attempted the questions.

Recording 6

Your teacher has just received a cassette from a Spanish teacher at your exchange school with various items recorded for your class. The Spanish teacher has recorded an interview with a girl who wants a penfriend. Listen for some personal details for your friend who is interested in writing to her.

8 What year is Mariluz in at her Spanish school?   (1)
9 For how long has she been learning English?   (1)
10 Name two kinds of pet she keeps in the house.   (2)
11 Where do her parents work now?   (1)
12 Why is Mariluz unable to help her parents much?   (1)
13 Describe one of the jobs she does for her parents. Give full details.   (1)

ULEAC 1992

Recording 7

On a school exchange visit to Spain, you listen to some Spanish students and teachers talking about their meal times and preferences. You have to note down some details for a report you have been asked to write for your school magazine. Answer the following questions.

6 When does José have breakfast?   (1)
7 What is Ana's favourite food?   (2)
8 What sort of wine does Don Miguel prefer?   (1)
9 Doña Blanca has been asked whether she likes cooking. Who does the cooking in her house in the evenings during the week?   (1)

Finally, the headmaster is asked when and where he eats in a normal working day. Where does he have the following meals?

10 Breakfast   (1)
11 Lunch   (2)
12 Supper   (1)

ULEAC 1993

Recording 8

While on holiday in Spain, you go by bus with your Spanish friend to meet some of his relatives. He doesn't know this part of the city well and needs to ask the bus driver for some information.

1 What will the bus do before it gets to the Barrio de Miralbueno? Give full details.   (1)
2 How much do you each have to pay for your ticket?   (1)
3 According to the driver where, in the Calle del Ebro, is the Bar Miralbueno? Give full details.   (2)

ULEAC 1992

Recording 9

1 Your family has rented a villa in Spain and you have called at the owner's house to collect the key. He is explaining some things to you.

   (a) What is the large key for?   (1)
   (b) What is the small key for?   (1)
   (c) What has the owner done to welcome you?   (3)
   (d) Where is the telephone?   (2)

NICCEA 1992

Recording 10

1 You are travelling on a ferry to Spain when you hear the following announcement.

   (a) What two things are you told you can choose in the cafeteria?   (2)
   (b) What type of service is provided in the restaurant?   (1)
   (c) When do the cafeteria and restaurant close?   (3)

NICCEA 1992

Recording 11

1 You have gone with your penfriend to her school in Spain. In class the teacher is speaking to one of her pupils.

   (a) What did Ignacio not have with him in school?   (2)
   (b) Explain exactly why he did not have it.   (3)

NICCEA 1992

Recording 12

You have gone to the cinema in Spain with your penfriend. She is buying tickets at the box office.

1 **(a)** At what time does the film start? (1)
  (b) Where do they want to sit? (1)
  (c) How much do the tickets cost? (1)

NICCEA 1992

Recording 13

You are watching a Spanish TV programme for young people. Youngsters are being asked how they would cope on a desert island.

They are asked three things ... how they would spend the time ... any particular item they would take with them ... and what they would miss.

Now look at the notes below. Listen to the recordings and fill in the gaps. Some of the gaps have been filled in for you.

	Way of spending the time	**Article to take**	**What they would miss**
Juan	sunbathing	sleeping bag	bed
Nacho	1	2	studies
Dolores	reading	3	4
Conchita	5	6	7
Pablo	8	9	10

(10)
MEG 1994

Recording 14

1 Your penfriend's brother talks to you about Northern Ireland.
  (a) What has your penfriend's brother heard about the countryside? (Give full details.) (4)
  (b) What does he say about the climate? (2)

NICCEA 1993

Recording 15

1 Your penfriend's brother tells you about his father.
  (a) When did his father change his job? (2)
  (b) What is the father's new job? (2)
  (c) What problem does the job have? (2)

NICCEA 1993

Recording 16

1 Your penfriend's brother tells you about his daily routine during the holidays.
  (a) What does your penfriend's brother usually do after lunch? (1)
  (b) What does he do after 4 o'clock? (2)
  (c) Why must he return home by 8.30 p.m.? (2)

NICCEA 1993

Recording 17

You are spending a few days in Spain. You have iust arrived at the railway station with two Spanish friends, Pedro and Ana.

1 At what time does your train leave? (1)

2 Where does Ana suggest you go? (1)

3 What does Pedro think you should do first? (1)

4   What does Ana want to know?   (1)

5   Where *exactly* do you have to go?   (1)

6   How many tickets do Ana and Pedro decide to buy?   (1)

Now Ana asks you a question.

7   What does she want to know?   (1)

NEAB 1992

Recording 18

You are sitting in a bar in Spain with three Spanish friends, Ana, José and Roberto.

1   What is Ana asking?   (1)

2   What *two* things does Roberto ask for?   (2)

3   Why is Ana paying for everything?   (1)

4   What does Roberto want to know?   (1)

5   What does Ana say about her Saint's Day? Mention *two* things.   (2)

6   **(a)** Why does José think he is lucky?   (1)
    (b) What present does he usually get for his birthday?   (1)

Roberto changes the subject.

7   What does he say to José?   (1)

8   Why does Roberto want to go to San Rafael?   (1)

9   How is Roberto going to travel to San Rafael? Mention *two* ways.   (2)

This summer Ana is going to work with children.

10 What country does Ana want to work in?   (1)

11 Why hasn't she used an agency to find a job?   (1)

NEAB 1991

Recording 19

You are talking to your exchange partner's mother in the kitchen of her home. She talks about the soup she is making and about how she likes going to restaurants.

Answer the questions below in *English*. There will be pauses for you to write your answers.

Now read through the questions.

1   In the soup she is making she has put

    one   (1)

    half a kilo of   (1)

    one   (1)

2   What kind of restaurants does she like to go to?   (1)

3   What is her favourite dish?   (1)

4   How much does she pay for her favourite dish?   (1)

5   What does she drink with the meal?   (1)

6   Where exactly is the nearest restaurant?   (1)

7   Why does she like the people who work there?   (1)

8   What is the thing about the restaurant that she does *not* like?   (1)

MEG 1993

Recording 20

You are on a cycling holiday with a Spanish friend in Spain. You arrive at a campsite. Your friends in England have asked you to look out for a good campsite, so you make notes of the conversation between Iyour friend Band the campsite owner. Look through the notes below and complete each one with the information required.

1   Price per person per night.   (1)

2   Opening time of the shop.   (1)

ABCABCABCABCABCABCABC

3 Closing time of the shop. (1)
4 Any day when the shop is closed. (1)
5 Best place to leave bikes is (1)
6 How often buses go to Cercedilla. (1)
7 The first bus leaves at (1)
8 Food sold in the bar. (1)
9 On arrival at the reception you have to (1)
10 Weather over the last week. (1)

MEG 1990

5.6 Transcripts

Recording 1: transcript

1 **F** Lo siento, no encuentro tu carta. ¿Me puedes dar tu nombre de nuevo, por favor?

2 **F** Sí claro, aquí está. ¿Puedo confirmar los detalles? ¿Cuántas personas sois? ¿Cuántas noches queréis pasar? Tenéis una tienda, ¿no?

3 **M** Vuestro sitio está muy cerca de la piscina grande. Las duchas y los servicios están a unos diez metros. Es un sitio muy bonito, creo que os gustará.

4 **F** ¡Ah! Un momento, por favor. ¿Puedes darme tu pasaporte? Lo puedes recoger mañana aquí.

5 **M** Mira este plano del camping. Aquí están los teléfonos. Tu sitio está enfrente de los teléfonos. Busca la plaza número cincuenta.

Recording 2: transcript

– Pues, quiero escribir a tus padres así que fui a correos. Allí, compré un sello de cuarenta pesetas.
– Luego, fui a una papelería y compré sobres. Costaron doscientas cincuenta pesetas.
– Como mañana es el cumpleaños de mi hija, fui a comprarle un regalo.
– Fui a una tienda de ropa y le compré una falda. Costó dos mil pesetas.
– Después, como necesitamos algo para el cuarto de baño, fui al supermercado. Compré pasta de dientes por ciento veinte pesetas.
– Mi marido va a Barcelona mañana en coche así que fui a una librería y le compré un mapa de carreteras. Costó quinientas pesetas.

Recording 3: transcript

Now read through questions one and two.

Allí a la izquierda podéis ver la torre del oro. Históricamente, es muy importante y muy interesante. Vale la pena subir en ascensor hasta el balcón … Mirad … mirad … allí …¿veis el balcón? … desde allí hay vistas magníficas de la ciudad y del río. ¡Es precioso!

Now read through questions three and four.

¡Mirad! Ésta es una iglesia muy famosa … Se llama la iglesia de María de los Ángeles. Es muy vieja … construida en el siglo trece, creo … Si vais a visitarla, os doy un consejo. ¡Es mejor ir por la mañana! Lo que pasa es que a mediodía, suelen llegar los autocares de los turistas americanos … y a partir de las doce y pico … ¡hay tanta gente!

Now read through questions five and six.

Estamos ahora cerca del centro de la ciudad … Aquí hay otro embotellamiento … ¡qué barbaridad! … y ¿sabéis la causa de estos problemas? … pues ¡son los semáforos! … en cada cruce tenemos semáforos … y el tráfico tiene que esperar … ¡sin razón! Lo que necesitamos es una autopista que cruce el centro de la ciudad.

Now read through question seven.

Allí podéis ver el parque central. Es famoso por los árboles extranjeros que cultivan allí … Pero ¡cuidado! hay muchos ladrones.

Now read through question eight.

En un momento, llegaremos a vuestro hotel. ¡Mirad aquel restaurante! Para mí, es el mejor de toda la ciudad. Cuando voy allí, siempre como el pescado … es muy rico.

Recording 4: transcript

– CONTINENTE – El Supermercado más grande de la Costa Blanca – Continente a su servicio. Más de mil artículos a los precios más bajos. Cafetería y Restaurante.
Aparcamiento gratis.
Túnel de Lavado.
Aceptamos Tarjeta Visa.
Abierto de 10 a 22 horas de lunes a sábado.
CONTINENTE Costa Blanca a su servicio.

Recording 5: transcript

13 F_1 Usted perdone. ¿Puedo interrumpir un momento? Sólo quiero hacerle una pregunta, señorita.

F_2 Usted dirá.

14 F Soy profesora de geografía. ¿Tiene usted folletos turísticos y pósters para usar en clase? A los alumnos les gustan mucho los folletos, y los pósters son para decorar la clase.

15 F_1 Lo siento, no tenemos, pero vaya usted a la oficina de turismo. Ellos sí tienen.

F_2 ¿Podría decirme dónde está la oficina de turismo?

F_1 Sí, claro. Siga todo derecho hasta el final de la calle. Al final de la calle tuerza a la izquierda y está allí mismo.

F_2 Muchas gracias. Perdonen que les haya interrumpido.

F_1 No importa.

F_2 Muchas gracias.

16 F Enrique, ¿te has fijado qué cortés era esa señora? Dijo gracias, dos o tres veces.

17 F ¿Ya ha tomado una decisión? Le gusta la oferta del Arenal. Entonces le reservo tres plazas. Tiene que traerme el dinero antes del miércoles. No podré guardar la reserva durante más tiempo.

18 F Si quiere, puede pagar con cheques de viajero. Y si quiere pagar con cheques de viajero tiene que traer su pasaporte.

Recording 6: transcript

8 & 9 – Hola, amigos. Empezamos este casete con una entrevista. Os presento a Mariluz Hernández. Es alumna del tercer curso de BUP, y estudia inglés desde hace cuatro años.

10 – Dime, Mariluz, ¿tienes hermanos?
– Pues no, soy hija única aunque en mi casa tengo dos gatos y tres perros … y mis padres tienen muchas vacas en los campos …

11 – ¿Cómo dices? ¿Dónde vives?
– ¡En una granja, naturalmente! Mis padres son granjeros. Compraron la granja hace unos diez años porque les gusta el campo. Antes trabajaban en la ciudad, como todos mis parientes.

12 – Y, Mariluz, ¿tienes que ayudar a tus padres en la granja?
– Bueno, sólo tengo tiempo para ayudarles un poco, a causa de los deberes que me dan en el instituto.

13 – ¿Qué haces, entonces?
– Doy la comida a los cerdos, y a veces ayudo a hacer queso con la leche de las vacas.
– Muy bien, Mariluz. Muchas gracias.

Recording 7: transcript

6 – Bueno, yo desayuno antes de lavarme por la mañana.

7 – A mí me gusta todo, pero sobre todo me gusta la tortilla de jamón.

8 – En general, prefiero beber vino, especialmente el blanco.

9   – A mí no me gusta cocinar – pero a mi marido, sí. Prepara la cena todos los días - pero yo cocino los fines de semana.

10, 11   – Yo desayuno en un café, a mediodía como en mi restaurante favorito y ceno en casa.
& 12

Recording 8: transcript

1   – Oiga, por favor, ¿este autobús va al barrio de Miralbueno?
         – ¡Claro! Después de cruzar el río.

2   – ¿Cuánto vale el billete? Queremos dos, por favor.
         – Cincuenta y cinco pesetas cada uno – entonces son ciento diez.

3   – ¿Me puede decir dónde está el Bar Miralbueno?
         – Vamos a ver … está cerca del puente, ¿no? No, es otro … bueno, está en la calle del Ebro, antes del banco.

Recording 9: transcript

Bueno, la llave grande es para la puerta principal y esta llave pequeña es para el garaje. He puesto algunos comestibles en la nevera. Y hay un teléfono cerca de la escalera.

Recording 10: transcript

Señores pasajeros, queremos informarles que la cafetería ya está abierta. Se puede escoger una comida ligera y un refresco. En el restaurante hay servicio de camareros que les ofrece una variedad de platos ricos y vinos interesantes. Les recordamos que los dos sitios cierran media hora antes de la llegada del barco al puerto.

Recording 11: transcript

– Ignacio, ¿no tienes tu cuaderno de historia?
– No, señorita.
– Pues, ¿por qué no?
– Bueno, lo dejé en la cocina esta mañana.
– Vale. Voy a hablarte más tarde.

Recording 12: transcript

– ¿Hay entradas para la película de las siete y cuarto?
– Sí, quedan algunas.
– Deme dos entradas, por favor.
– ¿Dónde las quiere?
– En las butacas de atrás, por favor.
– Muy bien. Son cuatrocientas pesetas.
– Vale. Aquí las tiene.
– Gracias.

Recording 13: transcript

– Y tú, Juan. ¿cómo pasarías el tiempo?
– ¿Para pasar el tiempo? No hay problema. Tomaría el sol todo el día … Pero no me gusta la idea de tener frío por las noches así que llevaría conmigo un saco de dormir … No me gusta la idea de dejar mi cama. No quiero dormir en el suelo.
– Y tú, Nacho … ¿unos días en una isla desierta?
– Y yo para pasar el tiempo, nadaría mucho en el mar. Y llevaría conmigo un abrelatas para …pues … para abrir las latas … claro. No me gustaría dejar mis estudios. Me gusta mucho estudiar.
– ¿Y tú, Dolores?
– Yo leería todo el día … Me encanta la lectura … Y llevaría conmigo muchas cerillas para poder hacer fuego … No me gusta la idea de dejar mi ordenador. Me encanta jugar con mi ordenador.
– Conchita ¿cómo pasarías tú el tiempo?
– Yo jugaría a las cartas incluso si tengo que jugar sola. Y llevaría un barco para poder pescar. Y no me gusta la idea de dejar mi moto … no quiero ir a pie todo el día.
– Y tú, Pablo, ¿cómo pasarías el tiempo?

– Yo cocinaría mucho … me encanta … Y llevaría una caña de pescar. No me gustaría dejar mi guitarra en casa.

Recording 14: transcript

Me gustaría visitar tu país alguna vez. Nuestra profesora de inglés estuvo allí el año pasado. Nos dijo que el campo es más verde y que hay muchos bosques y colinas. Y el clima es menos seco.

Recording 15: transcript

Mi padre era mecánico pero el mes pasado empezó a trabajar como conductor de camión. Le gusta mucho pero el problema es que viaja los fines de semana.

Recording 16: transcript

Normalmente, después de almorzar, descanso hasta las cuatro más o menos. Luego, doy una vuelta por la ciudad pero tengo que volver a las ocho y media porque la cena está preparada a esa hora.

Recording 17: transcript

1   F   Bueno, ya hemos llegado.
    M   ¿A qué hora sale el tren?
    F   Sale a las tres y media.

2   M   Ah, entonces todavía falta media hora.
    F   Sí. ¿Por qué no vamos a la sala de espera?

3   M   A la sala de espera podemos ir después. Yo creo que es mejor comprar primero los billetes.

4   F   Vale, los compramos ahora. Oye, y ¿dónde están las taquillas?

5   M   ¿No las ves? Allí … a la izquierda de la escalera.

6   F   ¿Y qué hacemos? ¿Le compramos también un billete a Manuel?
    M   Pero todavía no ha llegado. Si compramos cuatro y no viene ¿qué haremos con el billete? Es mejor comprar sólo tres.
    F   No, estoy segura de que va a venir. Manuel no falta nunca a una cita. Compremos cuatro.
    M   Vale, pues, si tú estás tan segura.

7   F   Oye, ¿Has traído dinero? Los billetes costarán ochocientas cincuenta pesetas cada uno. ¿Tienes bastante dinero?

Recording 18: transcript

1   F   ¡Venga!, que hoy invito yo. ¿Qué queréis tomar?

2   M₁   ¡Qué amable eres! Para mí una coca cola. Y tú Roberto, ¿qué quieres?
    M₂   Yo quiero una naranjada y un helado, si no te importa invitarme a dos cosas.

3   F   No, no me importa. Os invito a lo que queráis porque hoy es mi cumpleaños.

4   M   ¡Feliz cumpleaños Ana! ¿Cuántos años tienes?
    F   18 años, ya soy muy mayor.

5   M   ¿Y cómo vas a celebrarlo? ¿Vas a dar una fiesta?
    F   No, en mi familia somos muy tradicionales y celebramos poco el cumpleaños. Nosotros celebramos más el santo. Para mí el día de mi santo es más importante. Voy a dar una fiesta. Ya os invitaré, no os preocupéis.

6   M   Pues yo tengo suerte, en mi casa celebramos los dos y recibo regalos para mi cumpleaños y para mi santo. Ahora generalmente me dan dinero y lo gasto como quiero.

7   M   Oye, José, hablando de dinero, necesito dos mil pesetas. ¿No podrías dejarme dos mil pesetas?

8   M₁   Hombre, no sé ¿Para qué las quieres?
    M₂   Es que quiero ir a San Rafael para buscar trabajo. Me han dicho que en San Rafael hay un hotel que necesita un recepcionista para este verano. Y a mí me iría muy bien trabajar porque no tengo ni un duro.

9   M₁   Y las dos mil pesetas, ¿para qué son?
    M₂   Para el viaje, hombre. Primero el autocar y luego voy a tener que tomar un taxi, porque el hotel está un poco lejos.

10 **M** En ese caso sí que te las dejo. Tú también vas a trabajar este verano, ¿verdad, Ana?
    F Sí, no es del todo seguro, quiero ir a Alemania a cuidar niños.

11 **M** ¿Fue muy difícil encontrarlo?
    F Sí, es difícil encontrar estos trabajos. Si los buscas a través de una agencia tienes que pagar mucho dinero. Después de dos meses, un amigo de mi profesora de alemán me encontró el trabajo.

Recording 19: transcript

1 – Ésta es mi sopa favorita.
  – Pongo una cebolla entera, medio kilo de tomates y un huevo.

2 – Me gusta salir a comer …
  – Me gusta ir a los restaurantes franceses; los platos son muy ricos.

3 – El plato que me gusta más son las tortillas. Los franceses las hacen muy bien.

4 – Pago cuatrocientas pesetas por una tortilla … no es caro.

5 – Nunca bebo vino. Siempre bebo agua mineral.

6 – No tengo que ir lejos. Hay un restaurante en la esquina.

7 – Y me gustan los franceses que trabajan allí … son muy corteses.

8 – Pero lo que no me gusta es que este restaurante se cierra a las once y media. ¡Qué raro!

Recording 20: transcript

– Buenos días. Bienvenidos. ¿Queréis acampar aquí?
– Sí ¿Cuánto cuesta por noche?
– 250 pesetas por persona.
– ¿Y hay una tienda de comestibles?
– Sí. Se abre a las 8 de la mañana y se cierra a las 6 de la tarde. Y está cerrada los domingos.
– Muy bien. ¿Y dónde podemos dejar las bicicletas?
– Pues … en mi despacho … es lo mejor.
– Ya … esto … ¿hay autobuses a Cercedilla?
– Sí. Hay un autobús cada hora. El primero sale a las 7 y media.
– Estupendo. Y ¿venden comida en el bar?
– Hay solamente bocadillos de jamón.
– Vale.
– Muy bien. Vamos a ver. ¿Queréis llenar estas fichas?
– Sí. ¿Y qué tal el tiempo recientemente?
– ¿El tiempo? Pues hoy hace buen tiempo, pero durante la semana pasada, ha llovido.

5.7 Suggested answers

Recording 1

1 She wants my name.
2 **(i)** How many of us are there.
  (ii) How many nights will we stay.
  (iii) If we have a tent.
3 **(i)** Swimming pool.
  (ii) Showers.
  (iii) Toilets.
4 **(a)** Passport.
  (b) Tomorrow.
5 **(a)** Our pitch is opposite the phones.
  (b) 50.

Recording 2

1 Post office.
2 40.
3 Stationer's.
4 Envelopes.
5 Clothes shop.
6 Skirt.
7 Tooth paste.
8 120.
9 Book shop.
10 Road map.

Recording 3

1 The tower.
2 **(a)** The city.
  (b) The river.
3 Thirteenth.
4 Go in the mornings.
5 The traffic lights.
6 A motorway that crosses the city.
7 **(a)** Foreign trees.
  (b) Robbers.
8 Fish.

Recording 4

1 **(a)** It's the biggest.
  (b) It's the cheapest.
  (c) It's free.
  (d) From 10am till 10pm Monday
      till Saturday.

Recording 5

13 To ask a question.
14 **(i)** Brochures.
   (ii) Posters.
15 **(a)** To the tourist office.
   (b) Go straight on to the end of the street then
       turn left.
16 She is very polite.
17 Before Wednesday.
18 **(a)** By traveller's cheque.
   (b) My passport.

Recording 6

8 Third.
9 Four.
10 Cats, dogs.
11 On a farm.
12 Because of her homework.
13 She feeds the pigs and helps to make
   cheese with the cows' milk.

Recording 7

6 Before getting washed.
7 Ham omelette.
8 White wine.
9 Her husband.
10 In a café.
11 In his favourite restaurant.
12 At home.

Recording 8

1 Cross the river.
2 55.
3 Before the bank.

Recording 9

1 **(a)** Front door.
  (b) Garage.
  (c) He has put some food in the
      fridge.
  (d) Near the stairs.

Recording 10

1 **(a)** A light meal and a drink.
  (b) Waiter service.
  (c) Half an hour before the arrival
      of the ship in port.

Recording 11

1 **(a)** His history exercise book.
  (b) He left it in the kitchen that
      morning.

Recording 12

1 **(a)** 7.15.
  (b) At the back.
  (c) 400 pesetas.

Recording 13

1 Swimming.
2 Tin-opener.
3 Matches.
4 Computer.
5 Play cards.
6 Boat.
7 Motorbike.
8 Cooking.
9 Fishing rod.
10 Guitar.

Recording 14

1 **(a)** The countryside is green and
      there are many woods and hills
  (b) It is wetter.

Recording 15

1 **(a)** Last month.
  (b) Lorry driver.
  (c) He travels away at weekends.

Recording 16

1 **(a)** He rests till 4.00.
   (b) He goes for a walk round the city.
   (c) His evening meal is ready.

Recording 17

1 3.30.
2 Waiting room.
3 Buy the tickets.
4 Where is the ticket office.
5 To the left of the stairs.
6 Four.
7 If I have enough money.

Recording 18

1 What do we want to have.
2 **(i)** Orangeade.
   (ii) Ice cream.
3 It is her birthday.
4 How old she is.
5 **(i)** For her it is more important than her birthday.
   (ii) She is going to have a party.
6 **(a)** He celebrates both his birthday and his saint's day.
   (b) Money.
7 He asks for 2000 pesetas.
8 To look for work.
9 **(i)** Coach.
   (ii) Taxi.
10 Germany.
11 It is too expensive.

Recording 19

1 Onion, tomatoes, egg.
2 French restaurants.
3 Omelettes.
4 400.
5 Mineral water.
6 On the corner.
7 They are very polite.
8 It closes at half past eleven.

Recording 20

1 250.
2 8am.
3 6pm.
4 Sundays.
5 In his office.
6 Every hour.
7 7.30am.
8 Ham sandwiches.
9 Fill in forms.
10 Rain.

Chapter 6
Listening: Higher Level

6.1 Introduction

This is what you need to know about the exam:

- Whereas the Basic Level was compulsory, the Higher Level is optional. However, you have absolutely nothing to lose by attempting it even if you score zero.
- The recordings will be faster, the vocabulary will be from the full range of vocabulary (and not just the basic range outlined by your exam board).
- The full range of topics and settings can be included in the exam at Higher Level (at Basic Level they are restricted).
- As at Basic Level, the recordings will be of native Spanish speakers and there will be background noises.
- The recordings are longer and, as you would imagine, harder. They may be split into sections. Then you will either hear the whole recording through in sections and then the whole recording repeated in sections or you will hear one section and then that section repeated, then the second section and the second section repeated and so on. Listen out for the instructions.
- In addition to the types of settings you can expect at Basic Level, there are likely to be more:
  long conversations and dicussions
  arguments
  requests and instructions
- The major difference between Basic and Higher is that at Higher Level you will be asked to demonstrate Higher Level Skills. Let's look at this.

6.2 Higher Level skills

The person who wrote your exam paper is under instructions to include at least 40% of what is known as 'Higher Level Skills' questions. These questions test your ability to:

- Draw conclusions. For example if the recording is about a student who goes out every night till late and never buys any books, you might be asked a question like 'What conclusion can you draw about the student's commitment to his studies?'
  You would answer that he/she seems to ignore his studies.
- Identify attitudes and emotions. For example if the recording is about a man who is in tears and says that he should never have left the house that day, then you might be asked a multiple-choice question like:
  What emotion does the speaker feel? Tick one box only.
- (a)   He is quite happy with things.   ☐
- (b)   He is very angry.   ☐

(c)   He is proud of his achievements.   ☐

(d)   He is regretting something.   ☐

You would obviously tick the last box.

● Identify the important themes. For example if the recording is about a weather forecast which forecasts terrible weather every day except one, you might be asked 'Which day is the best day to go to the beach?'

6.3 In the examination

These are what you need to remember on exam day. This advice is similar to the advice given for Basic Level Listening.

● Do attempt the Higher Paper if you feel you have the slightest chance of scoring a point.
● Listen carefully to the recorded instructions and read the instructions and settings on the paper carefully.
● Remember that the mark allocation for each question will give you a clue as to what information and how much information is required.
● Always attempt each question even if you have to guess.
● If the question asks you to detect an emotion, you might be able to guess it from the tone of the speaker even if you do not understand what he/she has said.
● Remember that questions asking for specific detail follow the order of the information in the recording. However a question testing Higher Level Skills may often be the last question on a recording because to draw the correct conclusion, you may need information given throughout the recording. You may have to remember things from the beginning, middle or end of the recording.

6.4 Examination questions

The following extracts are on the cassette which can be bought with the book. They are all past GCSE papers. If you have the cassette, play the cassette over and over again. If you do not have the cassette, either get a friend to say the text to you or record it yourself onto a cassette and then listen to it. **Remember that the numbers mentioned are those on the original exam paper.** Also remember that in your exam each extract will be repeated after a pause. On the accompanying cassette the recordings are not repeated so when you have listened to a recording, rewind and listen again.

Recording 21

Read the setting and questions below. Then listen to the recording. The transcript is on page 93. Do not look at the transcript until you have attempted the questions.

Questions

You are staying with your Spanish friend. He is talking to you. There will be pauses during which you can write your answers.

Answer the questions in *English* in the spaces provided. You will hear the conversation twice. Now read through the questions.

1 How is your friend's mother feeling?   (1)

2 What happened yesterday?   (1)

3 How did your friend's mother try to solve the problem?   (1)

4 What did your Spanish friend learn a few moments ago?   (1)

5 Where is your friend going now?   (1)

MEG 1994

Student's answers

1 She is fed up.

2 There was a breakdown.

3 She called a mechanic.

4 The mechanic can't come.

5 To the launderette.

Examiner's comments

1 This answer is not enough to score. It is not an acceptable translation of **enfadada.** 'Angry' is the best answer. You must try and use standard English in your answers rather than colloquial English.

2 There *was* a breakdown but you have not mentioned the washing machine so you do not get the mark.

3 Correct.

4 Correct.

5 No. This is probably a guess. The correct answer is 'to a neighbour's house'.

Recording 22

Read the setting and questions below. Then listen to the recording. The transcript is on page 93. Do not look at the transcript until you have attempted the questions.

Questions

You overhear a Spaniard talking about a recent visit to England. Answer the questions in English. Answer Question 2 by ticking the appropriate box. Now read through the questions.

1 How did the speaker try to solve his problem?   (1)

2 Which statement best describes the progress the speaker made? Tick one box only.

    (a) He made poor progress.   ☐

    (b) He made fair progress.   ☐

    (c) He made good progress.   ☐

    (d) He made excellent progress.   ☐   (1)

3 What conclusion did the speaker draw about life for young people in England?   (1)

4 What advantage did the speaker see for young people in England?   (1)

5 What disadvantage did the speaker see?   (1)

MEG 1994

Student's answers

1 He studied English.

2 C.

3 They have more independence.

4 Young people in England learn to live without their parents.

5 Young people usually end up in gaol.

Examiner's comments

1 This answer is incomplete. The speaker did study but he went on a course in London. You must mention this.

2 No. This is one of the Higher Level Skill questions (see page 87). If you study the transcript you will see that you have drawn the wrong conclusion. The correct answer is D.

3 Correct.

4 Correct but you did not have to include the first four words of your answer as they are in the question.

5 If you study the transcript you will see that the speaker does not say that young people *usually* end up in gaol. You have understood nearly all the recording but the addition of 'usually' has denied you the mark.

Recording 23

Read the setting and questions below. Then listen to the recording. The transcript is on page 94. Do not look at the transcript until you have attempted the questions.

Questions

You are in Gerona airport in Spain. Your Spanish friend, Jaime, has not yet arrived to meet you so you ring up his home.

1 Jaime's mother answers the telephone. Why is she surprised that you are phoning? (1)

2 She tells you Carmen, Jaime's friend, is coming to meet you.
   (a) Where will she be parked? Mention *one* thing. (1)
   (b) How will you recognise her? Mention *two* details. (2)

3 You meet Carmen. What does she ask you? Mention *one* thing. (1)

4 You are in the car on the way to Jaime's house.
   (a) What does Carmen apologise for? (1)
   (b) Why is Jaime working overtime today? (1)

5 Carmen tells you more about Jaime's job.
   (a) Why does Jaime have a summer job? (1)
   (b) What does Carmen say about the job situation in the area? (1)

6 You are concerned that you won't see much of Jaime if he's working.
   (a) How does Carmen try to reassure you? (1)
   (b) When exactly does he work? (1)

NEAB 1994

Student's answers

1 Because I have been waiting for a long time.

2 (a) In the car park.
   (b) (i) She is tall.
       (ii) She has blonde hair.

3 How am I?

4 (a) She apologizes for Jaime not coming.
   (b) Because he has had flu.

5 (a) He is saving for something.
   (b) It is difficult to find a job.

6 (a) She says that Jaime only works afternoons.
   (b) He only works afternoons and Saturday mornings.

Examiner's comments

1 No. You have homed in on the wrong part of the recording. She has left a message at the information office.

2 (a) Yes but there is more information and to be sure of the mark you should include it. She will park near the car hire facility.
   (b) (i) Correct.
       (ii) No. **Moreno** means 'dark' not 'blonde'.

3 This is a guess. She asks if you remember her.

4 (a) Correct.
   (b) No. His workmates have had flu but he has not.

5 (a) Yes but you should have given more information. Mention the trip to America.
   (b) Correct.

6 (a) It is obvious if you think about it that you are giving the information required for **6(b)** here. She says 'Don't worry'.
   (b) Not quite. He only works alternate Saturday mornings.

6.5 Examination practice questions

For each of the following recordings read the setting and questions, then listen to the recording. The transcripts are on pages 94–7. Do not look at the transcripts until you have attempted the questions. Suggested answers are provided at the end of this chapter.

Recording 24

You arrive at a Spanish youth hostel with your Spanish friend, Carlos. He offers to sort out the accommodation for you both.

Answer the questions in *English*. Now read through the questions.

1 What problem do you discover on arriving at the youth hostel? (1)

2 What does Carlos do to try to remedy the situation? (1)

3 What new suggestion does Carlos have? (1)

4 What will happen in half an hour? (1)

5 What does Carlos want to do? (1)

MEG 1993

Recording 25

You are helping your Spanish friend to make a survey on the educational progress of young Spanish students. Five students are asked about their progress and attitudes to study. You will hear their answers. Listen to what they say and then select from List 1 the *topic* which best fits what the student has said and then write either letter **A, B, C, D, E** or **F**. You will not need to use every topic on the list.

Also for each student select from List 2 the word that best describes the speaker's attitude and write either letter **G, H, I, J, K** or **L**. You will not need to use every word in the list.

So if you feel that the **Student 1** is talking about a *clash of personalities* and is *ambitious*, you should write **A** and **G** for Question 1.

You will hear each student twice. Now read through the questions.

List 1 – Topics		List 2 – Attitudes	
A	a clash of personalities	G	ambitious
B	work before pleasure	H	having regrets
C	bad decisions	I	feeling victimized
D	a family illness	J	indifferent
E	duty to one's family	K	helpful
F	leaving education behind	L	grateful

Student 1
He is talking about (1)
He is (1)

Student 2
She is talking about (1)
She is (1)

Student 3
He is talking about (1)
He is (1)

Student 4
She is talking about (1)
She is (1)

Student 5
He is talking about (1)
He is (1)

MEG 1993

Recording 26

You have complained to a friend, Maribel, about a visit to the hospital where you had to queue for two hours to see a doctor. You have to go back there tomorrow. Maribel phones you.

13 Why is Maribel phoning? (1)

14 Maribel tells you what to do.
 (a) How do you spell the doctor's name? (1)
 (b) Why should you see this doctor? Give *both* reasons. (2)

15 Maribel then talks about two films. What do these Spanish films have in common? Mention *two* points. (2)

16 Why does Maribel want you to phone? Give *both* reasons. (2)

NEAB 1993

Recording 27

Your school has invited in three Spanish speakers, María, Juanita and Nicolau to answer a few questions. First your teacher talks to you.

 1 Today's session will be different. In what way? (1)

 2 What is the second difference? (1)

 Your teacher introduces María to the class.

 3 Write down *four* things the teacher tells you about María. (4)

 Now your teacher introduces Juanita, María's daughter.

 4 What does Juanita tell you about her Spanish? Mention *two* things. (2)

NEAB 1992

Recording 28

At home you and Elena are listening to a Spanish programme which she has managed to pick up on your radio. This is the listeners' problem section. First, Marisol, who is the person who answers the letters, talks to the presenter.

11 (a) Why does Marisol enjoy this work so much? (2)
 (b) How does the presenter react to the use of the word **problemitas**? (2)

12 (a) Why has Marisol used the word **problemitas**? (2)
 (b) What type of problem does the programme specialize in? Give one example. (1)

 This problem is from Victoria.

13 Why is Victoria worried? (2)

14 (a) Why should Victoria not be too concerned? (1)
 (b) What has Marisol told the listeners in previous programmes about keeping birds? (1)

NEAB 1991

Recording 29

Your parents have found the following recorded message on their Answerphone. The message is quite urgent: you help them to pick out the important points.

16 Where did Mariano find your home telephone number? Give *two* details. (2)

17 Why was Mariano away from home last week? (1)

18 Where is he being sent to in Madrid? (1)

19 What is the reason for the move? (1)

20 Why can't your parents phone Mariano at his home immediately? Give full details. (1)

ULEAC 1993

Recording 30

One of your teachers has interviewed a Spanish student who has spent a year in the United Kingdom. They discuss traditional festivals in Spain and the United Kingdom; you listen to the recording they made in order to compare traditions in the two countries.

21 What does the student not like about British weather? (1)

22 According to the student, to what extent are the British and Spanish aware of each other's traditional festivals? Give full details. (2)

23 Which British festival did this student find most strange? (1)

24 Describe *two* of the ways in which this festival was celebrated, as described by the student. (2)

ULEAC 1993

Recording 31

While you are staying with a Spanish family you fall ill and are visited by the family doctor. You need to be sure that you fully understand his comments and instructions.

1 What two things does the doctor think may have affected your stomach directly? (2)

2 What other reason is suggested for your feeling ill? (1)

3 Give full details of how you should take the medicine he prescribes. (3)

4 What two steps should you take to get your money back? (2)

5 What two pieces of advice does he give you for tomorrow? (2)

ULEAC 1992

Recording 32

Your Spanish penfriend talks to you about her future plans.

1 (a) Where was your penfriend called to? (2)

(b) What career was she advised to choose? (1)

(c) What aspects of the job appeal to her? (2)

NICCEA 1993

Recording 33

While on a camping holiday in Spain you are asked to help another English-speaking family who require the services of a local doctor for one of their children. You listen to what the doctor has to say.

1 (a) What has happened to the boy? (2)

(b) How does the doctor say he will treat him? (2)

(c) Why, according to the doctor, are children liable to have this kind of accident? (3)

NICCEA 1993

Recording 34

You receive a taped message from a friend you have made in a Spanish school. Your new friend is introducing herself and her family.

1 (a) What does Elena say about her age? (2)

(b) Where exactly does she live? (2)

(c) What two things are we told about her brother? (2)

(d) Give two details of Elena's personality. (2)

NICCEA 1992

Recording 35

You are interested to hear your penfriend's father in Spain telling you about a fishing trip he made with his son, Pedro.

1 (a) When did the father and son go fishing? (1)

(b) How did they keep themselves warm and dry? (2)

2 (c) What was especially suitable about the place where they stopped? (2)

(d) What were the only signs of movement? (3)

3 (e) How do we know that the father must have fallen asleep? (2)

(f) Where did he put the fish? (1)

(g) Why do you think the father probably ate what he caught? (1)

NICCEA 1992

Recording 36

In this section, you will hear part of an interview given by a Spanish lady who has just returned to Spain after spending three years teaching abroad. Look at the questions below.

Now listen carefully to the interview and answer the questions by either ticking the appropriate box or by answering in English. You will hear the interview twice.

1 Why did the lady go abroad?   (1)

2 Why did the lady return to Spain?   (1)

3 Which statement best describes the lady's impression of the people in the country where she worked? Tick one box only.

       fun-loving and friendly   ☐

       fun-loving but wary of foreigners   ☐

       miserable and unfriendly   ☐

       welcoming but very serious about life   ☐   (1)

4 Which statement best describes the headmistress of the lady's school? Tick one box only.

       She enjoyed good relationships with her pupils and imposed strong discipline. ☐

       She enjoyed good relationships with her pupils but did not have strong discipline. ☐

       She imposed strong discipline but had no links with her pupils. ☐

       She did not impose strong discipline and had no strong links with her pupils. ☐ (1)

5 Which statement best describes the headmistress's attitude to the learning of French? Tick one box only.

       All pupils had to learn French. ☐

       Those who wanted to could learn French. ☐

       Only those who studied English could learn French. ☐

       French should not be taught at school. ☐ (1)

MEG 1991

6.6 Transcripts

Recording 21: transcript

Oye ¿sabes qué ha pasado? Mi madre está muy enfadada. (pause) La lavadora no funciona … Ayer cuando mi madre estaba usándola hubo una avería … (pause) Mi madre telefoneó en seguida a un mecánico.

El mecánico dijo que vendría hoy para repararla. (pause) Llamó hace unos momentos … no puede venir hasta pasado mañana. (pause) Como mi hermana necesita ropa limpia para una fiesta esta tarde, voy a usar la lavadora de la vecina … ¿Vienes?

Recording 22: transcript

Siempre he tenido problemas con el inglés. Me cuesta mucho. Luego un día vi un anuncio para una escuela de idiomas en Londres. Decidí hacer un curso allí. Al principio no entendía nada … o casi nada. Pero a los diez días entendí casi todo lo que me decía el profesor. Y hasta conseguí hablar casi perfectamente. No puedes imaginarte cuánto aprendí en diez días.

Tuve también la oportunidad de ver un poco de la vida de los jóvenes en Inglaterra. Allí en Inglaterra entre los jóvenes hay un nivel distinto de independencia y de libertad.

Esto me parece bien y me parece mal a la vez. Por una parte, los jóvenes aprenden a vivir sin la ayuda de sus padres. Por otra parte, algunos hacen tantas tonterías que al final se encuentran en la cárcel.

Recording 23: transcript

1 **F** ¡Ah! ¿Todavía estás en el aeropuerto? ¿Has estado esperando mucho rato? Dejé un recado para ti en información, ¿no te lo dieron?

2 **F** Es que Jaime no puede ir a recogerte pero su amiga, Carmen, te esperará en el aparcamiento. Va en un Seat Málaga de color negro. Me ha dicho que estará cerca del alquiler de coches. Seguro que no la puedes perder. Es alta, de pelo moreno y rizado. Lleva puesta una camiseta roja y unos pantalones cortos blancos.

3 **F** ¡Hola! ¿Te acuerdas de mí? Nos conocimos en una fiesta el año pasado, ¿no te acuerdas?

4 **F** Siento que Jaime no haya podido venir a buscarte hoy. No es culpa suya. Es que le ha tocado trabajar horas extra porque mucha gente en su oficina tiene la gripe.

5 **F** Sabes que Jaime se va a los Estados Unidos el año que viene, así que tiene que ahorrar para poder pagar los gastos. La verdad es que ha tenido mucha suerte en encontrar ese trabajo para el verano. Mucha gente aquí no tiene empleo. Hay menos turismo, sabes.

6 **F** ¡Ah! ¡No te preocupes! El sólo trabaja por las tardes y los sábados por la mañana de manera alternativa, es decir un sábado sí, uno no. Seguro que tendréis mucho tiempo de estar juntos.

Recording 24: transcript

1 – Buenos días. ¿Hay camas?
   – Sí, tenemos camas libres pero solamente en el dormitorio de las chicas. El dormitorio de los chicos está lleno … lo siento.

2 – Lástima. Bueno, voy a buscar en la guía telefónica a ver si hay otro albergue por aquí.

3 – No encuentro nada. Mira. Tengo una tía que vive cerca de aquí. Voy a llamarla a ver si podemos dormir allí.

4 – Todo está arreglado … No te preocupes … Tenemos tiempo para tomar un refresco … mi tía viene a buscarnos en coche dentro de media hora.

5 – ¿Te gusta el refresco? Estoy un poco preocupado … no sé si mi tía va a encontrarnos aquí en el bar. ¡Vamos a esperarla en la calle!

Recording 25: transcript

Student 1

Pues yo tengo malas notas. Y ¿sabes por qué? Pues por culpa de mi padre. Yo quise estudiar idiomas y mi padre me dijo que no. Me dijo que con idiomas no voy a conseguir trabajo. Por eso, escogí química y física y no entiendo … nada … nada … nada … He escogido mal.

Student 2

Esto … tengo que decirte que me encantan todas mis asignaturas salvo una … la geografía. Y por una razón. La profesora me odia. Y yo la odio a ella también. Siempre me critica … siempre me hace preguntas dificilísimas … el antiguo profesor de geografía era tan simpático …

Student 3

Mis padres fueron muy pobres, sabes, a decir la verdad son campesinos … ellos no fueron a la escuela … bueno … fueron muy raramente … pero mis padres me dieron a mí la oportunidad de mejorar mi vida futura … estudio … no sólo porque me gusta sino porque se lo debo a mis padres.

Student 4

Oye … no sé por qué quieres hablar conmigo … habla con los otros porque yo me iré pronto … mi padre me ha encontrado trabajo en una fábrica cerca de aquí … Podría estudiar más pero no me apetece mucho. A ver como voy con el trabajo.

Student 5

Mira … cuando tenía doce años vi una película sobre la vida de un abogado … y desde aquel momento, supe lo que quería hacer … ser abogado … no un abogado corriente sino el mejor abogado del mundo … por eso estudio tanto … mis amigos salen a beber cerveza … salen a las discotecas … pues yo no … yo tengo una ambición … y la voy a conseguir … seguro.

Recording 26: transcript

13 **F** ¡Hola! Soy Maribel. Me dijiste que fuiste al médico y que tuviste que hacer dos horas de cola, ¿no? Pues mira, creo que te he arreglado el problema.

14 F Oye, ¿tienes un bolígrafo? Creo que te he solucionado el problema. Apunta: cuando llegues al hospital pregunta por el doctor Aguilera, A-g-u-i-l-e-r-a. Es un buen amigo de la familia y te está esperando. Espero que no sea nada grave.

15 F Oye, hablando de otra cosa. ¿Te acuerdas que me dijiste que querías ver una película española de calidad? Pues mira, ahora ponen dos muy buenas. La primera se llama *La Línea del Cielo* y ha tenido mucho éxito, tiene momentos muy graciosos, trata de un fotógrafo español que quiere aprender inglés y tiene muchos problemas. La otra se llama *La Mano Negra*, … también ha tenido éxito … y … también es bastante cómica … pero … bueno … no sé qué decirte, trata de un cantante que no tiene inspiración y ya no puede escribir canciones nuevas. Mejor que no te diga cuál prefiero y así decides tú. ¿Qué te parece?

16 F Bueno, pues, ya me llamarás para decirme cómo te ha ido en el hospital y qué película prefieres. Hasta luego.

Recording 27: transcript

1 F Hola, bienvenidos a todos. Ya os dije que la sesión de hoy sería un poco diferente. En primer lugar, será diferente porque vamos a hablar en español desde el principio hasta el final.

2 F En segundo lugar, la sesión será diferente porque durará media hora más que de costumbre.

3 F Ahora os voy a presentar a los invitados. Primero, María Torrente. María es sudamericana, es de Chile, pero lleva muchos años viviendo aquí en Inglaterra. Trabaja de secretaria en un centro de educación de adultos. Y nos conocemos porque su hija y la mía van al mismo instituto.

4 F1 Bien, y también está aquí la hija de María ¿Cómo te llamas?
F2 Me llamo Juanita.
F1 Y hablas un español perfecto, ¿verdad?
F2 Pues mi madre siempre me riñe y me corrige. Pero hablar es fácil, sólo me equivoco algunas veces, pero pocas. En cambio, siempre tengo dificultades para escribir.

Recording 28: transcript

11 F ¿Qué tal Marisol?
F Feliz de estar en la radio, como siempre. Ya sabes que me encanta estar aquí con vosotros, porque sois gente estupenda y me lo paso muy bien en el programa, además me encanta ayudar a nuestros oyentes con sus problemitas.
F Pues nosotros tenemos que agradecerte tus visitas y ya sabes que aquí en la radio todos te queremos mucho. Pero oye, ¿por qué siempre dices 'problemitas' cuando te refieres a las consultas de nuestros oyentes? ¿No te parece que sus problemas son importantes?

12 F Mujer, claro que lo son. Pero recuerda que el 'Consultorio del hogar' tiene como objetivo el aconsejar y ayudar a solucionar los problemas de todos los días. Nos especializamos, sobre todo, en los problemas que tienen nuestros oyentes porque se han acostumbrado a tener animales de compañía en la casa, y plantas, que es una cosa muy agradable, muy bonita y que forma una parte importante de sus vidas. Pero no es tan importante como el paro, el divorcio, la droga, por mencionar algunos, que me parece que son problemas mucho mayores, pero que nosotros no tocamos. Por eso digo 'problemitas'. No me interpretes mal.

13 F Desde hace unos meses mi canario me tiene muy preocupada. Come bien y come de todo lo que le pongo, pero ni se mueve ni canta, se pasa el día sentado al lado del comedero y nada más.

14 F En primer lugar, Victoria, tiene que tener en cuenta que es lógico que el animalito no cante, porque este tiempo no es muy adecuado para el canto de los pájaros. En segundo lugar, no sé si Victoria escucha habitualmente este programa, pero ya hemos dicho otras veces que los pájaros en esta época no deben estar en habitaciones muy calurosas y ésta podría ser simplemente la causa de la pasividad de su pájaro. Colóquelo en un sitio de la casa en donde esté fresco.

Recording 29: transcript

16 & 17 Pues, soy Mariano López, y os llamo desde Sevilla. Encontré vuestro número de teléfono en la guía telefónica cuando estaba en Londres la semana pasada en viaje de negocios.

18 & 19 Lo que pasa es que la empresa donde trabajo – me va a mandar a la oficina central allá en Madrid. En efecto voy a ser jefe de la Sección de Exportación. Os llamo para daros mi nueva dirección para que podáis mandarme los documentos que os pedí.

Mis señas serán: Avenida de Italia -14, Sexto B, Madrid. No olvidéis el código postal que es – vamos a ver – 28033.

20 Si queréis alguna vez llamarme por teléfono, no me llaméis a la oficina, sino a casa. A partir de la semana que viene mi número personal será el 413 - 65 - 82, con el prefijo 91.

Recording 30: transcript

21 & 22 – Dime, ¿qué te parece Inglaterra? ¿Cuáles son las cosas que te han gustado, y cuáles no?
– Con la excepción del clima, que parece cambiar de un momento a otro, me ha gustado todo. Lo que me ha resultado sorprendente son las fiestas y los festivales … Nunca había oído hablar de las fiestas inglesas: todos conocéis las nuestras, y aquí en Inglaterra se dice que en España hay fiestas casi todos los días. Pero aunque en Inglaterra no tengáis tantas, las que he visto son muy interesantes.

23 & 24 – ¿Cuáles te han gustado más?
– Navidad, Semana Santa, la Víspera de Todos los Santos. La más curiosa fue unos dos meses después de mi llegada en septiembre a vuestro país. No recuerdo bien el nombre, pero creo que se trataba de un tío que trató de asesinar al rey y destruir el Parlamento. Aquella noche en la escuela hubo fuegos artificiales y comimos hamburguesas al aire libre. También recuerdo los muñecos grandes que hicieron los niños de ropa vieja.

Recording 31: transcript

1 & 2 Bueno, me parece sobre todo que te está resultando un poco difícil acostumbrarte a la vida aquí en España. En cuanto al dolor de estómago, la comida y el agua son distintas, las horas que guardamos también … y tal vez te sientes enfermo porque echas de menos un poco a tu familia …

3 La receta que te voy a dar … es una medicina que pronto te quitará el dolor de estómago. Tienes que tomar dos cucharadas antes de cada comida hasta que se acabe la botella.

4 Tendrás que pagar la medicina en la farmacia, pero si tienes seguro de viaje, podrás pedirles el dinero al volver a tu país. ¡No pierdas el recibo!

5 Realmente no hace falta que guardes cama mañana … de todas formas, a lo mejor te sentirás muchísimo mejor. Pronto olvidarás eso, y ¡lo más importante es que te diviertas!

Recording 32: transcript

El otro día, en el instituto, me llamaron al despacho del director para hablar de mis estudios. Él me felicitó por mis buenas notas en lengua española y me aconsejó pensar en la carrera de periodista. Yo le dije que me encantaba la idea de escribir artículos y hacer entrevistas.

Recording 33: transcript

Mire, afortunadamente no es muy grave. Se ha cortado el pie, nada más. Le pondré una venda y le daré unas aspirinas. Me parece que ha pisado una botella rota o algo así. Siempre pasa igual. A los niños les gusta quitarse los zapatos cuando juegan.

Recording 34: transcript

Hola. Me llamo Elena Moreno Suárez y acabo de cumplir los quince años. Vivo en una finca en los alrededores de Sevilla con mis padres y mi hermano mayor, el que no está casado. Mis amigos dicen que soy muy guapa. Según mi madre, tengo un temperamento alegre y abierto.

Recording 35: transcript

1 Un día de primavera yo fui a la sierra con Pedro. Pusimos las cañas de pescar en el coche, y, por supuesto, llevábamos una chaqueta gruesa y botas.

2 Al llegar a un buen sitio para las truchas montamos las cañas y esperamos. Durante media hora no pasó nada. Se veían sólo los pájaros que volaban por encima de los árboles.

3 De repente mi hijo me despertó. Tiré de la caña y allí había un pez. Era una hermosa trucha grande. La metí en mi mochila. ¡Me gusta mucho el pescado!

Recording 36: transcript

– ¿Por qué fue Vd. al extranjero para trabajar?
– Fue una decisión dificilísima. Mis niños ya habían empezado en un colegio local ... estaban contentos allí pero cuando oímos la noticia de que la empresa de mi marido había ganado el contrato de construir un puente en aquel país ... no había más remedio ... tuvimos que ir también.
– Y ¿por qué volvió Vd. a España?
– Pues ... pasé tres años allí ... me lo pasé muy bien ... fue una experiencia enriquecedora ... pero al final de tres años ... aunque no habían terminado el puente ... aunque mi marido aún está allí ... echaba de menos España.
– Y ... dígame. ¿Cómo era la gente de allí?
– La gente allí era ... ¿como lo puedo explicar? ... una gente triste y seria.
No les gusta la risa ni diversiones ni nada de esto. Sólo les gustaba el trabajo ... y el dinero ... cosas materiales ... Me parece que para la mayoría, la vida era bastante aburrida. Y yo ... como española ... pues al final había conocido a muy pocos amigos ... es más fácil hacer amigos en España.
– ¿Conoció Vd. a alguien interesante allí?
– Sí ... una persona que no olvidaré nunca era la directora. Era una persona impresionante. Ella sabía los nombres de todas las alumnas ... sin excepción. Y esto en un colegio de quinientas alumnas. Y además, podía reconocer a la mayoría de los padres. Siempre se preocupaba por los problemas de las alumnas ... siempre les preguntaba si tenían problemas ... si los estudios iban bien. Pero en lo de la disciplina, me parece que la directora no era bastante severa. Cuando las alumnas llegaban sin libros ... llevaban ropa extravagante ... llegaban hasta fumando ... su reacción era ... pues ... increíble. No gritaba ... no se enfadaba ... ¡sonreía! Luego hablaba aparte con la alumna ... sin dar voces. Y claro, esta táctica tenía muy poco éxito.
– ¡Qué raro! ¿De dónde era la directora?
– No sé pero había vivido muchos años en Francia y sabía hablar francés perfectamente. Ella era de la opinión que sus alumnas podían aprender mucho de los franceses, su cultura, y su lengua. Las alumnas podían escoger las asignaturas que querían estudiar ... con una excepción ... el francés. La directora insistió que todas las alumnas tenían que estudiar francés. Esto era poco popular con las alumnas ... la mayoría se interesaba más por el inglés ... pero ella insistía ... y los que querían hacer inglés tenían que hacer francés también.

6.7 Suggested answers

Recording 21

1 Angry.
2 The washing machine broke down.
3 The phoned a mechanic.
4 The mechanic could not come.
5 To a neighbour's house.

Recording 22

1 He went on a course in London.
2 D.
3 They are more independent.
4 They learn to live without their parents.
5 Some young people end up in gaol.

Recording 23

1 Because she had left a message for me at the information desk.
2 (a)   Near the car-hire facility.
   (b)   (i)   Tall.
         (ii) She has dark curly hair.

3 She asks if I remember her.

4 **(a)** Because Jaime could not come to meet her.
  (b) Because many of the people in his office have flu.

5 **(a)** To pay for his journey to the USA.
  (b) There is a lot of unemployment.

6 **(a)** She says 'Don't worry'.
  (b) In the afternoons and alternate Saturday mornings.

Recording 24

1 The boys' dormitory was full.

2 He looks in the phone book for another youth hostel.

3 He calls his aunt.

4 His aunt is coming to pick you up.

5 He wants to wait in the street.

Recording 25

Student 1	C H
Student 2	A I
Student 3	E L
Student 4	F J
Student 5	B G

Recording 26

13 She thinks she has sorted out the problem.

14 **(a)** A-G-U-I-L-E-R-A
  (b) (i) He is a good friend of the family.
    (ii) He is expecting me.

15 **(i)** They are both successful.
  (ii) They are both funny.

16 **(i)** How I got on at the hospital.
  (ii) To tell her which film I want to see.

Recording 27

1 We will speak in Spanish from the beginning to the end.

2 It will last half-an-hour longer than normal.

3 **(i)** She is South-American.
  (ii) She is from Chile.
  (iii) She has lived a long time in England.
  (iv) She works as a secretrary in an Adult Education Centre.

4 **(i)** She finds speaking Spanish easy.
  (ii) She only makes mistakes occasionally.

Recording 28

11 **(a)** She enjoys being on the programme and she enjoys helping the listeners with their problems.
  (b) The presenter thinks that the listeners' problems are important.

12 **(a)** Because the problems they deal with are not as serious as unemployment, divorce or drugs.
  (b) Problems with pets.

13 Her canary does not move or sing.

14 **(a)** It is not the right time of year for the bird to sing.
  (b) They should not be kept in rooms which are too hot.

Recording 29

16 In the phone book when he was in London.

17 He was away on business.

18 In the central office.

19 He is going to be head of the export department.

20 Because the number won't be valid till next week.

Recording 30

21 It changes from one moment to the next.

22 Spaniards don't know about English festivals. English people know about Spanish festivals.

23 Guy Fawkes Night.

24 Fireworks and eating hamburgers in the open air.

Recording 31

1 The food and the water.

2 Because I miss my family.

3 Take two spoonfuls before each meal until the bottle is finished.

4 Apply to the insurance company when back in England. Don't lose the receipt.

5 Don't stay in bed. Have a good time.

Recording 32

1 **(a)** The headmaster's office.
(b) Journalist.
(c) Writing articles and doing interviews.

Recording 33

1 **(a)** He has cut his foot.
(b) He will put on a bandage and give him some aspirins.
(c) Children like to play without their shoes on.

Recording 34

1 **(a)** She has just reached her 15th birthday.
(b) On a farm on the outskirts of Seville.
(c) He is older than she is and is not married.
(d) Happy and frank with people.

Recording 35

1 **(a)** One day in spring.
(b) They wore thick jackets and boots.

2 **(c)** It was good for trout.
(d) The birds flying above the trees.

3 **(e)** Because his son had to wake him.
(f) In his rucksack.
(g) Because he says that he likes fish.

Recording 36

1 To be with her husband.

2 She missed Spain.

3 Miserable and unfriendly.

4 She enjoyed good relationships with her pupils but did not have strong discipline.

5 All pupils had to learn French.

Chapter 7
Speaking: Basic Level

7.1 Introduction

This is what you need to know about the Basic Level Speaking exam:
- It is compulsory; you cannot opt out of it.
- The speaking test in Spanish is the equivalent of the course-work that you do in other subjects.
- It is made up of two parts: role-play tests and a simple conversation.
- The exam will take place between March and June.
- It will be conducted by your teacher, who will usually be the one who decides when and where the exam takes place.
- It will be recorded on cassette and either marked by your teacher or marked by an external examiner.
- It will last about ten minutes.
- You will have time before the exam to prepare the role-play situations.
- You can keep the role-play cards in front of you during the exam.
- Your teacher will play the role of a sympathetic native speaker who speaks no English. This means you cannot ask him/her what words mean.

7.2 Role-play situations

The role-play situations will be based on the topics and settings laid down by your board. However there are certain situations which lend themselves to role-play and you should be aware of this. These situations are:

> at cafés and restaurants
> asking the way
> public transport
> at the customs
> at the campsite, youth hostel, hotel
> at the doctor's/scene of an accident
> shopping for food/drink/clothes
> at the post office
> on the telephone
> at the bank/exchange office
> lost property
> tourist information office
> at the cinema
> visiting and receiving an exchange partner

When you are revising for or attempting role-plays you should be aware of the following points:

- Do not be confused by the wording of the role-play prompt. If the prompt says 'Find out whether your friend has arrived or not' you may panic because you do not know 'find out' or 'whether' or 'or not'. Actually all you need to say to get full marks is 'has my friend arrived?' (**¿Mi amigo/a ha llegado?**). The skill lies in identifying what are the *key words* in the prompt. If you can communicate the key words then you will almost certainly gain full marks even if you make grammar mistakes.
- If you cannot communicate a key word, maybe you know the opposite word. For example if the prompt is: 'Say that it is cheap' and you do not know the word for 'cheap' but you do know the word for expensive, then **no es caro** will score the same as **es barato**.

7.3 Examples of Basic role-plays

Here are some role-play situations taken from past GCSE papers. After the role-plays, there are suggested answers. You must remember that these suggested answers are not the only way to score full marks nor are they answers suggested by the exam boards.

Role-play 1

You see this menu outside a restaurant in Spain. You and your Spanish friend decide to eat there.
  The waiter (your teacher) speaks to you.

(a) Order a meal from the menu for you and your friend.
    Do you want a dessert?
(b) Say yes and ask what there is.
    Jelly, custard or fruit.
(c) Say you prefer some grapes.
    Certainly. What do you want to drink?
(d) Ask if they have mineral water.
    Yes, of course.

NEAB 1991

Role-play 2

You are in Spain, staying with your exchange partner. Your teacher will play the part of the exchange partner. You want to write a letter home.
(a) Ask if he/she has a pen.
(b) Ask for a pencil.
(c) Say you are writing a letter to your parents.
(d) When he/she suggests you phone, say it is expensive.
(e) Ask your friend if he/she has any stamps.

MEG 1994

Role-play 3

You are in Spain and you enter a café. Your teacher will play the part of the waiter/waitress.
(a) Find out if they sell food.
(b) Ask for a ham sandwich.

(c) Ask for some milk.

(d) When he/she suggests you have lemonade, say you do not like it.

(e) Find out if there is another café nearby.

MEG 1994

Role-play 4

You are staying with a Spanish family. One evening you are not feeling very well. Your Spanish friend (your teacher) asks you what the matter is.

(a) Say you feel ill.
What's wrong exactly?

(b) Say you have a headache.
Can I get you something?

(c) Ask if he/she has an aspirin.
Of course. Anything else?

(d) Ask for a glass of water.
Here you are.

NEAB 1992

Role-play 5

You are staying with your Spanish friend (your teacher) who is asking you about your school holidays.

(a) Say you have six weeks.
In Spain they are longer.

(b) Ask what he/she does during the holidays.
I go to the beach. What about you?

(c) Say you are going to work in August.
What will you do with the money?

(d) Say you want to buy a computer.
Good idea.

NEAB 1993

Role-play 6

You see a bus trip advertised in the tourist office in Madrid. You go up to the assistant (your teacher) who asks if he/she can help.

(a) Ask how much it costs.
3,500 pesetas per person.

(b) Ask what there is in Segovia.
A Roman aqueduct.

(c) Say you want two seats for tomorrow.
Very well.

(d) Ask at what time the bus returns.
At 8 o'clock.

NEAB 1993

Role-play 7

You are at a sports centre in Albacete and you go to the ticket office with another English friend. The examiner will play the part of the clerk and will speak first. Your tasks are:

(a) To say you want to play tennis.

(b) To say you want to play for one hour.

(c) To ask how much it will cost.

(d) To ask if you can hire some balls.

(e) To say thank you and goodbye.

SEG 1994

Role-play 8

While visiting Madrid, a person in the street hands you this card. You show it to your Spanish friend (your teacher) who says he/she knows the Risco Bar.

MESON-BAR

EL RISCO

Especialidad en raciones de cocina

HAMBURGUESAS Y SANDWICHES

Calle Santa Ana, número 40

PEDRO BERNARDO

(a) Ask if the food is good.
Yes, it's very good.
(b) Ask if he/she is hungry.
Yes, very.
(c) Say you'd like to go.
Fine, let's go.
(d) Ask if it's far.
No, about ten minutes on foot.

NEAB 1992

Role-play 9

You are in a tourist information office in a Spanish town. The part of the person behind the counter will be played by the examiner. You will begin the conversation.

(a) Ask for a list of hotels.
(b) Ask for a plan of the town.
(c) Ask if you have to pay.

ULEAC 1994

Role-play 10

You are staying with your Spanish friend (your teacher) who tells you he/she is getting ready for school.

(a) Ask your friend how he/she goes to school.
I walk.
(b) Ask at what time it starts.
9 o'clock.
(c) Ask what the first class is.
English. Do you want to come?
(d) Say you are going shopping.
O.K., see you later.

NEAB 1993

Role-play 11

You are in Spain, in a railway station. Your teacher will play the part of the railway official.

(a) Ask where you can leave your suitcase.
(b) When he/she suggests the left luggage office, find out what time it closes.
(c) Say you want to go to Valencia this afternoon.
(d) Ask for a return ticket.
(e) Find out what platform it leaves from.

MEG 1994

Role-play 12

You are on holiday in Spain. You want to write some postcards to your friends in England. You go into a souvenir shop. The assistant (your teacher) asks you what you want.

(a) Say you want a pen.
O.K.
(b) Ask how much it is.
100 pesetas.
(c) Ask if they sell stamps.
Yes, how many do you want?
(d) Say five, for England.
300 pesetas altogether.

NEAB 1994

Role-play 13

You go into a bar with your Spanish friend. Your friend (your teacher) asks what you want to eat.

(a) Ask what he/she recommends.
   The ham.
(b) Say you don't have much money.
   I'll pay. What do you want to drink?
(c) Say fizzy mineral water.
   O.K.
(d) Ask if there is a telephone here.
   Yes, by the toilets.

NEAB 1994

Role-play 14

You are about to leave your penfriend's home in Spain. You are explaining your travel arrangements to him/her. Your teacher will play the part of your penfriend and will start the conversation.

(a) Say yes, the plane leaves at 11 o'clock.
(b) Ask your penfriend if he/she is going to the airport.
(c) Say you want to buy some magazines there.
(d) Say you hope to eat on the plane.
(e) Say your brother is going to meet you.

NICCEA 1992

Role-play 15

During a visit to Spain, you and your family are being shown round a village by a local guide. You are asking the guide some questions so that you can explain everything to your parents. Your teacher will play the part of the guide and will start the conversation.

(a) Say the square is very beautiful.
(b) Ask if there is a museum in the village.
(c) Say there are not many cars in the streets.
(d) Ask how people live there.
(e) Say you would like to see the church.

NICCEA 1992

Role-play 16

On arriving in a Spanish town you decide to take a taxi to the beach. The part of the taxi driver will be played by the examiner. You will begin the conversation.

(a) Say you want to go to the beach.
(b) Ask if it's very far.
(c) Say it's quicker by taxi.

ULEAC 1994

Role-play 17

You are at the Iberia check-in in Barajas airport, Madrid. You have an English friend with you. The examiner will play the part of the Iberia check-in clerk and will speak first. Your tasks are:

(a) To say you want to travel to London.
(b) To say you have tickets already.
(c) To ask if the plane will leave on time.
(d) To ask where they sell chocolate.
(e) To say thank you and goodbye.

SEG 1994

Role-play 18

One evening, you are feeling unwell. Your Spanish friend (your teacher) asks you what the matter is.

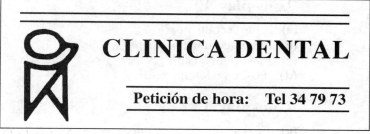

CLINICA DENTAL

Petición de hora: Tel 34 79 73

(a) Say you have toothache.
Can I get you anything,?
(b) Ask for two aspirins.
Here you are.
(c) Say you want to see a dentist.
I'll ring the clinic in the morning.
(d) Say you are going to bed.
That might be best.

NEAB 1994

Role-play 19

You are staying with your penfriend in Spain. He/she is asking you about your bedroom at home. Your teacher will play the part of your penfriend and will start the conversation.
(a) Say it is on the first floor.
(b) Say it is next to your parents' room.
(c) Say a bed, a wardrobe and a table.
(d) Say you watch television in the evenings.
(e) Say you also have a lot of records.

NICCEA 1992

Role-play 20

You are staying on a campsite in Spain when your young brother disappears. You are describing him to the manager/manageress at Reception. Your teacher will play the part of the manager/manageress and will start the conversation.
(a) Say he is called Richard.
(b) Say he is nine.
(c) Say he is slim and has fair hair.
(d) Say he is wearing his bathing costume.
(e) Say you are going to look for him there.

NICCEA 1992

7.4 Suggested answers

Role-play 1

(a) Quiero pollo, patatas y ensalada para mí y para mi amigo/a.
(b) Sí. ¿Qué hay de postre?
(c) Prefiero uvas.
(d) ¿Hay agua mineral?

Role-play 2

(a) ¿Tienes un bolígrafo?
(b) ¿Tienes un lápiz?
(c) Escribo una carta a mis padres.
(d) Es caro.
(e) ¿Tienes sellos?

Role-play 3

(a) ¿Vende comida?
(b) Un bocadillo de jamón, por favor.

(c) Leche, por favor.
(d) No me gusta.
(e) ¿Hay otro café por aquí?

Role-play 4

(a) Me siento enfermo/a.
(b) Tengo dolor de cabeza.
(c) ¿Tiene aspirina?
(d) Un vaso de agua, por favor.

Role-play 5

(a) Tengo seis semanas.
(b) ¿Qué haces durante las vacaciones?
(c) Voy a trabajar en agosto.
(d) Quiero comprar un ordenador.

Role-play 6

(a) ¿Cuánto cuesta?
(b) ¿Qué hay en Segovia?
(c) Quiero dos asientos para mañana.
(d) ¿A qué hora vuelve el autobús?

Role-play 7

(a) Quiero jugar al tenis.
(b) Quiero jugar una hora.
(c) ¿Cuánto cuesta?
(d) ¿Puedo alquilar pelotas?
(e) Gracias. Adiós.

Role-play 8

(a) ¿La comida es buena?
(b) ¿Tienes hambre?
(c) Me gustaría ir.
(d) ¿Está lejos?

Role-play 9

(a) Una lista de hoteles, por favor.
(b) Un plano de la ciudad, por favor.
(c) ¿Tengo que pagar?

Role-play 10

(a) ¿Cómo vas al colegio?
(b) ¿A qué hora empieza?
(c) ¿Cuál es la primera clase?
(d) Voy de compras.

Role-play 11

(a) ¿Dónde puedo dejar mi maleta?
(b) ¿A qué hora cierra?
(c) Quiero ir a Valencia esta tarde.
(d) Un billete de ida y vuelta.
(e) ¿Sale de qué andén, por favor?

Role-play 12

(a) Quiero un bolígrafo.
(b) ¿Cuánto cuesta?

(c) ¿Vende sellos?
(d) Cinco para Inglaterra, por favor.

Role-play 13

(a) ¿Qué recomienda?
(b) No tengo mucho dinero.
(c) Agua mineral con gas, por favor.
(d) ¿Hay un teléfono aquí?

Role-play 14

(a) Sí, el avión sale a las once.
(b) ¿Vas al aeropuerto?
(c) Quiero comprar revistas allí.
(d) Espero comer en el avión.
(e) Mi hermano va a buscarme.

Role-play 15

(a) La plaza es muy hermosa.
(b) ¿Hay un museo en la aldea?
(c) No hay muchos coches en las calles.
(d) ¿Cuánta gente vive allí?
(e) Quiero ver la iglesia.

Role-play 16

(a) Quiero ir a la playa.
(b) ¿Está muy lejos?
(c) Es más rápido en taxi.

Role-play 17

(a) Quiero viajar a Londres.
(b) Tengo ya los billetes.
(c) ¿El avión saldrá a la hora?
(d) ¿Dónde se vende chocolate?
(e) Gracias. Adiós.

Role-play 18

(a) Tengo dolor de muela.
(b) Dos aspirinas, por favor.
(c) Quiero ver a un/una dentista.
(d) Voy a la cama.

Role-play 19

(a) Está en el primer piso.
(b) Está al lado de la habitación de mis padres.
(c) Una cama, un armario y una mesa.
(d) Veo la televisión por la tarde.
(e) Yo también tengo muchos discos.

Role-play 20

(a) Se llama Richard.
(b) Tiene nueve años.
(c) Es delgado y tiene el pelo rubio.
(d) Lleva un traje de baño.
(e) Voy a buscarle allí.

7.5 Conversation

This is what you need to know about the Basic Conversation:

- The number of questions you will be asked depends on your exam board but there will be between 10 and 20 simple questions.
- You are not allowed to know beforehand exactly which questions you are going to be asked.
- The questions will be straightforward and of the type that you have practised with your teacher.
- Your teacher is allowed to 'nudge' you; this means if you make a mistake he/she might ask you to repeat what you have said or express surprise thus guiding you to the right answer. So if he/she asked you **¿A qué hora llegas al colegio por la mañana?** and you reply **A las seis**, he/she might express astonishment and alert you to the fact that you have given the wrong time.
- Avoid giving just **sí** or **no** for an answer. You cannot expect high marks unless you offer a bit more than this.
- Your answers do not have to be factually correct! If you are asked what you have in your bedroom and you do not know the word for a stereo (which you have in your bedroom) but you do know the word for a television (which you do not have in your bedroom) then answer **tengo una televisión**. The exam board is unlikely to check physically that you have a TV in your room. What is important is that you have been able to communicate something in Spanish.
- The topics and settings for the conversations will be those laid down by your exam board for Basic Level. However some topics lend themselves more than others to a basic conversation. The likely topics are:

you and your family	your pastimes and interests
your house and home	school
your region	daily routines
holidays	

- The conversation will be based on a number of these topics not just on one of them.
- You should take every opportunity to practise questions with a friend or a parent. Why not record questions onto a cassette, leaving a few seconds' pause for each answer? Then play the cassette and see if you know the answer without looking at any book or notes.
- Speak Spanish as often as possible. You could even imagine the conversations if you have no-one to help you!

7.6 Example questions and answers

YOU AND YOUR FAMILY

¿Cómo te llamas?	Me llamo …
¿Cuántos años tienes?	Tengo … años.
¿Cuántos sois en tu familia?	Somos …
¿Quiénes son?	Son mi padre, mi madre, mi hermano y yo.
¿Qué hace tu padre?	Es …
¿Qué hace tu madre?	Es …
¿En qué año naciste?	Nací en mil novecientos ochenta y siete.
¿Cuánto mides?	Mido un metro ochenta.
¿Tienes animales en casa?	Tengo un perro/un gato.
¿Cuándo es tu cumpleaños?	Es el veintisiete de setiembre.

HOUSE AND HOME

¿Vives en una casa o un piso?	Vivo en una casa/un piso.
¿Cómo es tu casa?	Mi casa es pequeña y cómoda.
¿A qué distancia se encuentra tu casa del colegio?	Se encuentra a cinco kilómetros de mi colegio.
¿Cuántas habitaciones hay en tu casa?	Hay … habitaciones.

¿Qué ves por la ventana de tu dormitorio?	Veo las casas de mis vecinos.
¿Qué hay en tu jardín?	Hay flores y árboles.
¿Qué hay en tu dormitorio?	Hay una cama, una mesa y una silla.

YOUR REGION

¿Qué sitios de interés hay cerca de tu casa?	Hay una iglesia interesante y un parque.
¿A qué distancia se encuentra tu casa de Londres/del mar?	Se encuentra a cien kilómetros de Londres/del mar.
¿Cuál es la población de tu pueblo/ciudad?	Hay ocho mil habitantes más o menos.
¿Qué hay que hacer en tu pueblo/ciudad?	Hay cines, discotecas y un club para jóvenes.

YOUR PASTIMES AND INTERESTS

¿Cuál es tu pasatiempo favorito?	Me gusta jugar al tenis.
¿Dónde juegas al tenis?	Juego en el parque.
¿Con quién juegas?	Juego con mi amigo/a.
¿Sabes tocar un instrumento musical?	Sé tocar el piano.
¿Qué programa prefieres en la televisión?	Prefiero 'vecinos'.
¿Vas al cine algunas veces?	Sí, voy cuando tengo dinero.
¿Te gusta la jardinería?	Odio la jardinería.
¿Qué deportes practicas?	Juego al hockey/al fútbol.
¿Qué tipo de música te gusta?	Me gusta la música pop.

SCHOOL

¿Qué asignatura prefieres?	Prefiero el español.
¿Por qué?	Me gusta el/la profesor/a.
¿Qué asignatura te gusta menos?	Me gusta menos el francés.
¿Qué deportes practicas en el colegio?	Juego al fútbol/al tenis/al hockey.
¿Cómo vienes al colegio por la mañana?	Vengo a pie/en coche/en autocar.
¿Cómo viniste al colegio esta mañana?	Vine a pie/en coche/en autocar.
¿A qué hora llegas?	Llego a las nueve menos cuarto.
¿A qué hora empiezan las clases?	Empiezan a las nueve y veinte.
¿Cuántas clases tienes cada día?	Tengo cinco clases cada día.
¿Cuánto tiempo dura cada clase?	Cada clase dura una hora.
¿A qué hora es el recreo?	El recreo es a las once y veinte.
¿Quánto tiempo dura el recreo?	El recreo dura veinte minutos.
¿Qué haces durante el recreo?	Hablo con mis amigos/as y como un bocadillo.
¿Cuántos alumnos hay en tu colegio/en tu clase de español?	Hay seiscientos alumnos en mi colegio/ hay veinte alumnos en mi clase de español.
¿Cuántos profesores hay en tu colegio?	Hay cuarenta profesores.
¿Qué haces durante la hora de comer?	Como mis bocadillos y juego al tenis.

HOLIDAYS

¿Adónde fuiste de vacaciones el año pasado?	Fui a España.
¿Has visitado otros países?	He visitado Francia, España y Alemania.
¿Con quién fuiste?	Fui con mi familia.
¿Cómo fuiste?	Fui en avión/en barco/en coche.
¿Has visitado España?	Sí, visité España el año pasado.
¿Dónde te alojaste?	Me alojé en un hotel.
¿Cuánto tiempo estuviste en España?	Estuve en España dos semanas.
¿Qué tiempo hizo?	Hizo sol todos los días.
¿Qué hiciste allí?	Tomé el sol y nadé en el mar.
¿Adónde irás este verano?	Iré a España otra vez.

DAILY ROUTINE

¿A qué hora te despiertas?	Me despierto a las siete.
¿A qué hora te levantas?	Me levanto a las siete y cuarto.
¿Qué haces para prepararte?	Me lavo, me visto y tomo el desayuno.
¿A qué hora sales para el colegio?	Salgo a las ocho y media.
¿A qué spora vuelves del colegio?	Vuelvo a las cuatro.
¿Qué haces al volver a casa?	Hago mis deberes.
¿A qué hora cenas?	Ceno a las seis y media.
¿Qué haces después de cenar?	Miro la televisión.
¿A qué hora te acuestas?	Me acuesto a las diez.

Chapter 8
Speaking: Higher Level

8.1 Introduction

This is what you need to know about the exam:

- The Higher Level Speaking test is not compulsory; you can opt out of it.
- You will have to perform role-plays which are harder than at Basic Level. The full range of Topics and Settings for your board may be encountered and the role-play may well have an unprepared element (see below).
- You will have to take part in a conversation which is more complex than what you experience at Basic Level. Communication and the quality of your language will be assessed.
- At Basic Level, most of the questions asked during the conversation will not be open-ended. For example you may be asked when your birthday is; when you have given the date, there is nothing much more that you can say. However at Higher Level, you will be asked open-ended questions. For example 'What did you do on your holidays?' and you will be expected to give a lot of information.
- The *MEG* Higher Level Speaking test is different to that of other boards. You have to do a *Narrator* which means you have to tell a story based on a series of pictorial or verbal clues (see below).
- As with the Basic Level test, you will be given time to prepare and you may keep your role-play cards and narrator card with you during the actual exam.
- Your teacher usually decides on the order of the different items in the test.

8.2 Higher Level role-play

You need to be aware that at Higher Level your syllabus allows for extra topics and settings to be tested. The most likely extra topics are:

> work and future
> emergencies (accidents and medical emergencies)
> services (repairs, complaints, lost property)

There is no better preparation for role-play than practising on exam-type questions!

- Use the role-play situations in this book.
- Make sure you know the *kind* of vocabulary that is likely to come up in these situations:

food	drink	clothes
public transport	garage	campsite, hotel and youth hostel
shopping	café/restaurant	post office/telephone/bank
asking the way	cinema	visiting and receiving an exchange partner

- Ask your teacher for past papers and materials which can provide you with practice.
- There is a book which specializes in role-play. It provides about 600 role-play questions and also provides a suggested answer. It is called Role-Play Revision for GCSE Spanish (ISBN 0 304 31874 4) and is available from book-shops.

8.3 The 'unprepared' questions

You may well have to face a role-play question which you do not know beforehand. On your card it will say something like: 'Be prepared to respond to what your teacher says', or 'Answer the person's question'. Your teacher will have a script which tells him/her what to ask you. You have to understand what your teacher says so be ready for it! There are several ways you can prepare for these questions:

- Read the setting carefully. For instance if the setting says: 'You get oil on your jeans while cleaning your bicycle so you take them to the cleaner's', there is a good chance that the 'unprepared' question will ask you how you got your jeans dirty.
- The majority of 'unprepared' questions are linked to the previous role-play command. Think carefully. Can you predict what it will be? For instance if the prompt is: 'Say that you have lost your suitcase', you can be fairly sure that the examiner will ask you to describe the suitcase or say what was in it or describe how you lost it.
- Remember that a short answer scores full marks and you have no need to use a full sentence. So have a short answer ready for 'what time?', 'when?', 'how much ?' 'where?' 'what did you buy?' 'what did you do?' 'what did you eat? drink?'.

  For example:

¿A qué hora te levantarás?	A las ocho.
¿Cuándo llegas? ¿cuándo llegaste?	Mañana/ayer.
¿Cuánto dinero quieres cambiar?	Veinte libras.
¿Dónde lo perdiste?	En la playa.
¿Qué compraste?	Un libro.
¿Qué comiste/bebiste?	Pescado/leche.

8.4 Examination role-play questions

The following are a selection of Higher Level role-play questions taken from past papers. These are followed by suggested answers. Remember that these answers are not recommended by the exam board nor are they the only way to answer the questions.

Role-play 1

You are looking at videos in a shop in Spain. Your Spanish friend (your teacher) asks you which one you want.

(a) Ask which videos he/she has already seen.
  Not many.
(b) Ask what 'Un trío de locos' is about.
  Three men on holiday.
(c) Offer to pay for it, and give a reason.
  Thanks.

NEAB 1994

Role-play 2

SITUATION	You are in Madrid. You have missed your coach to Valencia because of a strike on the underground. At the coach station, you go to the ticket office where the assistant (your teacher) asks if he/she can help.
YOU MUST	(a) Say you have missed your coach and explain why. (b) Express disappointment and ask if you can reserve a seat on another coach. (c) Answer any questions put to you and give a reason.
REMEMBER	You have to catch a boat from Valencia to Ibiza tomorrow morning.

Teacher's instructions
(a) Set the scene by saying:
   Estamos en la taquilla en la estación de autocares en Madrid. Yo soy el empleado/la empleada. ¿En qué puedo ayudarle?
(b) Allow the candidate to explain what happened and why it happened. Say you are sorry, but you cannot do anything about it.
(c) Allow the candidate to ask if he/she can reserve a seat on another coach. Say yes, there is a coach at 4 o'clock this afternoon and one at 11 o'clock tomorrow morning which is much quicker.
(d) End the conversation by making a reservation for the candidate on the 4 o'clock coach.

NEAB 1994

Role-play 3

Before setting out on a trip to Northern Spain, you see the weather forecast in the newspaper. Your Spanish friend (your teacher) asks if you're ready to leave.
(a) Express disappointment, and say you think it is going to rain.
   Why do you say that?
(b) Say you have seen the weather forecast in the newspaper.
   We can take an umbrella.
(c) Say you prefer to stay at home, and suggest another activity for the day.
   O.K.

NEAB 1994

Role-play 4

SITUATION	You ordered a taxi to the airport for 4 o'clock. At 4.20, you are still waiting. You ring the taxi firm again and the receptionist (your teacher) answers.
YOU MUST	(a) Explain why you are ringing. (b) Ask at what time the taxi will arrive. (c) Answer any questions put to you and give a reason.
REMEMBER	Your flight is at 6 o'clock but you have to be at the airport one hour before departure.

Teacher's instructions
(a) Set the scene by saying:
   Vd. llama a una parada de taxis en España.
   Yo soy el/la recepcionista.
   ¡Dígame!

(b) Allow the candidate to explain exactly why he/she is ringing.
   Say you're sorry, there has been a delay.
(c) Allow the candidate to ask when the taxi will arrive.
   Say at about 5 o'clock and ask if that is all right.
(d) End the conversation by saying that you will send a taxi as soon as possible.

NEAB 1994

Role-play 5

While on holiday in a Spanish seaside town you injure your arm, so you go to the hospital. The part of the doctor will be played by the examiner, who will begin the conversation.

(a) Say your arm hurts a lot.
(b) Say you twisted it when you were playing on the beach.
(c) Say it's very difficult to move it.
(d) Say you think it's broken.
(e) Answer the doctor's question. (The teacher will say '¿Dónde te quedas en la ciudad?')
(f) Give a reason why you can't return to the hospital tomorrow.
(g) Ask if you can have some tablets for the pain.

ULEAC 1994

Role-play 6

One morning your Spanish friend (your teacher) shows you this postcard from Wales.

(a) Express amusement and ask who has sent it.
My brother. What's Wales like ?
(b) Say it is a very mountainous country.
I'd like to go there.
(c) Say which other country you'd like to visit and give a reason.
Good idea.

NEAB 1993

Role-play 7

You have just arrived at your Spanish penfriend's house. You need to find out various things. The part of your penfriend will be played by the examiner, who will begin the conversation.

(a) Say you have put your things in your room.
(b) Ask if you can hang your clothes in the wardrobe.
(c) Ask if there is hot water for a shower.
(d) Say you would like to phone home later.
(e) Ask what time you have to be back if you go out.
(f) Answer your penfriend's question. (The teacher will say '¿Cómo vas a volver a casa?')
(g) Suggest one way you could help in the house.

ULEAC 1994

Role-play 8

One evening, at your Spanish friend's house, you are feeling hungry. Your friend (your teacher) shows you this advertisement for a home delivery pizza service.

(a) Express interest and ask if he/she has tried their meals.
Yes, they're good.
(b) Ask how long you have to wait.
About half an hour. Shall I telephone them?
(c) Say you prefer to go out to eat, and give a reason.
O.K.

NEAB 1993

Role-play 9

You are talking to your Spanish penfriend in Spain about last year's summer holiday. Your teacher will play the part of your penfriend and will start the conversation.

(a) Say you went to the south of France at the beginning of July.

(b) Say you stayed on a campsite near the coast.

(c) Describe the campsite. (Give two details.)

NICCEA 1994

Role-play 10

You are staying with your Spanish penfriend in Spain. You are talking to his/her father/mother about jobs you do at home. Your teacher will play the part of the father/mother and will start the conversation.

(a) Say last summer you painted the walls of your bedroom.

(b) Say it was difficult to choose a colour for the ceiling.

(c) Mention two jobs you do at home.

NICCEA 1994

Role-play 11

At home in England you receive a telephone call from your Spanish friend (your teacher) who tells you that he/she is in London.

(a) Express surprise and ask how long he/she has been in England.
   I arrived yesterday.

(b) Ask if he/she will have time to visit you.
   Sure, is Friday O.K?

(c) Ask him/her to come on Saturday, and give a reason.
   Fine, see you on Saturday.

NEAB 1992

Role-play 12

You are talking to your Spanish penfriend in Spain about presents. Your teacher will play the part of your penfriend and will start the conversation.

(a) Say you bought a tie for your father's birthday.

(b) Say there was a discount on men's clothes.

(c) Say what you will choose this year. (Give one detail about this item.)

NICCEA 1994

Role-play 13

During a visit to Spain you are talking to your Spanish penfriend's father/mother about a summer job. Your teacher will play the part of the father/mother and will start the conversation.

(a) Say your parents advised you to work during the summer.

(b) Say a teacher spoke to you about a job in an office.

(c) Say what you would like to do as a career.

NICCEA 1994

Role-play 14

You are staying with your Spanish penfriend in Spain. You are telling him/her about one of your uncles. Your teacher will play the part of your penfriend and will start the conversation.

(a) Say he has been living near Belfast for three years.

(b) Say you are not sure.

(c) Say why he is your favourite uncle. (Mention two points.)

NICCEA 1994

Role-play 15

You are on holiday with your family in Spain when you see advertisements for a circus. You go to the box office to get tickets. Your teacher will play the part of the ticket clerk and will start the conversation.

(a) Say how many tickets you want and for what time.

(b) Say in the third row or behind.

(c) Ask if you can see the animals afterwards.

NICCEA 1994

Role-play 16

While in Spain, you feel unwell and go to see a doctor (your teacher). He/she asks you what the problem is.

(a) Say that you have been unwell for two days.
   What's the trouble exactly?

(b) Say you have a cough and a high temperature.
   You've got 'flu – you'd better go to bed.

(c) Tell him/her that you have to be better before the weekend and say why.
   I'll give you a prescription.

NEAB 1992

Role-play 17

You have just arrived by coach from London to stay for the first time with a Spanish family in Ciudad Real. The examiner is the father/mother of the Spanish family. The examiner speaks first. Your tasks are:

(a) To thank them for their welcome and say how the journey was.

(b) To say that you ate all the time and are not hungry.

(c) To explain that you are very tired and hot after the journey.

(d) To ask where you can put your things.

(e) To ask where the nearest swimming pool is.

SEG 1993

Role-play 18

You were the witness of a traffic accident yesterday in the district of Los Asperones in Málaga. Today your Spanish friend (the examiner) brings you this photograph in *El País* and asks if it is the accident you witnessed. Your tasks are:

(a) To describe to your friend how the accident occurred.

(b) To say what you did when you witnessed it.

(c) To find out where your friend was at the time.

(d) To ask if you should go to the police.

SEG 1993

8.5 Suggested answers

Role-play 1

(a) ¿Qué vídeos has visto ya?
(b) Y 'Un trío de locos' ¿de qué se trata?
(c) Yo pagaré porque tengo mucho dinero.

Role-play 2

(In this type of role-play, you need to read the teacher's instructions.)
(a) He perdido mi autocar porque había una huelga en el metro.
(Lo siento pero no puedo ayudarle.)
(b) Estoy muy decepcionado/a ¿Puedo reservar un asiento en otro autocar?
(Hay dos autocares, uno a las cuatro de la tarde y el otro sale a las once, mañana por la mañana.
El autocar de las once es mejor porque es más rápido.)
(c) No. Tomaré el autocar de las cuatro porque tengo que tomar un barco de Valencia a Ibiza
mañana por la mañana.

Role-play 3

(a) No estoy contento/a. Creo que va a llover.
(b) He visto el pronóstico del tiempo en el periódico.
(c) Prefiero quedarme en casa. Podemos mirar la televisión.

Role-play 4

(In this type of role-play, you need to read the teacher's instructions.)
(a) Reservé un taxi para las cuatro. Todavía no ha llegado.
(b) ¿A qué hora llegará el taxi?
(c) Un taxi a las cinco es demasiado tarde. Tengo que estar en el aeropuerto a las cinco.

Role-play 5

(a) Me duele el brazo mucho.
(b) Lo torcí cuando estaba jugando en la playa.
(c) Es difícil moverlo.
(d) Creo que está roto.
(e) En el Hotel Sol.
(f) No puedo. Vuelvo a Inglaterra mañana.
(g) Me puede dar unas pastillas para el dolor?

Role-play 6

(a) Muy graciosa. ¿Quién la ha mandado?
(b) Es un país muy montañoso.
(c) Me gustaría visitar Francia también porque la gente es muy simpática.

Role-play 7

(a) He puesto mis cosas en mi dormitorio.
(b) ¿Puedo colgar mi ropa en el armario?
(c) ¿Hay agua caliente para una ducha?
(d) Quiero llamar a casa más tarde.
(e) ¿A qué hora tengo que volver si salgo?
(f) En taxi.
(g) Puedo ayudar a poner la mesa.

Role-play 8

(a) Sí, me interesa. ¿Has probado sus comidas?
(b) ¿Cuánto tiempo tendríamos que esperar?
(c) Prefiero salir a comer. Conozco un restaurante interesante.

Role-play 9

(a) Fui al sur de Francia a principios de julio.
(b) Me quedé en un camping cerca de la costa.
(c) El camping era estupendo. Había una piscina y un restaurante.

Role-play 10

(a) El verano pasado pinté las paredes de mi habitación.
(b) Era difícil escoger un color para el techo.
(c) Lavo el coche y arreglo mi habitación.

Role-play 11

(a) ¡Qué sorpresa! ¿Cuándo llegaste a Inglaterra?
(b) ¿Tienes tiempo para visitarme?
(c) ¿Puedes venir el sábado? Tengo todo el día libre.

Role-play 12

(a) Compré una corbata para el cumpleaños de mi padre.
(b) Había un descuento con la ropa de hombres.
(c) Este año escogeré un jersey porque son muy baratos.

Role-play 13

(a) Mis padres me dieron un consejo. Dijeron que debo trabajar durante el verano.
(b) Un profesor mencionó que había un trabajo en una oficina.
(c) Quiero ser dentista.

Role-play 14

(a) Lleva casi tres años viviendo cerca de Belfast.
(b) No estoy seguro/a.
(c) Me gusta mi tío porque es muy simpático y me da mucho dinero.

Role-play 15

(a) Quiero cuatro entradas para la sesión de las tres.
(b) En o detrás de la tercera fila.
(c) ¿Podemos ver los animales después?

Role-play 16

(a) Estoy enfermo/a desde hace dos días.
(b) Estoy tosiendo y tengo fiebre.
(c) Tengo que recuperarme antes del fin de semana porque hay una fiesta.

Role-play 17

(a) Gracias por la bienvenida. El viaje era muy largo y cansado.
(b) Comí todo el tiempo y no tengo hambre.
(c) Estoy muy cansado/a y tengo calor después del viaje.
(d) ¿Dónde puedo poner mis cosas?
(e) ¿Dónde está la piscina más cercana?

Role–play 18

(a) El coche iba demasiado de prisa. Chocó contra un camión en los semáforos.
(b) En seguida llamé a una ambulancia.
(c) ¿Dónde estuviste tú en aquel momento?
(d) ¿Debo ir a la policía?

8.6 Higher Level conversation

This is what you need to know about the exam:
- All the boards insist on this conversation.
- You will be assessed on your communication skills and also on the quality of your language.
- You may be asked to show your knowledge of tenses by being asked questions about what you did in the past, what you do normally and what you will do in the future.
- Your answers need to be longer than at Basic Level. You will be asked open-ended questions (questions that allow you to answer at length, e.g. **describe tus vacaciones**) and you must show that you can talk at length using impressive vocabulary and structures.
- You will not be allowed to give a pre-learnt speech. Your teacher will interrupt when he/she realizes this is what you are doing.
- Your teacher will have a list of topics on which the conversation will be based. He/she may give you a list of topics and questions and you should concentrate on these.
- The topics that you are most likely to encounter are:

family	your future plans
house and home	your hobbies
your village, town or region	your holidays
your school	

In the exam

- Try to give long answers.
- Try to use any impressive vocabulary that you know.
- Try to put expression into what you say.
- Prepare a few phrases and words that your classmates do not know. Spring them on your teacher in the exam (make sure they are right first!). He/she may be impressed to the point of increasing your mark.

8.7 Example questions and answers

Although your answers must not be a pre-learnt speech, it is nevertheless important that you are able to speak for about a minute on these topics. Why not record these answers on a cassette and listen to them as often as you can? Get a friend or parent to ask you the questions and see if you can talk for a minute. Ask them to interrupt you and ask you an unexpected question.

YOUR FAMILY
- Describe tu familia.
- En mi familia somos cuatro, mi madre, mi padre, mi hermana y yo. Tenemos también un perro. Mi padre trabaja en una oficina. No sé exactamente lo que hace. Mi madre es dentista.
- ¿Cómo es tu padre?
- Mi padre es grande y tiene los ojos negros. Tiene cuarenta y cinco años y le gusta leer periódicos y ver la televisión.
- ¿Cómo es tu madre?
- Mi madre es pequeña y bonita. Tiene los ojos marrones y el pelo largo y negro. Tiene cuarenta y dos años y le gusta trabajar en el jardín y salir con mi padre.

- ¿Cómo es tu hermana?
- Mi hermana tiene trece años y es muy simpática. Tiene los ojos azules, el pelo largo y rubio y lleva gafas. Le gusta la música pop y ver la televisión.
- ¿Tienes otros parientes?
- Sí, tengo otros parientes, muchos sobrinos, muchos tíos, muchos primos. Mis abuelos nos visitan a menudo.
- ¿Qué animal te gusta más?
- Me gustan los perros porque son muy cariñosos y limpios.

YOUR HOUSE AND HOME

- Describe tu casa.
- Mi casa es muy bonita. Hay tres dormitorios, una cocina, un comedor, una sala de estar y un cuarto de baño.
- Describe tu dormitorio.
- Mi dormitorio es muy cómodo. Hay una cama, una silla, una mesa, un estéreo, un televisor y muchos libros. Es mi habitación favorita.
- ¿Qué haces en tu dormitorio?
- Hago muchas cosas. Hago mis deberes, leo, escucho música, veo la televisión y duermo, por supuesto.
- Describe tu cocina.
- Mi cocina es muy moderna. Hay una nevera, un lavaplatos, una lavadora y una mesa con cuatro sillas. Desde la cocina se ve el jardín.
- Describe tu sala de estar.
- Mi sala de estar es muy cómoda. Hay un sofá, dos sillones, una alfombra roja, un televisor, un estéreo y cortinas muy bonitas.
- ¿Tienes un jardín?
- Sí, tenemos un jardín detrás de la casa. Es muy bonito. Hay un césped, árboles, plantas y flores. También hemos plantado patatas, cebollas, guisantes y zanahorias. A mis padres les gusta trabajar en el jardín.

YOUR VILLAGE/TOWN/REGION

- Describe tu pueblo/ciudad/ región.
- A mí me gusta esta región. Por aquí hay mucho de interés. Hay un canal, un río, un parque bonito y muchos campos de deporte y un cine. No lejos de aquí hay fábricas pero también hay campo bonito.
- ¿Dónde en Gran Bretaña se encuentra tu región?
- Se encuentra en el norte/sur/este/oeste/centro de Inglaterra/Gales/Escocia/Irlanda.
- ¿Desde hace cuántos años vives aquí?
- Vivo aquí desde hace quince años, es decir toda mi vida.
- ¿Cuáles son los edificios interesantes?
- Hay la biblioteca, el cine, el ayuntamiento, la vieja iglesia, la piscina y el hospital. También hay muchos edificios muy antiguos.

YOUR HOBBIES

- ¿Quieres describir tus pasatiempos?
- Tengo muchos pasatiempos. Me gusta jugar al fútbol/hockey/tenis/baloncesto. También me gusta leer, ver la televisión, ir al cine y salir con mis amigos.
- ¿Cuál es tu deporte favorito?
- Mi deporte favorito es la natación. Normalmente voy a la piscina los sábados con mis amigos.
- ¿Qué tipo de película te gusta?
- Me gustan las películas de aventura. No me gustan las películas románticas, las películas de horror ni las películas de guerra.
- ¿Qué cosas lees?
- Me gusta leer novelas pero también leo revistas y periódicos.
- ¿Tocas un instrumento musical?
- Toco la guitarra/el piano/el clarinete/el violín.
- ¿Qué haces normalmente por las tarde después de tus deberes?
- Leo, veo la televisión, escucho música, doy un paseo con el perro y visito a mi amigo.
- ¿Qué hiciste anoche después de tus deberes?

- Leí, vi la televisión, escuché música, di un paseo con el perro y visité a mi amigo.
- ¿Qué harás esta tarde después de tus deberes?
- Leeré, veré la televisión, escucharé música, daré un paseo con el perro y visitaré a mi amigo.

SCHOOL

- ¿Cómo te preparas para el colegio por la mañana?
- Me despierto a las siete, me levanto a las siete y cuarto, me lavo, me visto y tomo el desayuno. Luego preparo mis libros y salgo.
- Describe un día en tu colegio.
- Llego a las nueve menos cuarto. Voy a mi sala de clase y el profesor pasa lista. Luego voy a la primera clase. Hay otra clase luego es el recreo.
- ¿Qué haces durante el recreo?
- Charlo con mis amigos, como patatas y bebo limonada.
- Y ¿depués?
- Tenemos una clase más y luego es la hora de comer. A veces vuelvo a casa para comer, a veces como bocadillos y a veces como en la cantina. Luego hay dos clases más y vuelvo a casa y hago mis deberes.
- Describe tu colegio.
- Una parte del colegio es muy vieja y la otra parte es moderna. Hay terrenos de fútbol, pistas de tenis, laboratorios, un laboratorio de lenguas y una biblioteca. No tenemos piscina pero hay una muy cerca.
- Háblame de tus asignaturas y tus clases.
- Estudio ocho asignaturas, el inglés, las matemáticas, el español, la física, la química, la biología, la tecnología y el francés. Hay novecientos alumnos y sesenta profesores más o menos. Tenemos cinco clases diarias y cada clase dura una hora.
- ¿Desde hace cuánto tiempo estudias el español?
- Estudio el español desde hace tres años.

FUTURE PLANS

- ¿Qué vas a hacer el año que viene?
- Voy a seguir con mis estudios. Voy a estudiar el inglés, el francés, y por supuesto el español.
- Cuando termines tu bachillerato, ¿qué quieres hacer?
- Quiero ir a una universidad a estudiar idiomas.
- Y ¿después de la universidad?
- Quiero ser músico/a. Quiero hacer mucho dinero y ser muy famoso/a.

HOLIDAYS

- ¿Adónde fuiste de vacaciones el año pasado? ¿Qué hiciste allí?
- El año pasado fui a España con mi familia. ¡Lo pasé bomba! Comí muchísimo, bebí muchísimo, salí con mis amigos, bailé mucho y tomé el sol.
- ¿Qué tiempo hizo?
- Casi todos los días hizo buen tiempo. Hizo sol y calor. Sin embargo, un día llovió a cántaros y estuvimos mojados hasta los huesos.
- ¿Cómo viajaste a España?
- Fuimos en coche al aeropuerto, tomamos el avión y al llegar tomamos un taxi al hotel.
- ¿Adónde irás de vacaciones este año?
- Iré otra vez a España con mi familia.
- ¿Qué harás allí?
- ¡Lo pasaré bomba! Comeré muchísimo, beberé muchísimo, saldré con mis amigos, bailaré mucho y tomaré el sol.
- ¿Cómo viajarás a España?
- Iré en coche al aeropuerto, tomaré el avión y al llegar tomaré un taxi al hotel.

8.8 MEG Narrator Higher Level Part 2

This is what you need to know about this test:

- This exercise is a test on whether you can give an account of a day or an incident or a situation.
- It is scheduled to last three minutes.
- You need not mention every detail given on your card.
- You may invent and add extra details.
- To do this exercise successfully, you need to know your verbs, in particular your preterite tenses.

8.9 How to approach the Narrator exam

- Most of the Narrator tasks require you to talk about things that 'I' did or that 'we' did. So you should concentrate on those parts of the verb. If you want to make things simpler, then instead of saying 'we went' just say 'I went with my friend/family' so then you only have to concentrate on the 'I' part of the verb.

Learn this list of preterites and see how often they occur in the suggested answers that follow:

bebí *I drank*	fui *I went*
comí *I ate*	llegué *I arrived*
compré *I bought*	perdí *I lost*
decidí *(+ inf.)* *I decided*	tomé *I took*
di un paseo *I went for a walk*	vi *I saw*
empecé a *(+ inf.)* *I started to*	viajé *I travelled*
encontré *I found*	visité *I visited*
encontré a *I met*	volví *I returned*
entré en *I went in*	

- Try and introduce an imperfect tense into the account. If you find this difficult, just mention the weather or what you were wearing:

  Hacía buen tiempo. *It was nice weather.*
  Hacía sol. *It was sunny.*
  Llovía a cántaros y estábamos mojados *It was pouring and we were soaked to the skin.*
      hasta los huesos.
  Llevaba mi jersey nuevo. *I was wearing my new jersey.*

- Try to build up a collection of mark-winning phrases. For example:

al + inf.	para + inf.
al llegar *on arriving*	para reservar un billete *in order to book a ticket*
antes de + inf.	sin perder un momento *without wasting a moment*
antes de comer *before eating*	
después de + inf.	¡Qué día! *What a day!*
después de comer *after eating*	¡Qué barbaridad! *How awful!*

See how these expressions are used in the suggested answers that follow.

8.10 Example Narrator tasks and suggested answers

Here are three examples of Narrator tasks with suggested answers.

Narrator Task 1

You are staying with a friend in Spain. One day, you go out alone for a bike ride and have a puncture. Eventually, you meet someone who helps you to get home.

You tell your Spanish friend what happened.

You have made some notes to help you with the conversation (see below).

Your teacher will play the part of the Spanish friend.

You may add extra details, for example about the weather, the people involved, problems you encountered, other incidents, what you did on arriving home.

You do not have to use all the notes.

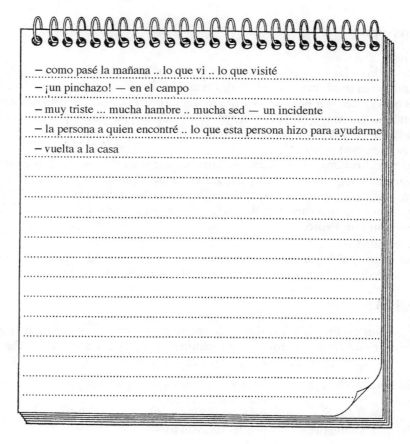

– como pasé la mañana .. lo que vi .. lo que visité

– ¡un pinchazo! — en el campo

– muy triste ... mucha hambre .. mucha sed — un incidente

– la persona a quien encontré .. lo que esta persona hizo para ayudarme

– vuelta a la casa

MEG 1993

Suggested answer

Examiner ¿Qué pasó?

– Esta mañana, fui de paseo en bicicleta. Lo pasé bomba. Hacía sol y hacía calor. Llevaba mi jersey amarillo. Vi muchos edificios interesantes y visité una iglesia vieja. Bebí una limonada y comí un bocadillo en un café.

Examiner ¿Qué pasó después?

– Después de salir del café, decidí volver a casa. Desgraciadamente cinco minutos más tarde tuve un pinchazo. Estaba en el campo y no había nadie para ayudarme.

Examiner ¡Qué barbaridad!

– Empecé a andar con la bicicleta. Dos horas más tarde, estaba triste, tenía hambre y sed. Luego hubo un incidente. Un perro me atacó y tuve que huir. Más tarde encontré a un hombre muy simpático. El hombre me ayudó. Puso mi bicicleta en su coche y me llevó a casa.

Examiner ¡Qué bien! ¿Cómo era el hombre?

– Era bastante viejo, tenía los ojos azules y el pelo largo y negro. Llevaba gafas. Era muy simpático. ¡Qué día!

Narrator Task 2

The notes below give an outline of an evening that you spent with another Spanish family while staying in Spain on an exchange.

You tell another Spanish friend about the evening. The Examiner will play the part of the other Spanish friend.

You need not mention every detail and you may add extra information.

| 19.00 | llegada a su casa ... descripción de la familia |
| | ¡Que casa más bonita! |

20.00–21.00	lo que hicimos antes de cenar
21.00	la cena … ¡Cuantos platos!
23.00	un paseo … la ciudad de noche
	un incidente
24.00	vuelta a la casa … problema con las llaves

MEG 1994

Suggested answer

Examiner ¿Qué pasó?
- Llegué a casa de Pedro a las siete. Llevaba mi jersey nuevo. Bebí una coca cola y hablé con la familia. Los padres eran muy simpáticos y Pedro tenía una hermana muy guapa. Era bastante joven, tenía los ojos azules y el pelo largo y negro. Llevaba gafas. Era muy simpática.
   La casa también era muy bonita con cuatro dormitorios y un jardín pintoresco. Antes de cenar, fui en el jardín con Pedro y jugamos al tenis.

Examiner ¿Qué pasó después?
- A las ocho cenamos. Primero, tomé mariscos. Luego tomé sopa de tomate. Luego tomé chuleta de cerdo con patatas. Luego comí queso y fruta. Bebí agua mineral con la cena. ¡Cuántos platos! Era una cena magnífica. Después de cenar, di un paseo por la ciudad con Pedro. Había mucha gente, muchos coches y mucha animación. Desgraciadamente hubo un incidente. Un perro me atacó y tuve que huir con Pedro.

Examiner ¡Qué barbaridad!
- Volví a casa con Pedro y al llegar tuve un problema con las llaves. ¡Había perdido mis llaves! Afortunadamente Pedro tenía una llave y entré con él. ¡Qué día!

Narrator Task 3

The notes below give an outline of a few days that you spent touring in Spain with your family.
   You tell a Spanish friend about the tour. The Examiner will play the part of the Spanish friend.
   You need not mention every detail and you may add extra information.

Llegada a Madrid	el viaje … la hora de nuestra llegada
	los sitios de interés
	visita a una discoteca
Viaje a Salamanca	por las montañas
	mal tiempo
	un restaurante inolvidable
Viaje a Burgos	la catedral
	recuerdos y tarjetas postales
	una persona a quien encontramos
Viaje a Pamplona	problema con el coche
	lo que perdimos

MEG 1994

Suggested answer

Examiner ¿Qué pasó?
- Después de viajar dos horas, llegué a Madrid en coche con mi familia a las dos de la tarde. Sin perder un momento, encontré un hotel y fui a visitar los sitios de interés. Visité la catedral y vi el palacio real. Más tarde fui a una discoteca y bailé y charlé con la gente.
   Al día siguiente, viajé con mi familia en coche a Salamanca. Fuimos por las montañas y llovía a cántaros. ¡Estábamos mojados hasta los huesos! Fuimos a un restaurante inolvidable. Comí mariscos, una chuleta de cerdo con patatas, queso y fruta. Bebí agua mineral.

Examiner ¿Qué pasó después?
- Al día siguiente, viajamos a Burgos. Visité la catedral y compré recuerdos y tarjetas postales. También compré regalos para mis amigos en Inglaterra. Encontré a mi amigo por correspondencia en Burgos. Vive allí y fuimos al cine juntos.

Examiner Fuisteis a Pamplona, ¿no?
- Sí pero cerca de Pamplona tuvimos un problema con el coche. Tuvimos un pinchazo pero mi padre lo reparó. Pero más tarde perdió las llaves del coche. ¡Mi madre las encontró en su bolsillo! ¡Qué día!

Chapter 9
Reading: Basic Level

9.1 Introduction

This is what you need to know about the exam:
- Basic Level Reading is one of the compulsory tests (Higher Level Reading is optional).
- Most people consider reading as the easiest of the four skills.
- You will have to deal with authentic material, i.e. material that you might expect to encounter in Spain rather than material written by an English person. The exam boards are under instructions to set questions on:
  > public notices and signs (e.g. menus, timetables, advertisements)
  > simple brochures
  > guides
  > letters
  > imaginative writing (of the sort a sixteen-year-old would read)
- Dictionaries are not allowed.
- Spelling and bad handwriting is not penalized unless it is so bad that the meaning of what you try to say is obscured.
- Each exam board has a restricted number of topics and settings for Basic Level and a larger number for Higher Level.
- You are only expected to understand the main points or specific details of these materials; you do not need to understand every word.
- The questions are in English and you answer in English (or Welsh).

9.2 How to prepare

You can often guess what kind of questions are going to appear. You must learn all the words from the vocabulary section in this book which could be used as signs. If you look through past papers there are words that always seem to be cropping up. Here are some guidelines:

Learn all the names of the shops, e.g. **carnicería** – butcher's.

Learn all the places in a town, e.g. **ayuntamiento** – town hall.

Learn all the signs you might find in a bus or train station, e.g. **la salida** – exit.

Learn all the places and features of a hotel, e.g. **el ascensor** – lift.

Remember **abierto** (open) and **cerrado** (closed) are always cropping up.

The days of the week, the months and seasons of the year are always cropping up.

Learn all the words used in weather forecasts.

Learn all the foods and drinks that you are likely to find on a menu.

9.3 During the exam

- Remember to read the setting of each question. It can often give a clue to the answer – often there is information in the setting of the question which is essential for the understanding of the question. For instance the question might say 'You are in Spain and you have lost all your money'. This last piece of information tells you that a bank or a police station are probably going to be involved in the answer. If you do not read the setting (and many candidates do not!) then you are at a disadvantage.

- Remember to look at the mark allocation for each question. If two marks are allocated, you know that the examiner is looking for two elements.

- Keep your answers short. If the question is a sign pointing left to the town hall and you are asked which way is the town hall, do not write 'to go to the town hall, you must turn left'. 'Turn left' or even 'left' is sufficient and you can spend the time saved reading the next question.

- Always attempt each question even if you have to guess. But remember that if you have more than one guess, the examiner will only look at the first answer you write.

9.4 Examination questions

Reading Test 1

EL CORTE INGLES	
TODO PARA TUS NIÑOS	
ABRIGOS	8500
CALCETINES	450
BLUSAS	925
ZAPATOS	5300
GUANTES	975
Especialistas en ropa de invierno	

1 You see a leaflet advertising a store that sells children's clothes.
   (a) How much are gloves?   (1)
   (b) What kind of children's clothes does the store specialize in?   (1)

2 You are about to go onto the beach. You see this sign. What is forbidden apart from camping?(2)

3 While on holiday, you want to enrol on a tennis course run by your hotel.

HOTEL SOL
CLASES DE TENIS

¡GRATUITO!

NOMBRE ————————————

NACIONALIDAD ————————————

NUMERO DE HABITACION ————————

¿Desde hace cuántos años juegas al tenis?

————————————————————

¿Juegas en un equipo?

————————————————————

Apart from name, nationality and room number, what other information are you asked for? (2)

4 You are expecting your Spanish friend and all his family to visit you in England. You receive a letter from your friend's father.

Sevilla 19 de mayo de 1994

Querido amigo:

Esperamos nuestra visita con mucha impaciencia. En sólo veinte días estaremos en Inglaterra. ¡Qué bien!

¿Me puedes hacer un favor? ¿Puedes ir a la oficina de turismo de tu pueblo a buscar información sobre la región?

Mi esposa se interesa por muebles antiguos y a mí me gustan las iglesias viejas. A mi hijo le gusta el deporte, sobre todo el baloncesto. A mi hija no le gustan los deportes. Ella prefiere bailar.

¿Puedes buscar información sobre estas cuatro cosas?

Sin más

Juliano

el padre de tu amigo español

(a) What is the chief interest of the mother? (1)
(b) What is the father interested in? (1)
(c) What is the favourite sport of the son? (1)
(d) What is the favourite activity of the daughter? (1)

MEG 1994

Student's answers
1 (a) 975.
　　(b) Coats, socks, shoes and gloves.

2 (a) Dogs.
　　(b) Playing pelota.

3 **(a)**   How long do you want to play tennis?
   (b)   Do you play in a club?

4 **(a)**   Furniture.
   (b)   Churches.
   (c)   Basketball.
   (d)   Ballet.

Examiner's Comments

1 **(a)**   Correct.
   (b)   You have not read the question properly. Look again. The bottom line states that the store specializes in winter clothing.

2 **(a)**   Correct.
   (b)   Not the correct answer. **Pelota** means 'ball'. The correct answer is 'ball games'.

3 **(a)**   No. **¿Desde hace cuánto tiempo?** means 'how long?'
   (b)   No. **Un equipo** means 'a team'.

4 **(a)**   You have given only part of the answer. You should have written 'old furniture'.
   (b)   Again you have lost a mark because you have left out the word 'old'.
   (c)   Correct.
   (d)   No. **Baile** means 'dancing'.

Reading Test 2

You are in Spain. You are shopping in a department store, 'El Corte Inglés' with your penfriend Concha.

1 In the store an assistant gives you a free sample of tea in a packet. A message is on the packet.

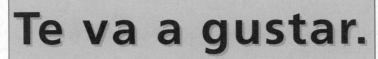

Te va a gustar.

C.P.C. Vía Augusta, 59-1. Planta 08006 Barcelona.

What does the message tell you?   (1)

2 On the way into the restaurant of the store, you see this sign.

> **Primeros platos de sopa, pasta o verdura, segundos de carne o pescado. Elija su menú**

What does the sign suggest you could have for:
(a)   a starter? Mention *one* thing.   (1)
(b)   a main course? Mention *one* thing.   (1)

3 You go to the music department of the store and buy a tape. This poster is on offer with the tape.

(a) What sports is the cartoon dog supposed to be doing? Mention *three*. (3)

(b) To get this poster you need to send off three things. One of them is your personal details. What are the other *two*? (2)

NEAB 1994

Student's answers

1 The message tells you that you will like it (the tea).

2 (a) Soup, pasta or vegetables.
(b) Meat or fish.

3 (a) Athletics, basketball and gym.
(b) (i) My address.
    (ii) The number of the shop where I saw the advertisement.

Examiner's Comments

1 Correct but your answer could have been much shorter leaving you more time for the harder questions later on. 'You will like it' would have been sufficient.

2 (a) Again your answer is too long. 'Soup' would have been sufficient.
(b) Correct but you need mention only one item.

3 (a) Correct. The other three you could have used are 'sailing' (**vela** means either 'sailing' or 'candle' – hence the picture!) 'swimming' or 'horse-riding'.
(b) (i) Correct.
    (ii) No. You have confused the French word **nombre** (which means 'number' in French) with the Spanish word **nombre** which means 'name'.

9.5 Examination practice questions

Here are some more past questions for you to practise on. Suggested answers are given at the end.

Reading Test 3

1 On a visit to Spain you see the following signs.
   (a) At a garage.

   What does this sign tell you?   (1)
   (b) At a railway station.

   (i) CONSIGNA   **(ii)** SALA DE ESPERA

   What do these signs tell you?   (2)

   (c) In a street.
   What does this sign tell you?   (1)   PASO DE PEATONES

2 You are exploring Spain by car with your parents. Your father, who does not speak Spanish, asks you about some signs that you see.
   (a) Why must you be careful on this road?   (1)

(b) Could you park here? (1)

ZONA DE APARCAMIENTO
RESERVADA A RESIDENTES
DISTINTIVO OBLIGATORIO

(c) You follow this sign, in what part of Villajoyosa would you find yourself? (1)

(d) What *two* things are you *not* allowed to do here? (2)

(e) Name *two* things advertised on this van. (2)

WJEC 1993

Reading Test 4

1 Travelling to Spain by car with your family, you see this sign while looking for a place to park in a Spanish town.

Why should you not park here? (1)

2 Later, at a junction, you see this sign:

Which vehicles are allowed to turn left, apart from buses and taxis? (1)

3 You see this advertisment in the window of a small supermarket.

What would you expect to be given free with a packet of Ariel washing powder?   (1)

4 You pick up an economy sized packet of RUFFLES crisps.

What gift will you find inside?   (1)

5 On the way out you see these notices at the check-out.

What are you being asked to do? (1)

6 Returning to your car, you find a handbill under the windscreen-wiper. Your parents ask you what it is advertising.

VEN A VERNOS...
Te veré en **Tevere**

EQUIPO PARA PESCA Y WINDSURF — ROPA DEPORTIVA
— EQUIPO DE CAMPING

Calle San Policarpo, 8 - B (frente Bar «Las Cañas»)

TORREVIEJA - ☎ **571 65 55**

(a) What sort of clothing does this shop sell? (1)
(b) What types of sports equipment can you buy here? Give *two* details. (2)

ULEAC 1994

Reading Test 5

1 One of your friends has to go home early to the U.K., and gets this leaflet from a travel agents.

(a) What discount is available for students? (1)

(b) What are the arrangements for luggage?
Give *full* details. (2)

Condiciones
– Billete válido 6 meses.
– Fecha de vuelta abierta o cerrada.
– Niños de   0 a 4 años GRATIS.
                    4 a 12 años 50% reducción.
– Estudiantes, menores de 27 años
   y 3.ª Edad: 10% descuento.
– Equipaje: 2 maletas gratis por pasajero.

2 While staying at an hotel, you and some friends decide to use the hotel tennis courts. Your friends ask you to explain the rules on the notice.

ATENCION

PARA JUGAR

– SOLO ZAPATILLAS DE TENIS

– EN LA PISTA DE TENIS SOLO LOS JUGADORES

– A LOS NIÑOS QUE NO SABEN JUGAR AL TENIS, NO ESTA
PERMITIDO JUGAR EN LAS PISTAS.

LAS PERSONAS QUE REALMENTE TIENEN INTERES EN PRACTICAR
EL TENIS PUEDEN JUGAR EN LAS PISTAS.

GRACIAS

(a)   What does the notice tell you about footwear? (1)

(b)   According to the notice, who is allowed onto the court at any one time? (1)

(c)   What does it say about children? Give *full* details. (2)

3 You and your friends decide to hire bicycles for a couple of days, and the hotel receptionist gives you this leaflet. Your friends need some help.

"DISFRUTE DE LA BICICLETA COMO DISFRUTAS DE LA VIDA".

ALQUILER, VENTA Y TALLER ESPECIALIZADO.

ESPECIALISTAS EN MOUNTAIN BIKE.

ACCESORIOS DE REGALO EN COMPRAS SUPERIORES A 50.000 pts.

SERVICIO POSTVENTA GRATUITO A LA COMPRA DE UNA BICICLETA.

TAMBIEN COMPRAMOS SU BICICLETA VIEJA.

ORGANIZAMOS EXCURSIONES

PRECIO ESPECIAL PARA GRUPOS.

¡GRACIAS!

BICISPORT "LAS AMERICAS"
Palmeras del Sur, L-I Tlfno: 75 18 29
Junto C/C. San Eugenio

(a)   What else does *Bicisport 'Las Americas'* offer in addition to bicycle hire? Give *two* details. (3)

(b)   What do you get if you spend more than 50.000 pesetas? (1)

(c)   What advantage will there be if you and your friends all hire bikes? (1)

4 In a Spanish magazine, you find this article entitled '*First Film for deaf people on TV3*'. Your friend does not understand fully and asks you for help with some details.

PRIMERA PELICULA PARA SORDOS EN TV3

El filme *Ghandi* será la primera película en TV3 con un sistema de teletexto; así las personas sordas podrán leer los diálogos mientras ven la película. Este avance tecnológico sigue al otro avance introducido hace varios días con la introduccion de un sistema dual que permite a los ciegos, y personas con problemas de los ojos, seguir las películas: además del diálogo de la película, pueden escuchar un comentario de las escenas (dado por un presentador). *Ghandi,* de **Richard Attenborough**, ganó ocho oscars en 1982. Está interpretada por **Ben Kingsley** y **Candice Bergen**. El líder indio, Ghandi, demostró a los ingleses cómo usar la paz en lugar de la violencia. Los ciegos pueden seguirlo, por fin, el martes que viene a las diecinueve horas.

(a) What is the TV3 channel going to do to help deaf people to enjoy films? Give *full* details. (1)

(b) When was similar help given to blind and visually handicapped people? (1)

(c) How exactly were blind or visually handicapped people enabled to enjoy films? Give *full* details. (2)

(d) When is the film due to be shown? Give *two* details. (2)

ULEAC 1993

Reading Test 6

1 You see this advertisement for a drink called Sinsa.

> **¡SED! ¡CALOR! ¡FATIGA!**
> beba **Sinsa**
> CON SABOR NARANJA
> ***
> **Apropiado para todas las edades**
> **De venta en farmacias**
>
> Necesario disolver el contenido del sobre en agua fría.

(a) What advice is given on line 2? (1)

(b) What flavour is the drink? (1)

(c) For what ages is the drink recommended? (1)

(d) Where can you buy the drink? (1)

(e) What advice is given about dissolving the contents of the envelope? (1)

2 A neighbour is intending to buy some property in Marbella. You are shown an advertisement and are asked questions about it.

> **_MARBELLA: 40 millones_**
>
> **CHALET NUEVO**
> Tres plantas, cuatro dormitorios, cinco cuartos de baño, salón y cocina. Garaje para dos coches. A 500 metros del mejor campo de golf de España. A dos kilómetros del centro de Marbella.

(a) How old is the villa? (1)

(b) How is the golf course described? (1)

(c) Where in Marbella is the villa situated? (1)

3 Your friend Tim has received the letter below from his Spanish penfriend. He asks you to help him understand it.

> Valladolid, 22 de mayo
>
> Querido Tim:
>
> ¿Cómo estás? Yo muy bien. Y mi familia también. En esta carta, voy a decirte lo que me gusta hacer. Es más fácil decirte lo que no me gusta hacer; no me gustan los deportes, no me gustan mis estudios, no me gusta la música clásica.
>
> ¡A mí me encanta cocinar! Me gusta cocinar platos de todos los países del mundo. Mi madre dice que mis platos son muy ricos; pero a veces mis padres no están muy contentos. ¿Sabes por qué? Pues dicen que los ingredientes son muy caros.
>
> ¿A ti qué te gusta hacer?
>
> Un abrazo,
>
> Elena.

(a) What is Elena's favourite pastime?   (1)
(b) Why are Elena's parents unhappy sometimes?   (1)

MEG 1992

Reading Test 7

1 Your Spanish penfriend's father is interested in learning English and shows you this advertisement for a course he is going to take.

(a) How long will the classes last each day?   (1)
(b) How long does the entire course last?   (1)
(c) According to the advertisement, what will the classes enable you to do?   (2)
(d) Apart from English, what other languages are offered?   (3)

> **NOVALINGUA**
> Clases intensivas de 3 horas diarias empezando el 18 de enero. Curso práctico de sólo 5 semanas que le permite hablar bien. Ofrecemos clases de inglés, francés, alemán e italiano.
>
> Diagonal, 600 (Francesc. Macía).
> T 200 11 12 y 209 77 30.

2 While reading a holiday magazine at your Spanish penfriend's house, you are interested to see the following article about Ireland.

Un lugar donde no hay bloques de apartamentos

Una casa en el campo. Una granja. Incluso, un castillo antiguo. En Irlanda es posible alojarse en plena naturaleza y admirar sus ríos, sus colinas, sus lagos, sus pueblos. Venga a Irlanda. Por aire con Aer Lingus (91–541 41 16). Desde Madrid. Por mar, con su coche, en los cómodos IRISH FERRIES (91–532 98 16). Desde Le Havre y Cherbourg.

Irlanda

(a) In what *three* types of accommodation might a tourist stay in Ireland.   (3)
(b) Name *three* aspects of the countryside which the tourist can admire.   (3)

3 While in a post office in Spain, your penfriend picks up a leaflet advertising a new telephone service which is available.

Con el servicio España Directo, España siempre responde. Con este servicio, usted puede comunicarse con España. No hay problemas de comprender ni de pagar. Desde cualquier teléfono público o privado. Contestamos directamente su llamada en español. Esta tarjeta contiene los prefijos que deben usarse desde los países extranjeros. Puede obtenerla en Correos. Y lleve siempre la tarjeta en el bolsillo.

Courtesy of Telefonica de España

(a) What problems will the new service help your penfriend avoid? (2)
(b) What does the España Directo card contain? (3)
(c) Where can the card be obtained? (1)
(d) What should your penfriend always do with the card? (2)

NICCEA 1994

Reading Test 8

1 You enter a launderette and see a list of the laundry services provided, together with prices.

ROPA DE SEÑORAS		ROPA DE CABALLERO	
Camisón	180	Camisas	175
Combinación	150	Pijama	220
Pantalones	240	Calzoncillos	120
Pañuelos	90	Calcetines	90
Blusas limpiar y planchar	195	Corbatas, limpiar y planchar	
Batas seda	270	Pañuelos corrientes	90
Albornoz	270	Toallas	120
		Camisetas	120
Vestido lana o abrigo corriente planchar		Pantalones, planchar	-
Vestido seda o terciopelo, planchar		Pantalones blancos, hilo o seda lavar y planchar	
Vestido noche, planchar		Chaquetas, planchar	240
Vestido Corriente limpiar y planchar	360	Chaquetas blancas, seda o hilo lavar y planchar	
		Traje completo, planchar	
Albornoz, lavar y planchar	270	Traje completo limpiar y planchar	
		Pantalón corto limpiar y planchar	210

How much would it cost
(a) for a lady to have her trousers laundered? (1)
(b) for a man's shirt to be washed? (1)
(c) for a pair of shorts to be washed and ironed? (1)

2   In a hotel you see these instructions about what to do in case of fire.

CASO DE INCENDIO No 340

SI DESCUBRE UN INCENDIO:

● Comunique rápidamente a RECEPCION la situación del FUEGO.

● Mantenga la calma: no grita ni corra.

● Abandone su habitación, CERRANDO la puerta. La escalera más próxima se halla a 5m. a la izquierda. Otra salida posible se encuentra a . . . m. a la derecha/ izquierda.

● Baje por una de las escaleras.

● NO UTILICE los ascensores.

SI LAS SALIDAS ESTAN BLOQUEADAS:

● Permanezca en la habitación.

● Hágase ver por la ventana.

(a) What is the *first* thing you should do on finding a fire? (2)

(b) If you want to show that you are remaining calm, what *two things* are you told *not* to do? (2)

(c) Where is the nearest staircase in relation to your room? (1)

(d) What advice are you given about what you should and should *not* do after leaving your room and shutting the door? (2)

(e) What *two things* are you told to do if your way out is blocked? (2)

3   Finally, in a magazine you read a series of brief interviews about fashion. This interview with Vicky Larraz about make-up is the first of them.

(a) With what does she compare make-up? (1)

(b) According to Vicky, who buys make-up nowadays? (1)

(c) How do you know she enjoys shopping for make-up? (2)

(d) What sort of make-up does she especially like to give away? (1)

(e) Why does she enjoy shopping for make-up in London? (1)

SEG 1992

ESTAR AL DIA

VICKY LARRAZ

El maquillaje para mí es como la ropa, es una forma de vestirse. Ante todo, es moda. Hoy, hay tantos colores diferentes que buscar cosas nuevas y maquillarse es una aventura para las mujeres y los hombres también. En mis viajes es lo primero que compro. Me encanta dar a mis amigas estuches con muchos colores para los ojos. En Londres sobre todo encuentro siempre colores fantásticos.

Reading Test 9

1 You see this letter in a comic which your Spanish penfriend has sent you.

TU CORREO AMIGO

Mi nombre es Sandra, tengo catorce años y me gustaría mantener una larga correspondencia con chicos y chicas. Cambio monedas y pósters de vuestros ídolos.
    Escribidme a: Sandra. c/ Hernán Cortés, 8, 5°-D- Raíces Nuevo. Castrillón. 33400 Asturias.

(a)   What age is Sandra? (1)
(b)   Who does she want to write to? (1)
(c)   Apart from posters, what does she want to swop? (1)
(d)   On which floor of the building does she live? (1)

2 You notice this item on shopping in a brochure which you received at the Tourist Office in Madrid.

---

ir de compras

Por la tarde los turistas que visiten Madrid quieren conocer y visitar los grandes almacenes y las calles del gran comercio.

En Madrid se pueden comprar artísticos objetos hechos en España: trabajos de madera, hierro, vidrio, porcelana, plata y oro. También se venden muchos artículos de cuero – zapatos, bolsos, maletas, guantes, etc. Los artículos de deportes de toda clase tienen dos importantes requisitos para el cliente: magnífica calidad y excelente precio.

(a)	Name *three* materials used in the manufacture of artistic objects.	(3)
(b)	Give *three* examples of leather goods.	(3)
(c)	Give *two* reasons why you should buy sports equipment in Madrid.	(2)

NICCEA 1993

Reading Test 10

1 You are on the Iberia flight to Bilbao and a steward first brings round newspapers and then a plastic packet containing this.

juego de la oca / parchís

What is it?   (1)

2 You also receive a Spanish magazine called *El tiempo* and to pass the time you start to read items in it. This one attracts your attention.

Recuerda que en el tema de la droga tú tienes siempre la última palabra.

What are you being advised to say 'no' to?   (1)

3 In a newspaper called *El país* you also see an advertisement for a film that is on Spanish television that evening.

Festival de Cine.
Cita en Las Vegas.
Una cantante española sale con un americano rico en Las Vegas. Muchos buenos números musicales.

Hoy a las 22h.

Para una inmensa minoría.

What is the film going to be about?   (1)

4 When you arrive in Bilbao with your family, you will be hiring a car. This item of publicity in *El país* is very important for you all.

EL CINTURON SIEMPRE.

DELANTE Y DETRAS. EN CIUDAD Y EN CARRETERA

LAS IMPRUDENCIAS SE PAGAN
...CADA VEZ MAS.

Dirección Gral. de Tráfico

Ministerio del Interior

(a) What is it advising you to do? (1)
(b) In which areas should you follow the advice given? (1)

SEG 1994

Reading Test 11

1 You read about a performer, a man called Guru Josh.

¡HOLA!
ME LLAMO
GURU JOSH

¿MI MEJOR PRENDA DE VESTIR?
Mis pantalones. Son cómodos, originales. Me los han conseguido unos amigos de Jersey. Son 'Instinct'.

'Instinct' hace ropa de surf. Yo hago surf, soy muy bueno, y nado también. Me gustan estos deportes. Todo eso viene de que yo nací cerca del mar.

(a) What is his favourite article of clothing? (1)
(b) Why? (1)
(c) What is he like at surfing? (1)
(d) What other sport does he like? (1)
(e) Why does he like these sports? (1)

2 You are leaving your hotel at the end of your holiday. The receptionist gives you a parcel and this note from your friend Juan.

> ¡Hola!
> ¡Qué lástima que no os viera antes de marcharos!
> Espero que os guste este pequeño recuerdo de España. Son unas castañuelas.
> ¿Podéis buscar un corresponsal para mi hermana menor? Tiene doce años. Es simpática. Se llama Carmen. Le gustan los animales y monta a caballo en sus ratos libres. Detesta leer. Prefiere ir al cine.
> Gracias por ayudarme.
> Bueno, escribidme pronto. Adiós y buen viaje.
> Juan

(a) What does he say is in the parcel? (1)

(b) He asks you to look for a penfriend for his sister Carmen. What does he tell you about her? Mention *four* things. (4)

NEAB 1993

Reading Test 12

1 Your teacher has given you a Spanish magazine to take home. Your friend who no longer studies Spanish is interested in the article below but does not understand all of it and asks you about some of the details of the story.

La señorita y el vagabundo

Ocurrió esta historia en la esquina formada por dos de las principales calles de Madrid, un día a las seis de la tarde. Cuando el semáforo estaba en rojo, un vendedor de pañuelos de papel – de los que abundan en las grandes ciudades de España – aprovechó para ofrecer a una señorita un paquete de estos pañuelos. Ella le dio 300 pesetas sin tomar su paquete de pañuelos. Un policía que vio la escena se acercó al vendedor y le preguntó cuánto le dio la señorita y si la reconoció. El joven 'vagabundo', que no tenía otro trabajo que esto, tuvo una sorpresa muy grande cuando el guardia le informó que le dio la propina de 300 pesetas la princesa Cristina, que viajaba por Madrid en su coche.

(a) Where exactly did this event take place? Give *full* details. (2)

(b) What was the young man selling? Give *two* details. (2)

(c) What was odd about the behaviour of the young woman driving the car? Give *full* details. (2)

(d) What *two* questions did the policeman ask the young man? (2)

(e) What was the reason for the young man's surprise? (1)

2 Your Spanish pen-friend has written to you in preparation for your going to stay with her. Your parents wish to know what she is telling you.

Oviedo
15 de mayo

¡Hola!

¿Qué tal estás?

Me parece que ésta será la última carta antes de tu viaje a España. Dentro de unas semanas nos veremos cara a cara por primera vez. ¡Qué bien!

Mis padres dicen que iremos al aeropuerto a buscarte. El aeropuerto está cerca de Avilés, a unos cuarenta kilómetros de aquí. No está muy lejos, y además hay autopista, de manera que sólo son treinta minutos de viaje. Nos acompañarán mis dos hermanos y una amiga. ¡Menos mal que el coche de mi padre tiene siete asientos!

Me hiciste unas preguntas sobre nuestra vida diaria: no te preocupes, aquí no nos levantamos temprano. Durante las vacaciones desayunamos a las ocho y media o así. Mis padres trabajan en Oviedo, y si queremos, nos llevarán todos los días al centro en coche.

Ya me parece que me suspenderán en los exámenes, pues casi no he estudiado nada en estos últimos meses. Si no apruebo los exámenes, tendré que buscar trabajo. Ya he hablado con el director de un banco de nuestro barrio, y parece que allí habrá un puesto libre a fines de agosto.

Bueno, escríbeme pronto para darme los detalles de tu viaje.

¡Hasta pronto!

Julia

(a) Why is this letter from Julia particularly important? (1)
(b) Where exactly is the airport? Give *full* details. (2)
(c) How many people will be there to meet you? (1)
(d) What does Julia tell you not to worry about? (1)
(e) How will you and Julia be able to get into the centre of Oviedo each day? (1)
(f) What is Julia worried about? (1)
(g) Where does she hope to get a job? (1)
(h) When might she be able to start? (1)

ULEAC 1992

Reading Test 13

1 Your friend invites you home for something to eat. You are going to have one of these pizzas.

¡¡SERVICIO A DOMICILIO GRATIS !!			
ESPECIALIDADES	**Masa Molde y Masa Fina** (Pan Pizza) (Thin'n'Crispy)	**MEDIANA** (2 personas)	**GRANDE** (3–4 personas)
MARGARITA: Doblo de queso		995	1.495
PIZZA VEGETARIANA: Aceitunas negras, pimiento verde, champiñones, cebolla.		1.295	1.795
PIZZA LOCA: Pepperoni, anchoas, ternera, guindilla		1.295	1.895
PIZZA MARINERA: Gambas, atún, anchoas, sardinas, pimiento verde, aceitunas		1.395	1.995
SUPREMA: Pepperoni, ternera, cordo al anís, cebolla, pimiento verde, champiñones.		1.295	1.895
SUPER SUPREMA: Aceitunas negras, cerdo al anís, pepperoni, jamón, cebolla, pimiento verde, champiñones, ternera.		1.395	1.995

(a) There is a delivery service. How much does it cost? (1)
(b) You order a large 'Pizza Vegetariana' to share between you. What will it have on it? Mention *three* things. (3)
(c) How much will your large 'Pizza Vegetariana' cost? (1)

2 You leave your friend and go back to your hotel. You need to get some clothes washed. The hotel has a laundry service. Here are the instructions.

SERVICIO DE LAVANDERIA
Por favor, deje la ropa con esta lista. La ropa tiene que estar delante de la puerta de su habitación a las 10:45 de la mañana. Puede recoger su ropa a partir de las 6:30 de la tarde del día siguiente.

☐ Vestidos   ☐ Pañuelos
☐ Pantalones Cortos ☐ Pijamas
☐ Camisas   ☐ Faldas

NOMBRE _____

HABITACION _____

FECHA _____

(a) Put a tick in the box on the list next to
(i) shorts
(ii) shirts
You should put only *two* ticks. (1)
(b) Where do you leave your washing at 10.45? (1)
(c) When exactly can you collect your washing? (1)
(d) What *three* pieces of information do you have to write on the bottom of the form? (3)

3 After you have returned to England, you receive this note from the friend you met in Mallorca.

> ¡Hola! Estoy pasando unos días en Canarias con mis padres. Me quedé muy triste cuando te fuiste pero puedo ir a visitarte el próximo verano ¡Fenomenal! ¡Ah! encontré tu reloj ¿Te lo mando o te lo llevo cuando te visite? Escríbeme pronto. Recuerdos a tus padres, fueron muy amables
>
> tu amiga española
>
> Ana

(a)	Why was your friend sad?	(1)
(b)	What is your friend going to do next summer?	(1)
(c)	What *two* suggestions does she make about your watch?	(2)
(d)	What does she say about your parents?	(1)

NEAB 1992

9.6 Suggested answers

Reading Test 1

1 (a) 975.
  (b) Winter clothes.

2 (a) Dogs.
  (b) Ball games.

3 (a) How many years have you played tennis?
  (b) Do you play in a team?

4 (a) Old furniture.
  (b) Old churches.
  (c) Basketball.
  (d) Dancing.

Reading Test 2

1 I will like it.

2 (a) Soup.
  (b) Meat.

3 (a) Athletics, basketball, gym.
  (b) (i) My address.
    (ii) The name of the shop where I saw this advertisement.

Reading Test 3

1 (a) Toilets.
  (b) (i) Left luggage.
      (ii) Waiting room.
  (c) Pedestrian crossing.

2 (a) Because lorries come out onto it.
  (b) No.
  (c) The port.
  (d) Bathe and go onto the boats.
  (e) Toys and presents.

Reading Test 4

1 It is reserved for motorcycles.

2 Two-wheeled vehicles.

3 A digital watch.

4 Earrings.

5 Show the inside of your bag to the cashier.

6 (a) Sports clothes.
  (b) Equipment for fishing and windsurfing.

Reading Test 5

1 (a) 10%.
  (b) Two suitcases free per traveller.

2 (a) You can only wear tennis shoes.
  (b) Only the players.
  (c) Children who can't play tennis are not allowed on the courts.

3 (a) They sell and repair bicycles.
  (b) Free accessories.
  (c) A reduction.

4 (a) Introduce teletext.
  (b) A few days ago.
  (c) In addition to the normal film dialogue there is a commentary.
  (d) Next Tuesday at 1900.

Reading Test 6

1 (a) Drink Sinsa.
  (b) Orange.
  (c) All ages.
  (d) At a chemist's.
  (e) Dissolve them in cold water.

2 (a) It is new.
  (b) The best in Spain.
  (c) Two kilometres from the centre.

3 (a) Cooking.
  (b) The ingredients are very expensive.

Reading Test 7

1 (a) Three hours.
  (b) Five weeks.
  (c) Speak well.
  (d) French, German and Italian.

2 (a) A house in the country, a farm or a castle.
  (b) Its rivers, its hills, its lakes.

3 (a) Problems of understanding or paying.
  (b) The codes to be used from foreign countries.
  (c) At the post office.
  (d) Always carry it with him/her in his/her pocket.

Reading Test 8

1 (a) 240
  (b) 175.
  (c) 210.

2 (a) Tell reception.
  (b) Do not shout or run.
  (c) 5 metres to the left.
  (d) Go down one of the stairways and do not use a lift.
  (e) Stay in your room and make yourself visible at the window.

3 (a) Like clothes.
  (b) Men and women.
  (c) It's the first thing that she buys.
  (d) Multicoloured eye make-up.
  (e) There are fantasic colours available.

Reading Test 9

1 (a) 14.
  (b) Boys and girls.
  (c) Coins.
  (d) Fifth.

2 (a) Wood, iron and glass.
  (b) Shoes, bags and suitcases.
  (c) Magnificent quality and excellent price.

Reading Test 10

1 A game.

2 Drugs.

3 A Spanish singer goes out with a rich American in Las Vegas.

4 (a) Fasten your seat-belt.
  (b) In the city and on the open road.

Reading Test 11

1 (a) His trousers.
  (b) They are comfortable and original.
  (c) He is very good.
  (d) Swimming.
  (e) He was born near the sea.

2 (a) Castanets.
  (b) **(i)** She is twelve.
      (ii) She is nice.
      (iii) She is called Carmen.
      (iv) She likes animals.

Reading Test 12

1 (a) On the corner of two main streets in Madrid.
  (b) Paper handkerchiefs.
  (c) She gave him 300 pesetas without taking the handkerchiefs.
  (d) How much the woman gave him and if he recognized her.
  (e) She was Princess Cristina.

2 (a) It is the last before I travel to Spain.
(b) Near Avilés, 40 kilometres from here.
(c) 6.
(d) Getting up early.
(e) By car with her parents.
(f) Failing her exams.
(g) In a bank in her area of the city.
(h) At the end of August.

Reading Test 13

1 (a) It is free.
(b) Olives, peppers and mushrooms.
(c) 1.795.

2 (a) Pantalones cortos, camisas.
(b) Outside the door of your room.
(c) After 6:30 in the evening.
(d) My name, my room number and the date.

3 (a) Because I left.
(b) Visit me.
(c) Shall she send it or bring it with her.
(d) They were very nice.

Chapter 10
Reading: Higher Level

10.1 Introduction

This is what you need to know about the exam. Much of the advice given in Chapter 6 about Higher Level Listening applies to Higher Level Reading.

- The questions will be in English (or Welsh) and you have to answer in English (or Welsh).
- As at Basic Level, you do not have to write in full sentences. Note form is fine and often a one-word answer suffices.
- Whereas the Basic Level was compulsory, the higher test is optional. However, you have absolutely nothing to lose by attempting it even if you score zero.
- The passages will be longer and more difficult than at Basic Level, the vocabulary will be from the full range of vocabulary (and not just the basic range outlined by your exam board).
- The full range of topics and settings can be included in the exam at Higher Level (at Basic Level they are restricted).
- As at Basic Level, the materials will be authentic and will be the kind of written material that you would expect to find in Spanish magazines, newspapers etc.
- In addition to the types of settings you can expect at Basic Level, there are likely to be more:
    imaginative writing
    formal letters (e.g. to a campsite, to a newspaper editor)
    informal letters (e.g. letters from Spanish friends)
    newspaper and magazine articles which may be in interview form and which may give
        someone's point of view or even two people's points of view
    guides and brochures but longer than at Basic Level.
- The major difference between Basic and Higher is that at Higher Level you will be asked to demonstrate *Higher Level Skills*. Let's look at this.

10.2 Higher Level skills

The person who wrote your exam paper is under instructions to include at least 40% of what is known as 'Higher Level Skills' questions. These questions test your ability to:

- Draw conclusions. For example if the passage is about a student who goes out every night till late and never buys any books, you might be asked a question like 'What conclusion can you draw about the student's commitment to his studies?'
    You would answer that he/she seems to ignore his studies.
- Identify attitudes and emotions. For example if the passage is about a man who is in tears and says that he should never have left the house that day, then you might be asked a multiple-choice question like:
    What emotion does the speaker feel? Tick one box only.

(a)   He is quite happy with things.   ☐   (b)   He is very angry.   ☐
(c)   He is proud of his achievements.   ☐   (d)   He is regretting something.   ☐
You would obviously tick the last box.

- Identify the important themes. For example if the material is a weather forecast which forecasts terrible weather every day except one, you might be asked 'Which day is the best day to go to the beach?'

  You should make sure that you have learnt the vocabulary section on emotions on page 55.

  There is no better preparation for this exam than reading regularly in Spanish. You can use the passages in this book or materials that your teacher will provide for you.

10.3 In the examination

These are what you need to remember on exam day.

   This advice is similar to the advice given for Basic and Higher Level Listening and Basic Reading.

- Do attempt the Higher Paper if you feel you have the slightest chance of scoring a point.
- Read the material carefully and read the instructions and settings on the paper carefully.
- Remember that the mark allocation for each question will give you a clue as to what information and how much information is required.
- Always attempt each question even if you have to guess.
- Remember that questions asking for specific detail follow the order of the information in the passage. However a question testing Higher Level Skills may often be the last question on a recording because to draw the correct conclusion, you may need information given throughout the passage. You may have to remember things from the beginning, middle or end of the passage.

10.4 Examination questions

The following questions are all past GCSE questions. Work through them carefully and only look at the answers when you have either got your own answer or are in total despair!

PÍDENOS LO QUE QUIERAS

Queridos Reyes Magos.
Desearía que me trajerais...

camiseta de manga corta
calcetines
cadena de oro
diccionario inglés
juego de ajedrez
botas de patinar sobre hielo

Reading Test 1

You are in Spain. You are spending Christmas with your friend, Jordi.

   Jordi shows you this list of the things he would like for Christmas.

   Mention *four* things on the list. (4)

NEAB 1994

Student's answers
(i)   T-shirt.
(ii)   Socks.
(iii) Chain.
(iv) An English dictionary.

Examiner's comments
(i)   You have not given enough information. You have not mentioned 'short-sleeved'.
(ii)   Correct.
(iii) Again not enough information. You should have mentioned 'gold'.
(iv) Correct.

Reading Test 2

Jordi's mother gives you this Christmas card.

From what she writes, Jordi's mother seems to be a thoughtful person. What gives this impression? Give *full* details. (2)

NEAB 1994

Student's answers

(i) She wishes my family all the best for Christmas.

(ii) She hopes I have a nice time with them.

Examiner's comments

(i) The first answer is obviously a guess. You have not understood **echar de menos** which means 'to miss'.

(ii) The second answer is correct.

Reading Test 3

As this is the last issue of the year, the magazine is offering you the chance to send away for some back copies.

(a) What are you told about copies 1 to 4? (1)

(b) What 'good ideas' can you read about in the following back copies?
   (i) Number 9.
   (ii) Number 11. (2)

NEAB 1994

Student's answers

(a)

(b) (i) How to talk in public.
   (ii) How to cure summer sickness.

Examiner's comments

(a) Here you were faced with a difficult question but you should never leave a blank. It is always worth a guess. Perhaps you could have guessed that **agotado** means 'unavailable'.

(b) (i) Correct.
   (ii) You have confused **invierno** and **verano,** a very common mistake. **Invierno** means 'winter' not 'summer'.

Núm.	Reportaje	Buenas Ideas
Los 4 primeros números están agotados		
5	Todo sobre EL AGUA	
6	Todo sobre EL AIRE	Conoce las estrellas
7	Nueva York	¡Qué sano es reír!
8	El Transiberiano	Buen regreso al cole
9	El esquí	Cómo hablar en público
10	Jerusalén	Recetas con chocolate
11	El rally París-Dakar	Cómo curar los pequeños males de invierno
12	Venecia	Consejos para cuidar a tu gato

10.5 Examination practice questions

Reading Test 4

You read in a Spanish newspaper about an incident at a power station (central nuclear) in France.

DRAMA EN UN PUEBLO FRANCES
INCENDIO EN UNA CENTRAL NUCLEAR

Hasta recientemente los habitantes de Mer en Francia estaban contentos con su central nuclear construida hace diez años a cinco kilómetros de sus hogares. La piscina en el pueblo recibe agua caliente de la central gratis, los habitantes gozan de una reducción del 10 por ciento por su electricidad y el viento casi siempre lleva el humo de la central en dirección contraria.

    Todo esto ha cambiado. Desgraciadamente hubo un incendio anteayer en la central ocasionando un muerto y varios heridos. El difunto, Francis Menard, soltero, empleado en la central, limpiaba máquinas cuando se produjo el incidente. Los bomberos le encontraron boca abajo en una oficina llena de humo. Los bomberos de Mer que respondieron a la llamada de la central no comprendieron el peligro de la situación. No llevaban equipo especial para hacer frente a un incendio de esta clase y emplearon agua para apagar el fuego en una zona eléctrica.

    El Alcalde, Pierre Rey, prometió una investigación para encontrar la causa del incendio.

---

1 Give *three* reasons why the people of Mer were happy to have a nuclear power station near their homes. (3)

2 What kind of incident changed their minds? (1)

3 According to the article, when did the incident take place? (1)

4 What personal detail is given about the power station worker, Francis Menard? (1)

5 What had Francis Menard been doing when the accident took place? (1)

6 Who were called to deal with the incident? (1)

7 What disadvantage did they have? (1)

8 What mistake did they make? (1)

MEG 1994

Reading Test 5

You would like to continue studying Spanish next year. A sixth form student, Catherine, is showing your class some of the work she did last year.

1 Catherine shows you this questionaire she completed. It is about the conversation classes she had with Alicia, a South American who was helping the teacher.

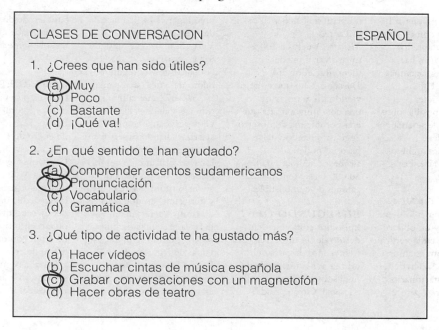

CLASES DE CONVERSACION   ESPAÑOL

1. ¿Crees que han sido útiles?
   (a) Muy
   (b) Poco
   (c) Bastante
   (d) ¡Qué va!

2. ¿En qué sentido te han ayudado?
   (a) Comprender acentos sudamericanos
   (b) Pronunciación
   (c) Vocabulario
   (d) Gramática

3. ¿Qué tipo de actividad te ha gustado más?
   (a) Hacer vídeos
   (b) Escuchar cintas de música española
   (c) Grabar conversaciones con un magnetofón
   (d) Hacer obras de teatro

(a) In number 1, what does Catherine say about the classes? (1)
(b) How did the classes help Catherine? (2)
(c) What did Catherine like doing best? (1)

NEAB 1993

Reading Test 6

1 While staying at your Spanish penfriend's house, you see the following interview with the Cuban singer Jon Secada in a pop music magazine.

Jon Secada es un cantante cubano que ahora vive en Miami. Hace más de un año, el auténtico descubridor de Jon, es decir, Emilio Estefan, el marido de Gloria, nos hablaba de él. En aquella época Jon escribía canciones que luego las cantaba Gloria.

Dice Emilio: 'Creo que he descubierto al mayor fenómeno de la música en toda mi vida. Jon compone maravillosamente y canta con una sensibilidad especial.'

Contesta Jon: 'Emilio siempre ha sido como un padre para mí. Me ha dado toda clase de consejos y yo siempre le he hecho caso.'

Julián Ruíz pasó un rato con Jon durante su reciente visita a España.

– Jon, tú naciste en Cuba. ¿No es cierto?

– Sí, pero no te puedo contar absolutamente nada de Cuba porque cuando salí de allí era muy pequeño. Emocionalmente Cuba no ha significado nada para mí.

– ¿Te sientes tú más cómodo en inglés o en español?

– La verdad es que no tengo ningún problema. Me da lo mismo un idioma que otro. Me siento cómodo en ambos.

– ¿Supongo que Gloria Estefan ha colaborado en tu disco?

– Claro, por supuesto Gloria es una persona estupenda. Estaba segura de que la canción 'Just another day' iba a ser un éxito mundial.

– ¿Sabías muchas cosas de España?

– Ya conocía España cuando vine aquí con Gloria. No me siento extraño. El idioma nos une mucho.

(a) What was Jon Secada doing when he was discovered by Emilio Estefan? (2)
(b) According to Jon, in what way has Emilio been like a father to him? (2)
(c) How has Jon responded? (1)
(d) Why does Jon not know much about Cuba? (2)
(e) What does he say about his ability in English and Spanish? (2)
(f) What is his opinion of Gloria Estefan? (1)
(g) What did she think of the song 'Just another day'? (3)
(h) Why does Jon feel at home in Spain? (1)

NICCEA 1994

Reading Test 7

1 You buy a copy of the magazine *Tribuna* and discover this article about unidentifed flying objects (UFOs).

Los informes secretos que prueban la presencia de 'ovnis' en España

El Ministerio de Defensa ha decidido acabar con el misterio que durante los últimos treinta años ha rodeado las investigaciones sobre los ovnis. Ha levantado el carácter clasificado que pesaba sobre tres de los más de sesenta informes oficiales escondidos en los archivos del ejército del aire. Por ejemplo:-

EL PRIMER OVNI

Duende 20: A ver si lo tiene en el radar. Hay un objeto no identificado en la vertical de nuestro avión; estamos dando vueltas a su alrededor y permanece estacionario. Tiene forma de ... parece

un platillo blanco y brillante.

Matador: Vuelva a 300 y mire a ver si puede identificar el objeto.

Duende 20: Lo que estamos viendo no es un avión; es una cosa muy extraña que está por encima de nosotros. Seguimos dando vueltas pero no podemos alcanzarlo. Ahora estamos a 36.000 pies y tenemos 320 galones de combustible.

EL SEGUNDO OVNI

Episodios como éste han dejado de ser un secreto casi treinta años después del primer avistamiento de un ovni sobre territorio nacional. Otro episodio

tuvo lugar el 14 de marzo de 1968 en el aeropuerto de Villa Cisneros en el antiguo Sáhara español. Ese día el comandante y el segundo piloto del vuelo de Spantax IB/371-372 que cubría la ruta Las Palmas-Villa Cisneros iban a empezar a aterrizar cuando observaron que no navegaban solos. Una luz brillante de color blanco se movía fuera de su avión, a su misma velocidad y dirección, sin que la torre de control detectara en el radar la presencia de ningún objeto extraño. Durante su vuelo de regreso a Las Palmas los dos pilotos lo observaron de nuevo, pero esta vez era observado

también desde el suelo, lo que indicaba que no podía ser solamente un reflejo en la cabina.

EL TERCER OVNI

Otro caso se produjo a catorce kilómetros de Burgos la madrugada del I de enero de 1975. Según un informe escrito por la Capitanía General de la VI Región Militar, aquella mañana cuatro soldados de la Academia de Ingenieros del Ejército observaron un objeto en forma de tronco de árbol con una luz muy fuerte de color amarillo que aterrizaba o quedaba en suspensión a unos pocos metros del suelo.

(a) Why could Alfonso Torres not have written this article before now? (2)
(b) Who are Duende 20 and Matador? (2)
(c) What do you learn about the position and the appearance of the first UFO? (2)
(d) Where had the Spantax plane started its flight? (1)
(e) Write down one similarity and one difference between the first and second UFOs. (2)
(f) Why was the first sighting of the second UFO particularly mysterious? (2)
(g) How does the author think people might explain away the sightings of the second UFO?(1)
(h) What would lead you to believe the Spantax pilots? (1)
(i) What was the doubt in the minds of the soldiers involved in the case of the third UFO near Burgos? (2)

SEG 1994

Reading Test 8

1 ATREVETE A ABRIRLO
In a Spanish Post Office, you pick up a leaflet which gives details of some of the services on offer. One of your companions asks you to explain certain points dealt with in the leaflet.

TELEGRAMA

Envía tu recado de una forma inmediata.

Utiliza el Telegrama.

Lo entregamos en mano.

Para mayor comodidad también lo puedes enviar por teléfono.

POSTAL EXPRES

Es nuestro servicio Postal más rápido. Puedes enviar tanto objetos como cualquier tipo de documento. De puerta en puerta, a cualquier parte del mundo o localidad española.

BUROFAX

Si tu correspondiente tiene FAX, puedes enviar copia exacta de cualquier documento desde nuestras oficinas y lo recibirá al INSTANTE. Si tu correspondiente no lo tiene, no importa; garantizamos llevárselo a casa.

FILATELIA

La Filatelia es el arte que trata del coleccionismo de los sellos. Suscribiéndote al Servicio Filatélico, recibirás en tu casa todas las nuevas emisiones que se pongan a la venta, al día siguiente de la emisión. COLECCIONAR SELLOS ES CULTURA.

**UN SERVICIO RAPIDO –
AL ALCANCE DE TODOS**

Tú eliges la rapidez, nosotros te ponemos los medios. Correos y Telégrafos es ante todo un servicio público, que está al ALCANCE DE TODOS. Mejorar día a día nuestro servicio, es sin duda alguna, nuestro principal objetivo; por eso queremos dar respuesta a tus posibles preguntas. ¡Siempre te escuchamos!

Puedes pedir más información en cualquiera de nuestras oficinas.

Correos y Telégrafos *Correos y Telégrafos*

(a) According to what is stated, why can you have total confidence in the telegram system? Give *two* details. (2)
(b) For what two types of material is the Postal Expres service designed? Give *two* details. (2)
(c) How can you be sure that something sent by Postal Expres will get to its destination? (1)
(d) What happens if you want to send a FAX to somebody who does not have a FAX machine? Give *full* details. (2)
(e) If you subscribed to the Philatelic Service, when would you expect to receive newly issued stamps? Give *full* details. (2)
(f) What promise is made about the quality of the postal services, and how does the Post Office hope to achieve this? (2)

ULEAC 1994

Reading Test 9

1 In *El país* you read the publicity printed below, dealing with an issue of great social significance.

En el bar él paga las copas. En casa lo paga ella

Esta imagen puede ser la de tu compañera. O la de un familiar cercano, la vecina con la que coincides en el ascensor o la mujer de algún amigo. Aunque tal vez sea la imagen que ves reflejada en el espejo cada día.

La imagen de alguien que es objeto de agresiones y vejaciones por parte de la persona con la que vive.

Cada mujer tiene derecho a ser defendida y protegida. Cada mujer maltratada física o psíquicamente tiene derecho a denunciarlo en defensa de su dignidad.

Todos nosotros tenemos el derecho y la obligación de informarnos y ayudar.

La resignación y el silencio son los mejores amigos de quienes maltratan. No callemos ante los malos tratos.

Ninguna mujer debe pagar en casa el precio de la irracionalidad. Siempre hay una salida.

Teléfono Emergencias Sociales 24h:

☎

900–100333
Llamada gratuita

No callemos ante los malos tratos.

Siempre hay una salida.

Campaña de sensibilización contra los malos tratos.

(a)	What two main social problems are highlighted in this publicity?	(2)
(b)	Explain why both he and she pay, according to the headlines.	(2)
(c)	Of whom does the article suggest that this might be a picture?	(5)
(d)	What does the article suggest that the woman has lost?	(1)
(e)	How can the general public become better equipped to help such people?	(1)
(f)	What is the worst thing we can do?	(1)
(g)	The article uses the word **salida** in two different senses. What are they?	(2)
(h)	What suggests that urgent help is easy to obtain?	(2)

SEG 1993

Reading Test 10

1 You know that Spaniards use their hands a lot when talking, so you are interested in this article.

Gestos,

UN IDIOMA SIN PALABRAS

Siempre se ha dicho que el lenguaje de los gestos es universal, pero viajeros y trotamundos saben que eso no es del todo cierto.

- Llevar el dedo índice a uno de tus ojos quiere decir 'cuidado' en España.

- Tocarse el lobillo de la oreja puede significar 'no me creo nada de lo que me estás diciendo' en Rusia o 'todo va bien' en Portugal.

- En Bulgaria se gira la cabeza de un lado a otro para decir 'sí' y para decir 'no' la mueven de arriba abajo.

(a)	What do Spaniards mean when they point to their eye?	(1)
(b)	What does touching your earlobe mean:	
	(i) in Russia?	(1)
	(ii) in Portugal?	(1)
(c)	What do people in Bulgaria do when they want to say 'no'?	(1)

NEAB 1992

Reading Test 11

1 You read this letter from the mother of a teenage girl.

Quiere estudiar, pero necesitamos que trabaje

Una hija mía termina este año el COU y tiene empeño en estudiar una carrera universitaria. Su profesor dice que está muy capacitada. El problema es que en casa tenemos una mala situación económica y necesitamos otro sueldo. Yo quiero que busque un trabajo. ¿Es la mía una proposición egoísta?

OPINION

Su hija podría buscar alguna pequeña ocupación a tiempo parcial, que suelen realizarse fuera del horario de estudios: clases particulares, cuidar algún niño..., así la carrera de su hija no supondría una carga para la economía familiar y realizar estudios superiores le permitiría, en el futuro, acceder a algún puesto de trabajo de mayor categoría.

(a) What does the daughter want to do when she leaves school? (1)
(b) What would her mother prefer her to do? (1)
(c) Why? (1)
(d) Do you think that the answer is biased towards the daughter or the mother or neither? Give a reason for your answer. (2)

NEAB 1992

Reading Test 12

1 LO QUE DEBE SABER EL CAMPISTA

During a camping holiday on the north coast of Spain, you and your friends are given this leaflet by the receptionist of a campsite. Your friends want to know about the campsite rules.

SE DEBE

☆ Entregar en la oficina de recepción su pasaporte, y firmar la ficha de entrada. Una vez cumplido esto, la documentación será devuelta.

☆ Informar a la Dirección del Cámping cualquier caso de enfermedad contagiosa.

☆ Pagar el precio de los distintos servicios usados al recibir la correspondiente cuenta.

NO SE DEBE

☆ Romper el silencio o perturbar el descanso de los demás campistas (en las horas detalladas en las Reglas del Cámping: entre las 22.00 y las 08.00 horas). Está prohibido por completo el uso de radios y transistores.

☆ Hacer fuego fuera de los lugares autorizados para ello. (En todo caso, se debe tomar las precauciones normales contra el incendio.) Siempre es mejor tener cerca del fuego un cubo de agua.

☆ Hacerse acompañar por animales que sean un peligro o inconveniente para los campistas.

☆ Abandonar basura en cualquier sitio, y especialmente en los arroyos, fuentes, vías públicas, o playas del cámping.

☆ Introducir en el cámping a personas no residentes en él sin obtener el permiso del personal del cámping.

☆ No se permite lavar ropa en los lavabos ni en las pilas destinadas para lavar platos.

☆ El campista que rompe alguna de estas reglas podrá ser expulsado del cámping.

(a)	When will they hand back your passports?	(1)
(b)	What does it say about illness?	(1)
(c)	When do you have to pay for each service?	(1)
(d)	What is the rule concerning the use of radios?	(1)
(e)	Where are you allowed to light fires?	(1)
(f)	What precaution are you advised to take when lighting a fire? Give *two* details.	(2)
(g)	What does it say about animals? Give *full* details.	(1)
(h)	Which areas of the campsite are the owners particularly anxious to keep clean? Give *full* details.	(4)
(i)	What are the rules about bringing guests on to the campsite? Give *full* details.	(2)
(j)	What are the rules concerning washing clothes? Give *two* details.	(2)
(k)	What happens if you break the rules?	(1)

ULEAC 1993

Reading Test 13

1 When travelling to Spain with your family, you encounter a problem at the airport. Your father is given the following document.

Estimado pasajero:

   Por favor, acepte nuestras más sinceras excusas por no entregarle el equipaje a su llegada a destino. Esperamos que esta pérdida sea sólo temporal, y así estamos haciendo todo lo posible para hallarlo. Ya hemos procesado una descripción de su maleta y una computadora a nivel internacional está intentando encontrarla.

   Esta búsqueda continúa durante 120 horas.

   En el caso improbable de que, dentro de tres días no se hubiera descubierto, su ficha será enviada a la correspondiente Oficina Central de Equipajes, donde se continuará la búsqueda.

   Por favor, tome nota de las horas y teléfonos indicados en este folleto; nuestro personal hará en todo momento lo posible por atenderle y se pondrá en contacto con usted tan pronto como su investigación haya tenido buen éxito.

   Lamentamos de nuevo el incidente causado, reiterándole nuestras excusas por las molestias que hayamos podido ocasionarle.

(a)	Why do the airport authorities apologize to the passenger?	(2)
(b)	What two facts indicate that the authorities are trying to resolve the problem?	(4)
(c)	What will happen if the matter has not been put right within three days?	(3)
(d)	What is the passenger asked to do?	(3)
(e)	When will the authorities be in contact with you again?	(2)

NICCEA 1993

Reading Test 14

1 Pepe, the perfect tourist, has published a humorous guide for holiday-makers. This is how it begins.

COMO COMPORTARSE EN LA PLAYA

Durante los meses de verano, millones de personas van de vacaciones, abarrotando las piscinas, los lagos, las playas … ¿Pero, existe algún libro que te diga cómo debes comportarte en esos lugares? ¡No, no lo hay! Aunque no debes preocuparte: las increíbles reglas de comportamiento de 'Pepe, turista modelo', te dirán como hacerlo.

REGLA 1: **PEPE conserva la calma cuando en la playa hay niños que no paran de jugar a su alrededor, gritando.**
En ningún caso es aconsejable seguir el ejemplo de un ciudadano de Colonia que pasaba sus vacaciones en una isla del Mediterráneo. Le prometió un helado al niño que más aprisa se comiera un pastel de arena que él mismo había hecho … y durante un rato tuvo paz y tranquilidad, pero se dice que algo más tarde mantuvo una ruidosa discusión con los padres del niño.

REGLA 2: **PEPE tiene siempre en cuenta que los demás veraneantes también tienen derecho a un ambiente tranquilo y relajado.**
Por lo que, con sumo cuidado, Pepe sube el volumen de su equipo de música en el que estaba escuchando un poco de 'heavy metal' sólo con la intención de que no se oiga el rumor de las conversaciones de los demás bañistas, que molesta un tanto …

(a) According to the title, what is the purpose of this guide? (1)
(b) What problem does Rule 1 deal with? (1)
(c) Pepe solved the problem by keeping calm. What exactly did another holiday-maker do? (2)
(d) Why didn't this idea work in the end? (1)
(e) Judging from Rule 2, Pepe is a considerate holiday-maker.
Do you agree? Give a reason for your answer. (2)

NEAB 1991

Reading Test 15

A Spanish friend shows you this letter. Answer the questions which follow.

Buenos Aires, 5 de junio

Querida Marta:

Espero que al recibir esta carta estés bien, así como toda tu familia. No sé por qué no he recibido ninguna contestación a la carta que te escribí en marzo. ¿Te has equivocado de dirección? Te escribo con un computador. Me lo prestó mi cuñado.

Ahora vivimos en Buenos Aires, en la ciudad misma. Antes, vivíamos en una granja pero como mis padres se envejecían y a mi padre le duele la espalda, de mala gana tuvieron que encontrar otra cosa. Yo echo de menos el aire libre.

Mis amigos y yo tenemos bicicletas. Como medio de transporte tiene muchas ventajas. Todos mis amigos trabajan en el centro. Aparte de permitirles llegar temprano a su trabajo, también les permite ahorrar los gastos de transporte. Como yo no trabajo, utilizo la mía menos que ellos. Sin embargo, realizo dos o tres paseos por semana y así me mantengo en buen estado físico.

Acabo de leer un libro sobre la historia de la bicicleta. ¡Qué historia! ¿Sabes que las primeras bicicletas eran empujadas con los pies, y que eran totalmente de madera?

Bueno, amiga, no te canso más con mi carta. ¿Por qué no vienes a verme? ¡En Buenos Aires el clima es templado en todas las estaciones!

Recibe un abrazo de tu amigo,

Felipe.

1 What question is Marta asked in the first paragraph? (1)
2 From whom did Felipe borrow his computer? (1)
3 Why did Felipe move house?
Tick one box only.

His parents wanted to live in the country. ☐

His parents wanted to be with him. ☐

His parents wanted to leave their farm. ☐

His parents were getting old and frail. ☐ (1)

4 What regrets does Felipe have about moving house? (1)
5 What *two* advantages does cycling have, according to Felipe's friends? (2)
6 What specific advantage does cycling have for Felipe? (1)
7 What *two* surprising facts has Felipe learnt about the first bicycles? (2)
8 Why might a tourist be attracted to Buenos Aires? (1)

MEG 1992

10.6 Suggested answers

Reading Test 1

(i) Short-sleeved T-shirt.
(ii) Socks.
(iii) A gold chain.
(iv) An English dictionary.

Reading Test 2

(i) She hopes that I do not miss my family.
(ii) She hopes I have a nice time with them.

Reading Test 3

(a) They are not available.
(b) (i) How to speak in public.
(ii) How to cure small winter ills.

Reading Test 4

1 (a) The swimming pool gets free hot water.
(b) They get 10% off their electricity bills.
(c) The wind almost always takes the smoke away from their home.

2 A fire.

3 The day before yesterday.

4 He was single.

5 Cleaning the machines.

6 The firemen.

7 They did not have the right equipment.

8 They put water in an electrical area.

Reading Test 5

1 (a) They have been very useful.
(b) To understand South-American accents and pronunciation.
(c) To record conversations with a tape-recorder.

Reading Test 6

1 (a) Wrote songs.
(b) He gave advice.
(c) He always heeded it.
(d) He left Cuba when he was very small.
(e) He speaks both equally well.
(f) She is a fantastic person.
(g) She thought it was going to be a world hit.
(h) The language unites them.

Reading Test 7

1 (a) The Ministry of Defence had forbidden it.
(b) Air-force pilots.
(c) It was stationary and was like a small white shiny saucer.
(d) Las Palmas.
(e) It was white and it was moving.
(f) It did not show up on the radar.

  (g) As a reflection.
  (h) It was seen from the ground as well.
  (i) Whether it landed or whether it hovered just above the ground.

Reading Test 8

1 (a) They deliver promptly into the hand of the recipient.
  (b) Objects and documents.
  (c) Door-to door service.
  (d) They will take the fax to their house.
  (e) The following day.
  (f) They want to improve by answering customers' questions; they always listen.

Reading Test 9

1 (a) Drinking too much and wife-beating.
  (b) He pays money in the bar but she pays in pain when he gets home and beats her.
  (c) A friend, a family member, the neighbour you meet in the lift or the wife of a friend or yourself.
  (d) Her dignity.
  (e) To be better-informed.
  (f) Show resignation and be silent.
  (g) Way to get out of the house and a solution.
  (h) There is a free help-line.

Reading Test 10

1 (a) Be careful.
  (b) **(i)** I do not believe you.
       (ii) All is well.
  (c) They nod their heads.

Reading Test 11

1 (a) Study at University.
  (b) She wants her to work.
  (c) The family needs the money.
  (d) No because it suggests a way that both family and daughter can benefit.

Reading Test 12

1 (a) When you have signed your form.
  (b) Contagious illnesses have to be reported.
  (c) When you receive the bill.
  (d) They are forbidden.
  (e) In authorized areas.
  (f) Have a bucket of water near the fire.
  (g) No animals which may be a danger or cause a nuisance.
  (h) Streams, fountains, public roadways, beaches.
  (i) Get permission from the staff.
  (j) Forbidden in the handbasins or in the sinks to be used for washing dishes.
  (k) You will be expelled.

Reading Test 13

1 (a) Not delivering luggage on arriving at destination.
  (b) They have a description of the luggage and they are searching by computer world-wide.
  (c) The information will be relayed to the Central Luggage Office and the search will continue.
  (d) Make a note of times and phone-numbers in this brochure.
  (e) As soon as the search has been successful.

Reading Test 14

1 (a) How to behave on the beach.
(b) Children who constantly play and shout on the beach.
(c) Told a child to eat a sand-cake.
(d) There was a row with the parents.
(e) No because he turns up the volume of his music to drown other noises.

Reading Test 15

1 Has she got his address wrong?

2 Brother-in-law.

3 His parents were getting old and frail.

4 He misses the fresh air.

5 They arrive early for work and they save money.

6 Keeps fit.

7 They were pushed along by your feet and they were made entirely of wood.

8 The climate was temperate all year round.

Chapter 11
Writing: Basic Level

11.1 Introduction

This is what you need to know about the exam:
- This is the only Basic Level paper which is optional. However you cannot get a grade C unless you attempt it.
- You lose nothing by attempting it even if you score zero.
- Your work will be mainly assessed on your ability to communicate. If you get the message across to a sympathetic native speaker then you score. The quality of your language is also taken into consideration but not as much as at Higher Level.
- A lot of marks are lost in Basic Level and Higher Level Writing by candidates who misread or ignore the instructions. There are certain tasks to be completed and marks are allocated to each of these tasks. If you omit a task, you lose those marks no matter how brilliant your Spanish is!
- Your handwriting is all–important. Your paper may be marked by a very tired examiner with a hundred or so papers to mark after yours. He/she does not have time to decipher your handwriting. If what you write is not immediately readable it may well be presumed to be wrong.
- The day of your GCSE exam is not the day to experiment. You must build up a stock of Spanish that you know is correct and on the day select from your stock.

11.2 The tasks you have to complete at Basic Level

There are considerable differences among the exam boards. Make sure you know what is required by *your* exam board.

> Writing a list
> Messages and notes
> Postcards
> Completion of letter
> Form-filling
> Diary entries
> Writing a letter (*MEG* requires you to write a letter at Higher 1 Level, not at Basic Level.)

Writing a list

This is one of the easiest of the tasks. The kind of questions asked are predictable. You may be asked for:

> a list of items of food and drink for a party or picnic
> a list of presents to take home from Spain
> a list of relatives and family members
> a list of clothes

a list of contents in a bag
a list of activities to be undertaken with a friend
a list of colours
a list of animals

Note that a one-word answer is enough to score. For instance on a shopping list you do not have to say **un kilo de manzanas**. **Manzanas** by itself is sufficient to score. In the same way, if you have to write a list of family members, **hermano** is enough to get the score. You do not have to write **mi hermano.**

- Make sure you do not repeat the same article.
- Make sure you do not write English words. 'Sandwich' and 'hockey' may be acceptable Spanish words in other contexts but not here!
- Make sure you know the vocabulary for the above list suggestions.

Writing messages

These are some of the things you may be asked to do:

Say that you have gone out, give a reason, say when you will be back and say how you will get back.
He salido. Voy a la discoteca con Juan. Volveré a las ocho en el autobús.

Say that you have gone to bed, give a reason and say when you want to get up in the morning and what you are going to do tomorrow.
Estoy en la cama. Estoy cansado/a. Quiero levantarme mañana a las ocho. Voy a la playa con Juan.

Give someone instructions on how to get to a place, e.g. tell someone to get bus number 8 to the cathedral. Cross the square and take the second road on the right.
Toma el autobús número ocho hasta la catedral. Cruza la plaza, y toma la segunda calle a la derecha.

Invite someone to join you, e.g. in the Mariposa disco in the main square.
¿Quieres venir? Estoy en una discoteca que se llama 'La Mariposa' en la plaza mayor.

Ask someone to do something, e.g. call Juana at eight o'clock.
¿Puedes llamar a Juana a las ocho?

Say where you have gone, e.g. to the beach/disco/Juana's house.
He ido a la playa/la discoteca/la casa de Juana.

Say that you are not hungry/thirsty.
No tengo hambre/sed.

Write down a phone message, e.g. Say Juan called at six o'clock. He will be in front of the cinema at eight o'clock. Say that his sister cannot come because she is ill.
Juan llamó a las seis. Estará delante del cine a las ocho. Su hermana no puede ir. Está enferma.

Candidates lose marks on these tasks because they do not indicate *who* is doing what and *whether it is in the past, present or future*. So the endings to your verbs are all-important.

Writing a postcard

Usually a blank postcard is printed on the exam paper and you have to fill it in. You are given a set of tasks to complete. These tasks are often fairly predictable:

Say where you are and who you are with.	Estoy en Málaga con mi hermano.
Say what the weather is like.	Hace calor todos los días.
Say what your hotel is like.	Mi hotel es moderno y cómodo. Hay dos piscinas.
Say what your campsite is like.	El camping es muy grande. Hay dos piscinas.
Say what the youth hostel is like.	El albergue juvenil es muy limpio y cómodo.
Say when you arrived or will arrive.	Llegué aquí ayer. Llegaré a Madrid mañana.
Say when you left or will leave.	Me marché de Madrid ayer. Me marcharé de aquí mañana.
Say how long you will stay.	Estaré aquí hasta el domingo.
Say what you have done.	He visitado los monumentos históricos, he hablado mucho español, he comido mucho, he bailado en las discotecas.
Say what you do during the day.	Visito los monumentos históricos, hablo mucho español, como mucho, bailo en las discotecas.

Say what you will do tomorrow.	Voy a ver los monumentos históricos, voy a hablar mucho español, voy a comer mucho y voy a bailar en las discotecas.
Say whether you like Spain and give reasons.	Me gusta España mucho. Me gusta el sol, la playa y la gente.
Say what you think of the food.	Me gusta la comida sobre todo las tortillas y los mariscos.
Describe a person whom you have met.	En la discoteca, encontré a un(a) español(a). Es muy guapo(a) y tiene el pelo largo y moreno.
Say what you have bought.	He comprado una guitarra y muchos discos y perfume para mi madre.
Say that you hope to visit a friend.	Espero visitar a un(a) amigo(a).

Completion of letter

These are very simple translation exercises. A letter is printed on the exam paper in Spanish and there are about ten words omitted. Under each gap is a word in English. You have to write the Spanish word for that English word in the gap. For example:

Tengo un gato y un ....
                                (dog)

You would obviously write **perro** in the gap.

Form-filling

You should always look at the mark distribution for this question. For some of the easy entries, no marks at all are awarded. On the other hand, some of the entries attract two marks so you should make sure you give two details in these questions.

The questions asked are usually fairly predictable. You should know the following vocabulary:

nombre *first name*
apellido *surname*
edad *age*
dirección *address*
fecha *date*
fecha de nacimiento *date of birth*
fecha de llegada *date of arrival*
fecha de salida *date of departure*
firma *signature*

Be prepared to answer questions like:
(suggested answers in brackets)

Nacionalidad (británica)
Profesión (estudiante)
Asignatura preferida (español)
Asignatura que no te gusta (inglés)
Pasatiempo favorito (tenis)
Comida favorita (patatas)
Comida que no te gusta (pescado)
Animales en casa (perro y gato)

Notice that **británica** always here has an **-a** ending even though it refers to a boy because it agrees with **nacionalidad** which is feminine.

Diary entries

Again the questions asked tend to be very predictable. You will have to give a list of things you plan to do on certain days or a list of things you did on certain days. Make sure you can muster ten things that you either did or will do. For example:

Fui/iré al campo.
Fui/iré a un concierto.
Fui/iré a un museo.
Fui/iré de compras.

Fui/iré a un restaurante.
Fui/iré al cine.
Fui/iré al teatro.
Fui/iré a ver a mi amigo.
Fui/iré al parque.
Fui/iré a una discoteca.

Letter-writing

NB: *MEG* asks you to write a letter in the Higher Level 1 exam not at Basic Level.

● Your letter should be about 60 or 70 words long except for *MEG* who specify 100 words.
● You must double-check and triple-check that you do not leave out a communication point. You may have to reply to a letter. If so make a careful list of the points you have to communicate. If the question sets out which points to make, be sure to include them all. Make a list and tick them off once you have completed the task.
● Your letter will be either formal (i.e. to a person that you do not know) or informal (i.e. to a Spanish friend). For formal letters, use **Usted.** For informal letters, use **tú.** Make sure you know how to change vocabulary accordingly:

	FORMAL LETTER	**INFORMAL LETTER**
Beginning:	Muy señor mío *(Dear Sir)*	Querido Juan/Querida Juana *Dear Juan/Juana*
Ending:	Le saluda atentamente *(Yours faithfully)*	Un abrazo de … *(a hug from …)*
Can you send me …?	¿Puede Vd. mandarme …?	¿Puedes mandarme …?
your	su/sus	tu/tus
I am sending you …	Le mando …	Te mando …

Informal letters

You should be able to predict at least some of the things you will have to write about. Make sure you have answers ready to the following:

Write about yourself.
Me llamo … Tengo dieciséis años. Vivo en Birmingham. Me gusta tocar la guitarra y leer novelas. Voy a una discoteca con mis amigos los sábados.

Write about your family.
Mi padre es mecánico y mi madre es dentista. Tengo una hermana de diez años. También tenemos un perro. Los domingos damos un paseo juntos cuando hace buen tiempo.

Write about your house.
En mi casa hay tres dormitorios, una cocina, un comedor y una sala de estar. También tenemos un pequeño jardín detras de la casa. Desafortunadamente no tenemos un garaje.

Write about your school.
Mi colegio es bastante grande. Hay quinientos alumnos más o menos y cuarenta profesores. Hay tres laboratorios, un campo de deportes, dos pistas de tenis pero desafortunadamente no hay piscina.

Write about the area where you live.
Cerca de mi casa hay cines, parques y un club de jóvenes. También hay fábricas y mucho tráfico. El campo no está lejos y me gusta dar paseos en el campo con mi familia.

Write about a family occasion.
Ayer era el cumpleaños de mi madre y fuimos a un restaurante. La comida era excelente. Tomé sopa de verduras, luego bistec con patatas y luego un helado enorme. Después fuimos todos juntos al cine a ver una película americana. ¡Lo pasé bomba!

Write about an incident at school.
Ayer hubo un incendio en mi colegio. Todos los alumnos tuvimos que salir y fuimos al campo de deportes. Los bomberos llegaron diez minutos más tarde y apagaron el fuego. El laboratorio de química fue destrozado.

Write about an incident involving your family.
Ayer fuimos a la playa en el coche de mi padre. Durante el día mi padre perdió las llaves del coche. Tuvimos que dejar el coche allí y volver en autobús.

Invite someone to come to England.

¿Por qué no vienes a Inglaterra en verano? Mi madre dice que puedes venir. Tenemos un dormitorio libre o quizás prefieres compartir conmigo? ¡Lo pasaremos bomba!

Accept an invitation.

Muchísimas gracias por tu carta y gracias por haberme invitado a España. Sí, mis padres dicen que puedo ir. ¡Lo pasaremos bomba! Llegaré en avión el tres de julio.

Decline an invitation.

Muchísimas gracias por tu carta y gracias por haberme invitado a España. Lo siento pero no puedo ir porque mis padres no tienen dinero y además tengo exámenes y tengo mucho que hacer.

Say thank you for something.

Muchas gracias por el regalo. ¡Qué camiseta más bonita! Cuando lo abrí ¡qué sorpresa! Voy a llevarla esta tarde en la discoteca.

Thank someone for their hospitality

Muchas gracias por todo lo que hiciste para mí durante mi estancia contigo. Gracias a tus padres también. Todo era excelente: la comida, mi habitacíon, las excursiones.

Say that you got home safely from Spain.

El viaje de regreso era muy agradable. No hubo retrasos y en el avión me dieron una comida excelente. Mis padres me esperaban en el aeropuerto de Londres.

Say what you will do when your Spanish friend visits you.

¡Lo pasaremos bomba! Iremos al campo, iremos a discotecas, veremos los museos, iremos al cine, conocerás a mis amigos, nadaremos en la piscina.

Formal letters

Again you should be able to predict at least some of the tasks you will be set.

Say that you were not happy with the hotel/campsite/youth hostel and give a reason.

Quiero quejarme. No me gustaba el hotel/camping/albergue juvenil. Los servicios estaban muy sucios.

Find out what there is to do in the city.

¿Qué se puede hacer en la ciudad?

Say you would like to book accommodation for the family.

Quiero reservar dormitorios/camas para toda la familia.

Find out what facilities there are in the hotel.

¿Qué facilidades hay en el hotel? ¿Hay una piscina?

Say you lost your watch while you were there.

Mientras estaba en su hotel, perdí mi reloj.

Give the dates of your arrival and departure.

Llegaré el dos de mayo y me marcharé el cinco de mayo.

11.3 Examination questions

Writing Test 1

While you are on holiday in Spain you receive this invitation. Your Spanish friend, Lola, wants you to go to her birthday party.

Write a note to Lola in Spanish.
Tell her that:
- you would like to come to the party;
- you are sorry, you cannot;
- you are visiting Granada on Saturday;
- you want to see a concert there;
- you bought the tickets this morning;
- you are going to telephone from Granada.

Write neatly and put down *all* the information you are asked to give. The number of words is not important.

NEAB 1994

Student's answers
Quiero venir a la fiesta.
No puedo.
Voy a Granada el sábado.
Quiero ver un concert.
Compra los billetes mañana.
Voy a llamar desde Granada.

Examiner's comments
On line 2, you have left out 'you are sorry'. You should have included **lo siento**.

On line 4, **concert** is French! You have left out 'there'. You should have written **quiero ver un concierto allí**.

On line 5, **compra** is wrong. That means you want someone else to buy the tickets. You need to know the endings of the verbs, even at Basic Level. **Billetes** is used for transport tickets and **entradas** for entertainment tickets. **Mañana** by itself means 'tomorrow'. You should have written **Compré las entradas esta mañana**.

Writing Test 2

You are in Spain and are staying with your Spanish penfriend. You are about to go out shopping for clothes. You make a list of the items of clothing that you want to buy and also the colour that you prefer. Do not write the same item or colour twice.

The first item and colour have been written for you.

Ropa		**Color**	
bañador		marrón	
(a)	(1)	**(f)**	(1)
(b)	(1)	**(g)**	(1)
(c)	(1)	**(h)**	(1)
(d)	(1)	**(i)**	(1)
(e)	(1)	**(j)**	(1)

MEG 1994

Student's answers

(a)	zapatos	**(f)**	negro
(b)	abrigo	**(g)**	blanco
(c)	sombrero	**(h)**	azul
(d)	T-shirt	**(i)**	amarillo
(e)	jupe	**(j)**	negro

Examiner's comments

For the fourth item you have used an English word. Although this word is used extensively in Spain, you would be wise to steer clear of English words here and in other parts of the Spanish GCSE.

For the fifth entry you have given a French word. You should have written **falda.** You have also thrown away a mark for using the same word twice. You have written **negro** twice.

Writing Test 3

You have received this note from your Spanish friend Marisa. She asks you to help her with some work she has to do for her English teacher. She wants to know what you usually do at the weekend.

> *Una tarjeta simpática*
>
> *¡Socorro!*
>
> *Tengo que escribir una descripción de un fin de semana típicamente inglés para mi profesor de inglés y no sé cómo. ¿Me puedes decir lo que haces tú normalmente el sábado y el domingo?*
>
> *Muchas gracias*
> *Un abrazo*
>
> *Marisa*
>
> *P.D. Te escribo más cuando tenga tiempo*

Write a letter to Marisa *in Spanish* telling her about a typical weekend in your life.

Tell her:
- what time you get up;
- what you have for lunch;
- what you do at the weekend (mention *three* things);
- if you have to do homework at the weekend.

Ask her:
- if she goes to school on Saturday;
- when her holidays start.

Write neatly and put down *all* the information you are asked to give. The number of words is not important.

NEAB 1993

Student's answers

Me lavo a las nueve.
Como bocadillos para la cena.
Salgo al cine y a discotecas los finales de semana.
Tengo muchos deberes los finales de semana.
¿Vas al colegio los sábados?
¿Cuándo empiezan tus vacaciones?

Examiner's comments

You have not written your reply in the form of a letter. You should write an opening and a closing expression.

On the first line **me lavo** means 'I wash'.

On the second line **la cena** means the evening meal.

Finales is wrong for a week-end. You are given the correct word in Marisa's letter. Also you have mentioned only two things.

11.4 Examination practice questions

Here are some more past questions for you to practise on. Suggested answers are given at the end.

Writing Test 4

Your parents want to send you to stay with a Spanish family, and they receive this model letter. Following the guidelines given in the words or questions below the spaces, write in the *words in Spanish* with which you would fill in the spaces, in order to send it back to the agency your parents are using.

27.5.94

Muy señores míos:

Deseamos mandar a nuestro/a...................................a quedarse con una
        (1) (son/daughter)

familia española para dos...
        (2) (weeks)

Tiene ....años, y buscamos una familia con ....de
    (3) (How old are you?)   *(4) (children)*

la misma ....Prefiere quedarse en un(a) ....
    (5) (age)   *(6) (do you prefer a house or a flat?)*

Para comer, le gusta(n) ....y no le
        (7) (what do you like to eat?)

gusta(n) ....
        (8) (what do you not like to eat?)

Le interesa(n) ....
        (9) (what are your interests?)

y le gusta ....
    (10) (what do you like to do?)

Le ruego me conteste cuanto antes.

Le saluda atentamente,

....(firma)

---

(10)

ULEAC 1994

Writing Test 5

You want a Spanish penfriend, and your teacher gives you a form issued by a Spanish magazine for teenagers. You simply have to fill in the form below, so that the magazine can publish your details.

Answer each point on the form below wherever possible *with words in Spanish*.

Nombre................................Apellido...

Edad............años................meses. Fecha de nacimiento........................

Familia...

.... (1)

¿Qué animales tienes en casa? ....

....(1)

¿Cómo eres tu? ....

....(2)

Estudios y trabajo:
La asignatura que prefieres:...(1)

La asignatura que no te gusta:..(1)

¿Qué haces para ayudar en casa? ....

....(2)

Intereses y pasatiempos
Me gusta más:..(1)

Me gusta bastante:...(1)

Firma...................................Fecha...

ULEAC 1993

Writing Test 6

Your family is planning to spend a holiday in Spain and wants to book accommodation at a small Spanish hotel. The Tourist Office of the town you are going to has sent this form, which you have to fill in on behalf of your family.

Fill in each point required on the form below wherever possible *with words in Spanish*.

Nombre...............................Apellido...

Dirección ....

....

Nacionalidad...(1)

Preferimos un hotel situado en...

....(2)

Tipo de habitaciones que queremos...

....(2)

Comidas que vamos a tomar en el hotel:

(a)..(1)

(b)..(1)

(c)..(1)

Fecha de llegada...(1)

Fecha de salida...(1)

Firma...................................Fecha...

ULEAC 1994

Writing Test 7

You have received this card from your Spanish friend Isabel wishing you good luck with your exams.

Write a letter *in Spanish* to Isabel.

Say:
- what subjects you are studying;
- when you finish your exams;
- what plans you have for the holidays (mention *two* things);
- what you are going to do after the holidays (mention *two* things).

Ask:
- what Isabel is doing at school;
- if she is going abroad this summer.

Write neatly and put down *all* the information you are asked to give. The number of words is not important.

NEAB 1991

Writing Test 8

While on holiday in Madrid, you and an English friend arrange to fly to Barcelona to visit a Spanish friend. Unfortunately, you have to postpone your visit because your English friend is ill. You send a telegram of about 25 words *in Spanish* to your Spanish friend to tell him/her of the new arrangements.
  Include the following points:
- say that you can't come tomorrow;
- say your friend is ill;
- say your sister is coming with you;
- say that you arrive on Monday morning;
- say you return to Madrid on Friday.

(10)

MEG 1992

Writing Test 9

While your Spanish penfriend is staying in your home, she decides one day to go shopping when you are at school. She offers to get you some things that you need. To make it easier for her, you write her a note in Spanish.

  Write in Spanish about 30 words.

  Say that it does not cost much to go by bus.

  Say that you would like a film for your camera.

  Say that you need a blue biro.

  Say that the supermarket is not far from your school.

  Ask if she can meet you after school.   (20)

NICCEA 1992

Writing Test 10

Your Spanish pen-friend has asked you what you do during the evenings. Write down one thing you do *each* evening, try to think of a different thing for *each* night. Monday's is done for you.   (8)

Día	Actividad
Lunes	limpiar mi dormitorio
Martes	
Miércoles	
Jueves	
Viernes	
Sábado	
Domingo	

WJEC 1993

Writing Test 11

During the summer you are going on a trip with your local youth club to stay at a large house on the coast in Northern Ireland. You decide to tell your Spanish penfriend about it.

  Write her a letter, in Spanish, *of about 60 words*.

  Include the following points:
- where exactly the house is located;
- the length of the stay and the cost of the trip;
- a brief description of the house you are going to stay in;
- leisure facilities on offer in the area. (Mention at least *two*.)

REMEMBER TO BEGIN AND END YOUR LETTER CORRECTLY.   (40)

NICCEA 1994

Writing Test 12

Your Spanish penfriend has asked you in his last letter to tell him what you do at home during the holidays.

  Write him a letter, in Spanish, *of about 60 words*.

  Include the following points:

(a) when you get up and go to bed

(b) meals at home (mention *two* and say briefly what you have)

(c) two leisure activities (give two details of each activity)

(d) two jobs you do about the house (give two details of each job).

REMEMBER TO BEGIN AND END YOUR LETTER CORRECTLY.   (40)

NICCEA 1993

Writing Test 13

You have decided to spend a fortnight's camping holiday on the Costa Brava. Write a letter to the Tourist Office in Gerona, in which you make the following points:
- you are hoping to go to the Costa Brava,
- the intended length of your stay,
- the sort of holiday you are planning,
- how many people there will be in your party,
- whether you want a first, second or third class campsite,
- where your ideal campsite will be,
- whether you intend to sleep in a tent or a caravan,
- the sort of thing you hope to do while you are there.

Remember to write your letter entirely in Spanish, to include a date, and to start and end your letter correctly. (20)

SEG 1993

Writing Test 14

While at home in England you receive a letter from a Spanish friend of which an extract is included here. Write a reply to it, making sure that you deal with all your friend's questions.

Remember to write your reply entirely in Spanish, to include a date, and to start and end your letter correctly.

Pamplona, 23 de mayo de 1992

¡Hola! ¿Qué tal estás?

Te escribo otra vez para contestar tu carta que recibí ayer. En tu primera carta me dices cómo te llamas y dónde vives, pero no me dices nada de tu familia ni de tu colegio.

¿Cuántos hermanos tienes? ¿Cómo se llama tu madre? ¿Cuántos animales hay en tu casa? ¿Cómo es tu colegio? ¿Cómo llegas allí todos los días?

Tengo muchas preguntas, ¿verdad? Y además también quiero saber algo sobre tus vacaciones. ¿Adónde vas a ir este verano? ¿Qué harás allí?

Marisol

(20)

SEG 1992

11.5 Suggested answers

Writing Test 1

Lola:
  Quiero venir a la fiesta.
  Lo siento pero no puedo.
  Voy a Granada el sábado.
  Quiero ver un concierto allí.
  Compré las entradas esta mañana.
  Voy a llamar desde Granada.

Writing Test 2

(a) zapatos   **(f)** negros
(b) abrigo   **(g)** blanco
(c) sombrero   **(h)** azul
(d) camisetas   **(i)** amarilla
(e) falda   **(j)** roja

Writing Test 3

Querida Marisa:
  Gracias por tu mensaje. Voy a contestarte:
  Me levanto a las nueve.
  Como bocadillos para el almuerzo.
  Salgo al teatro, al cine y a discotecas los fines de semana.
  Tengo muchos deberes los fines de semana.
  ¿Vas al colegio los sábados?
  ¿Cuándo empiezan tus vacaciones?
  Un abrazo
  Tu amigo inglés/amiga inglesa

Writing Test 4

  1 hijo/hija

  2 semanas

  3 dieciséis

  4 hijos

  5 edad

  6 casa/piso

  7 patatas

  8 pescado

  9 el tenis

 10 jugar a las cartas

Writing Test 5

The following are suggested answers to those questions which attract a mark.

  1 Vivo con mi padre y mi madre y mi hermana.

  2 Un gato y un perro.

  3 Soy alto/a, tengo el pelo negro.

  4 Español.

  5 Química.

  6 Lavo los platos y hago las camas.

  7 El baloncesto.

  8 Jugar a las cartas.

Writing Test 6

The following are suggested answers to those questions which attract a mark.

1 británica

2 la costa cerca de la playa

3 una habitación doble y dos habitaciones individuales

4 (a)   pollo con patatas
  (b)   pescado con guisantes
  (c)   bistec con zanahorias

5 el dos de mayo

6 el dieciséis de mayo

Writing Test 7

Manchester

2 de mayo

Querida Isabel:

Gracias por tu tarjeta. Eres muy bondadosa. Ya sabes que estoy estudiando el inglés, las matemáticas, la geografía, la historia, el francés y la religión. Terminaré mis exámenes el veinte de junio y quiero ir a Francia y luego iré a España a broncearme. Después de las vacaciones volveré al colegio a estudiar el español, el francés y el inglés. Quiero también aprender a tocar la guitarra.

    ¿Qué estudias en tu colegio?

    ¿Vas al extranjero este verano?

Un abrazo

Paula

Writing Test 8

No puedo venir mañana. Mi amigo está enfermo.
Mi hermana viene conmigo. Llego el lunes por la mañana.
Vuelvo a Madrid el viernes.

    John.

Writing Test 9

No cuesta mucho ir en autobús. Necesito una película para mi máquina fotográfica. También necesito un bolígrafo azul. El supermercado no está lejos de mi colegio. ¿Puedes encontrarme al final de mis clases?

Writing Test 10

hacer mis deberes
escuchar música
visitar a amigos
ir a la piscina
leer mi libro
salir a la discoteca

Writing Test 11

Belfast

23 de mayo

Querida Isabel:

Voy a decirte lo que hago en verano. Voy con mi club de jóvenes a una casa en la costa. Está a sesenta kilómetros al norte de Belfast. Nos quedamos dos semanas y cuesta solamente sesenta libras. La casa es cómoda y tiene dos pisos y un jardín. Hay un cine y un teatro cerca.

Un abrazo

Mary

Writing Test 12

Lurgan

12 de octubre

Querido Miguel:

Voy a contarte algo de mi vida. Me levanto a las ocho y me acuesto a las once. Desayuno a las ocho y diez y bebo un café solamente. A la una como mis bocadillos con mis amigos. Me gusta el fútbol. Juego los domingos y veo partidos en la televisión. Juego al ajedrez con mi padre por la tarde. Limpio mi habitación los lunes a las ocho y paso la aspiradora los sábados cuando mis padres trabajan.

Un abrazo

Paul

Writing Test 13

Liverpool

el 24 de mayo

Muy señor mío:

Espero ir a la Costa Brava y quiero pasar dos semanas allí. Vamos a acampar y seremos cuatro. Haga el favor de enviarme información sobre un camping de primera clase. El camping ideal estaría en la costa. Vamos a dormir en una tienda. Esperamos tomar el sol, ir a la playa y conocer a muchos españoles.

Le saluda atentamente

D. Ferguson

Writing Test 14

Stoke

30 de mayo

Querida Marisol:

Muchas gracias por tu carta. Voy a contestar las preguntas que me haces.

Tengo un hermano y se llama John. Mi madre se llama Sue. Tenemos un perro que se llama Toby. Es enorme y come muchísimo. Mi colegio es bastante tranquilo. Hay quinientos alumnos y es mixto. Hay campos de deportes y ordenadores en todas partes. Llego al colegio a pie porque está a dos minutos de aquí. Este verano espero ir a Francia con mi familia. Vamos a tomar el sol y comer y beber muchísimo. Me gusta la cocina francesa.

Un abrazo

Paula

Chapter 12
Writing: Higher Level

12.1 Introduction

Each exam board has different requirements and you need to know what your exam board requires:

MEG

Length of paper	Higher part 1 –	30 minutes
	Higher part 2 –	35 minutes
Number of questions	Higher part 1 –	one from a choice of two
	Higher part 2 –	one from a choice of two
Number of words per question	Higher part 1 –	100
	Higher part 2 –	150
Type of question	Higher part 1 –	choice of either a formal or an informal letter
	Higher part 2 –	choice of two accounts

NEAB

Length of paper	–	50 minutes (total of 65 including Basic)
Number of questions	–	Two (no choice)
Number of words per question	–	100 approx.
Type of question	–	Question 1 – Letter
	–	Question 2 – Account

NICCEA

Length of paper	–	50 minutes
Number of questions	–	One (choice of two)
Number of words per question	–	200
Type of question	–	Either a letter or a composition

SEG

Length of paper	–	60 minutes
Number of questions	–	Two (a choice is given in question)
Number of words per question	–	100
Type of question	–	Question 1 – either a composition or an account
	–	Question 2 – Task based on documents

ULEAC

Length of paper	–	60 minutes (total of 105 including Basic)
Number of questions	–	Two (from a choice of three)
Number of words per question	–	100
Type of question	–	Expansion of notes
	–	Composition
		Report

WJEC

Length of paper	–	70 minutes
Number of questions	–	Two (Question 1 may have a choice but no choice in Question 2)
Number of words per question	–	100–120
Type of question	–	Question 1 – Letter
	–	Question 2 – Composition

Number of words

- Do not write less than the number stipulated.
- Do not go over the number stipulated more than you need to make the last sentence make sense.
- The exam boards say a word is 'a group of letters with a space either side'. Count your words as you go and note the number.

Mark allocation

Marks for Higher Writing are allocated for:
- Communication (getting the message across).
- Accuracy – the fewer mistakes the more marks you get. But remember that your work will be marked positively. Your mistakes are not counted.
- Richness of your vocabulary and expressions.

Should you enter Higher Level Writing?

Yes! You have nothing to lose by attempting it and you cannot get a grade A or B unless you have attempted it. Some candidates have earned enough points from their other papers to gain a grade A but because they did not merely write their name on the Higher Writing paper, they were awarded a grade C. Be warned!!

12.2 Preparing for the examination

Check with the list above for the requirements for your board. Also check with your teacher. You will probably have to write a letter. If so, work through the advice given in the previous chapter. It is very likely that you will have to write an account. It could be a description of an event or an accident, it could be a report destined for the police or for your school magazine. Sometimes the instructions ask you to write an account as part of a letter. If this is the case, do not write the beginning or end of the letter or include letter-material expressions like ¿cómo estás? but go straight into the account that you have to write.
- For letter-writing, see the advice given in the previous chapter.
- For account or compositions, you need to build up a stock of Spanish that you know is correct and that you can use with just about any task you are set. You can call this stock of Spanish your *Survival Kit*.

12.3 Survival kit

You will find this list of preterites useful:

bebí *I drank*
comí *I ate*
compré *I bought*
decidí (+ inf.) *I decided*
di un paseo *I went for a walk*
empecé a (+ inf.) *I started to*
encontré *I found*
encontré a *I met*
entré en *I went in*
fui *I went*
llegué *I arrived*
perdí *I lost*
tomé *I took*
vi *I saw*
viajé *I travelled*
visité *I visited*
volví *I returned*

- Try and introduce an imperfect tense into your work. If you find this difficult, just mention the weather or what you were wearing:

  Hacía buen tiempo. *It was nice weather.*
  Hacía sol. *It was sunny.*
  Llovía a cántaros y estábamos mojados hasta los huesos. *It was pouring and we were soaked to the skin.*

  Llevaba mi jersey nuevo. *I was wearing my new jersey.*

- Try to build up a collection of mark-winning phrases:

  al + inf.
  al llegar *on arriving*

  antes de + inf.
  antes de comer *before eating*

  después de + inf.
  después de comer *after eating*

  para + inf.
  para reservar un billete *in order to book a ticket*

  sin perder un momento *without wasting a moment*
  ¡Qué día! *What a day!*
  ¡Qué barbaridad! *How awful!*
  desgraciadamente *unfortunately*
  afortunadamente *fortunately*
  luego *then*
  al día siguiente *on the following day*
  como estaba cansado/a *as I was tired*
  con mucho cuidado *with great care*
  dos minutos más tarde *two minutes later*

Look through the questions from past papers: after the questions there are suggested answers. These suggested answers are not super answers. They are not at a level that you cannot possibly hope to achieve. But they are at a level that can be reasonably expected of a student who has studied Spanish for two or three years and though they may not gain full marks, they are of good enough quality to earn the full points available for the questions.

12.4 In the examination

- Just before the examination, check the present, imperfect and preterite tenses of **mirar**, **comer** and **vivir**. As soon as you can after going into the examination room, after you have been given the signal to start, write them out on rough paper or on the actual examination paper. Then write out the expressions that you have learnt, e.g. **antes de comer**, **al llegar**, **llovía a cántaros** etc. During the exam, *tick them off as you use them*!
- Read through the questions carefully. Make a list of points you have to communicate or if you think that is too time-consuming underline them as they appear on the exam paper. *Tick them off as you answer them.*
- In your mock exam, you should have made a note of how long each question took you. You should have worked on this in the weeks before the exam. Now set yourself a schedule that will give you time to check what you have written. *Remember:* once you have written something it is very difficult to spot the error. Once it is down on paper, somehow it looks right! *Think* carefully before you write. *Check* each verb with the lists you have written for *tense* and *ending* before you write it down.
- Remember that what you write must be relevant to the question. Any material you have pre-learnt will not score any marks unless it is used in a question that is relevant to that material.
- It is a good idea to work through the suggested answers that follow and see if you can learn parts of them off-by-heart. But remember if you do use these selections, they must be relevant to the question.

12.5 Examination questions

Writing Test 1

You have just spent a fortnight on a visit to a Spanish friend during which several things went wrong and you were only able to cope thanks to the extreme kindness of your host/hostess and his/her friends and family. Write a letter to him/her remembering the problems and everyone's kindness and sending them a small gift as a means of thanking them for it.

In your letter you should:
- mention *three* different problems that arose. (items 1, 2, 3)
- IN EACH CASE, mention the help that you received. (items 4, 5, 6)
- thank them for the help given. (item 7)
- say you hope they like the present you are sending them as a small token of your gratitude. (items 8 & 9)
- express the wish that they enjoy the rest of their holidays. (item 10)

REMEMBER TO DATE, START AND END YOUR LETTER CORRECTLY. Write about 100 words and STATE AT THE END OF YOUR LETTER THE NUMBER YOU HAVE USED. (60)

SEG 1993

Student's answer

Estimado Pablo:

¿Cómo estás? Volví a Inglaterra sin incidente pero aquí hace muy mal tiempo.

Lo pasé muy bien en España; fui a discotecas, tomé el sol y bebí demasiado.

Estoy escribiendo para decirte gracias por todo lo que hiciste por mí. El primer desastre ocurrió cuando perdí mi dinero en la playa. Luego estuve enfermo y no podía hacer nada. Llamaste al médico.

Más tarde podía ir a la playa donde encontré a mucha gente interesante.

Te digo gracias sinceramente por todo. Espero que os guste el regalo. Espero que pases bien el resto de tus vacaciones.

Le saluda atentamente

A. Whittle

Examiner's comment

The candidate must realize that there are 10 items which he/she has to communicate. It is spelt out on the question paper. Yet only two problems are mentioned and for the first problem the help you received is not mentioned. Neither is the idea of a token of gratitude mentioned. So the maximum content mark is 6 out of 10. Moreover, the introduction and the end of the letter are more like a business letter than a letter to a friend. You would lose more marks here.

Some of the Spanish you introduce is perfectly correct but it is not relevant to the question. It is obvious padding. If the question had been to describe what you did in Spain this material would be perfectly acceptable. There is no date or town at the beginning.

Please see the suggested version later.

Writing Test 2

While on holiday in Spain, you are involved in a minor accident while crossing the road outside your hotel. You were not seriously injured, but you have to provide the local police with a written report *in Spanish*. Make sure you cover the following areas.

- The circumstances leading up to the accident, e.g. where you were going, why you crossed the road.
- The car which hit you and what the driver was like.
- Your injuries and how they were treated.
- The effect the accident is likely to have on the rest of your holiday. (40)

ULEAC 1993

Student's answer

Voy describir lo que ocurrió esta mañana. Estoy turista británica y mi hotel se llama el Hotel Sol. Mi madre me mandó al supermercado a comprar loción bronceadora. Para ir al supermercado tuve que cruzar la calle.

Encontré un paso de peatones y crucé. Un Ford Escort negro no paró. Frenó fuertemente pero el coche me volcó.

El conductor era joven, llevaba gafas de sol, tenía unos veinticinco años y tenía pelo largo y negro.

Al caerme, perdí dos dientes y me corté la cara. Afortunadamente no tenía huesos rotos. Una ambulancia me llevó al hospital pero salí dentro de dos horas.

El médico ha dicho que tendré que guardar cama durante dos días.

Examiner's comment

On line 1, there should be **a** between **voy** and **describir. Estoy** should be **Soy**. The candidate has obviously built up a survival kit of preterites, imperfects and expressions and I have underlined them in the text.

He/she has done well to do this: the expressions are all relevant to the question and so will score marks.

Perhaps the candidate could have written **sin perder un momento** before **encontré**, **desgraciadamente** before **Un Ford Escort** and **Después de examinarme** before **El médico**. All these are expressions from the survival kit mentioned above.

Writing Test 3

You have written on behalf of your family to the Tourist Office in Toledo and they have sent you the brochure you requested, which includes the map of the province and the information about hotels and useful addresses which are printed below. However, they have forgotten to send you a list of hotels and prices. As you haven't enough time to write again to the Tourist Office, you decide you had better stay in the Parador 'Conde de Orgaz', which is the only one mentioned by name.

CAPACIDAD – HOTELERA DE TOLEDO

LA CIUDAD de Toledo cuenta con 10 instalaciones hoteleras, con un total de 800 plazas, de las que 108 corresponden a un hotel de cuatro estrellas, Parador Nacional 'Conde de Orgaz'; 300 a hoteles de tres estrellas, 128 a hoteles de dos estrellas y 100 a hoteles de una estrella, correspondiendo el resto a hostales de dos y una estrella.

Write a letter *in Spanish* of about 100 words to the Parador in which you:
- say that you would like to occupy a room in ten days from now;
- tell them how long you wish to stay;
- tell them how many people will be with you;
- say what sort of room you require and ask its price;
- state *two* other requirements you have;
- ask how far it is from the Parador to the centre of Toledo;
- say how you will be travelling;
- ask the Parador to comment on a place on the map which you have chosen to visit.

STATE AT THE END THE NUMBER OF WORDS YOU HAVE WRITTEN   (60)

SEG 1991

Student's answer

Carlisle

20 de mayo

Querido señor:

Quiero reservar una habitación del treinta de mayo hasta el cinco de junio. Seremos dos, mi hermana y yo. Quiero una habitación con dos camas individuales y un cuarto de baño. ¿Puede decirme cuánto cuesta?

También quiero una habitación con vista al mar y en el primer piso.

¿A qué distancia está el Parador del centro de Toledo? ¿Hay un parking? Queremos visitar Madrid. ¿Vale la pena? ¿Tiene Vd. información sobre Madrid?

Adiós

P. Reid

Examiner's comment
Querido Señor and **adiós** are not the best ways to start and finish a formal letter. See the suggested answers for better versions. The candidate has used **quiero** three times. He/she would attract more marks if he/she used **quisiera** and **me gustaría** on the second and third occasion.

You are asked to say how you will be travelling; you have asked if there is a car-park. This is relying a lot on the examiner's good will. You could be travelling by train and thinking of hiring a car once you have arrived. It is much better to spell out what you are asked to communicate. See the suggested answer.

Apart from that the level of Spanish is excellent and should score full points.

12.6 Examination practice questions

Here are some more past questions for you to practise on. Suggested answers are given at the end.

Writing Test 4

You have just moved school. You have been asked to write an article for a Spanish school magazine about your old school. Include the following points:
- a description of your old school (ie buildings, location, facilities);
- a memorable event at your last school;
- a description of a teacher whom you will never forget;
- a reason why you moved school;
- your feelings about your present school.   (20)

MEG 1994

Writing Test 5

While in Spain on an exchange, you enter a competition and win first prize! The prize is a night out with Anita Suarez, a famous Spanish tennis star.

You have a pleasant evening with Anita and the following day, your Spanish exchange partner asks you to write an account of your evening *in Spanish* for his/her school magazine.

Write an account of your evening mentioning the *five* points below.

What you had to do to win the prize.

How you prepared for your evening out.

Where you went with Anita and what you did.

Describe Anita.

Your plans to see Anita play.

(20)

MEG 1993

Writing Test 6

You decide to spend the summer holidays working in Spain. You apply for the job advertised below.

> ### Spain
> HOTEL SOL: Ctra Nacional 232, 26200 Haro (la Rioja), Spain.
>
> HOTEL WORKERS (3): Duties, wages and period of work by arrangement. 6 days work a week. Knowledge of Spanish necessary. Knowledge of some French and English an advantage. Applications in Spanish to the hotel manager, Sr. Blanco, at the above address.

Write a letter in Spanish to the hotel manager.

Say:
- why you want to work in Spain;
- what sort of work you would be able to do in the hotel;
- what jobs or work experience you have had here in Britain;
- how well you speak Spanish and French;
- what else makes you think you would be good at the job.

Ask:
- if you can work for six weeks in July and August;
- how much you will earn;
- if you will have to pay for meals and acommodation.

Write neatly and put down *all* the information you are asked to give. The number of words is not important.

NEAB 1994

Writing Test 7

While on holiday in Galicia you bought a magazine about Spain called 'España Hoy'. In it you notice the competition overleaf.

You decide to enter the competition. You have to write an account in Spanish saying why you enjoyed reading the magazine and why you would like to win the trip around the world for three people.

Say:
- what you thought was interesting about this magazine;
- why you enjoy travelling;
- which *two* people you would take with you on the trip and why;
- which *two* places you would most like to visit and why;
- when you would most like to take the trip;
- why you think it should be *you* who wins the competition.

Write neatly and put down all the information you are asked to give. The number of words is not important.

EXCEPCIONAL CONCURSO Cuyo PREMIO será un:

VIAJE DE 23 DIAS ALREDEDOR DEL MUNDO *para tres personas*

- España • Bankok (Thailandia) • Hong Kong (SE China)
- Taipei (Formosa) • Tokyo (Japón) • Honolulú (Hawai)
- Los Angeles (California) • New York • España

En vuelo regular y hoteles de 1ª Superior.

Plan del viaje:

Día 1º:	España–Bangkok		Día 10º:	Taipei–Tokyo	A	Día 20º:	Los Angeles–New York	A
Día 2º:	Bangkok	AD	Día 11º:	Tokyo	A	Día 21º:	New York	A
Día 3º:	Bangkok	AD	Día 12º:	Tokyo	A	Día 22º:	New York–España	
Día 4º:	Bangkok–Hong Kong	AD	Día 13º:	Tokyo	A	Día 23º:	España	
			Día 14º:	Tokyo–Honolulú	A	(A: Alojamiento. D: Desayuno)		
Día 5º:	Hong Kong	AD	Día 15º:	Honolulú	A			
Día 6º:	Hong Kong	AD	Día 16º:	Honolulú	A	● Avión, vuelo regular, clase turista		
Día 7º:	Hong Kong–Taipei	AD	Día 17º:	Honolulú–Los Angeles	A	● Traslados.		
Día 8º:	Taipei	AD	Día 18º:	Los Angeles	A	● Hoteles 1ª Superior		
Día 9º:	Taipei	AD	Día 19º:	Los Angeles	A			

NEAB 1993

Writing Test 8

Your Spanish friend María is thinking of visiting the United States of America to attend an English language course in New York. She has written to ask for your advice.

Write a letter to María *in Spanish* and try to persuade her to come and visit you in Britain instead.

Tell her:
- what you think of her plans to spend the holidays studying;
- that there are similar courses in this country;
- that she could come and stay with you and your family;
- what sorts of things you can do if she visits you;
- why else you think she should come here instead of the United States.

Ask her:
- what her parents think about her going to the United States;
- how she feels about your ideas.

Write neatly and put down *all* the information you are asked to give. The number of words is not important.

NEAB 1992

Writing Test 9

You have just come back from a visit to Ibiza, where you stayed in the hotel Buenavista. On your return you discover certain problems. Write a letter to the management of the hotel explaining the problems and asking for their help.

In your letter you should mention the following items:

(a) Say that you have just spent a week in their hotel, giving the room number.
(b) Explain when you arrived and left.
(c) Explain that you left something behind in your room and say what it was.
(d) Give *two* details about it.
(e) Ask if someone can look for it.

(f) Tell them what you want them to do with it.
(g) Say that you have just discovered that an item of your clothing has been damaged.
(h) Say you never wore it, so it must have happened in your bedroom.
(i) Ask them to talk to the girl who cleaned your room.
(j) Explain what you expect them to do about this.

REMEMBER TO DATE, START AND END YOUR LETTER CORRECTLY. Write about 100 words and STATE AT THE END OF YOUR LETTER THE NUMBER YOU HAVE USED.

(60)

SEG 1994

Writing Test 10

Imagine you are 1 of the 2 young people in the pictures below. Write 100–120 words *in Spanish* to describe the incident.

(80)

WJEC 1993

Writing Test 11

You have been taking part in a school exchange trip to Southern Spain. When you travel to Málaga airport to catch the plane to Belfast, you find that it has been delayed. Write a letter, in Spanish, to your Spanish penfriend telling him about the journey home. Your letter should follow the outline given below:

(i) Describe the journey from your penfriend's house to Málaga airport.

(ii) Say how you heard about the delay, why it occurred and how long it lasted.

(iii) Say what you did at the airport during this time and describe your eventual departure.

(iv) Describe your arrival in Belfast, how you felt and your journey home.

NICCEA 1994

Writing Test 12

Your parents are planning a house/flat-swapping holiday in Spain, and ask you to prepare a description of where you live to send to the agency. Write a detailed description in Spanish covering the following elements suggested by the agency.

- descripción de la casa/del piso; tamaño; edad; número de habitaciones; otras cosas de interés
- muebles; número de camas; electrodomésticos etcétera
- ¿jardín? localidad; tiendas etcétera
- sitios de interés; diversiones; excursiones posibles; transportes   (40)

ULEAC 1994

Writing Test 13

You are going to visit a youth hostel in Spain. You write a letter to the youth hostel mentioning the following points:

- say you have visited Spain several times and say you have only stayed in hotels and camp sites;
- give the dates of your arrival and departure and the reason for your visit;
- ask for information about the youth hostel and local places of interest;
- ask for directions to help you find the youth hostel and ask if it is in the city centre;
- say you will arrive by car and ask where you should park.   (20)

MEG 1994

12.7 Suggested answers

Writing Test 1

Uttoxeter

9 de junio

Querido Pablo:

¿Cómo estás? Volví a Inglaterra sin incidente pero aquí hace muy mal tiempo.

Estoy escribiendo para decirte gracias por todo lo que hiciste por mí. El primer desastre ocurrió cuando perdí mi dinero en la playa. Afortunadamente me prestaste dinero. Luego estuve enfermo y no podía hacer nada. Llamaste al médico. Luego hubo un retraso con el vuelo de regreso y me dejaste quedar una noche más.

Te digo gracias sinceramente por todo. Espero que os guste el regalo que mando para deciros gracias.

Espero que pases bien el resto de tus vacaciones.

Un abrazo

A. Whittle

Writing Test 2

Voy a describir lo que ocurrió esta mañana. Soy turista británica y mi hotel se llama el Hotel Sol. Mi madre me mandó al supermercado a comprar loción bronceadora. Para ir al supermercado tuve que cruzar la calle. Encontré un paso de peatones y crucé. Un Ford Escort negro no paró. Frenó fuertemente pero el coche me volcó.

El conductor era joven, llevaba gafas de sol, tenía unos veinticinco años y tenía pelo largo y negro.

Al caerme, perdí dos dientes y me corté la cara. Afortunadamente no tenía huesos rotos. Una ambulancia me llevó al hospital pero salí dentro de dos horas.

El médico ha dicho que tendré que guardar cama durante dos días.

Writing Test 3

Carlisle

20 de mayo

Muy señor mío:

Quiero reservar una habitación del treinta de mayo hasta el cinco de junio. Seremos dos, mi hermana y yo. Quiero una habitación con dos camas individuales y un cuarto de baño. ¿Puede decirme cuánto cuesta?

También quiero una habitación con vista al mar y en el primer piso.

¿A qué distancia está el Parador del centro de Toledo? Vamos a llegar allí en coche. ¿Hay un parking?

Queremos visitar Madrid. ¿Vale la pena? ¿Tiene Vd. información sobre Madrid?

Le saluda atentamente

P. Reid

Writing Test 4

Mi primer colegio era bastante viejo. Había laboratorios, un laboratorio de lenguas pero desafortunadamente no había una piscina. El colegio se encontraba en el campo y había vistas maravillosas.

Un día ¡hubo un incendio! El incendio tuvo lugar en el laboratorio de química y tuvimos que salir al campo de deportes. Había mucho humo. Los profesores pasaron lista y cinco minutos más tarde los bomberos llegaron y apagaron el fuego sin perder un momento.

No olvidaré nunca a mi profesor de español. Era muy simpático e hizo mucho para nosotros. Organizó un intercambio con España y fuimos todos a Granada. ¡Lo pasé bomba! Nuestro profesor de español nos acompañó y nos compró helados todos los días.

Desgraciadamente tuve que cambiar de colegio. Mi padre cambió de trabajo y tuvimos que mudar de casa.

Me encanta este colegio y tengo muchos amigos aquí. Las facilidades son muy buenos pero echo de menos a mis amigos de allí ... y a mi profesor de español.

Writing Test 5

Cuando estuve en España, gané un concurso de tenis y el premio era una tarde con Anita Suárez. ¡No podía creerlo! Para prepararme para la tarde con Anita, fui a las tiendas y compré mucha ropa nueva. Fui a la peluquería y también le compré flores. Nos encontramos en El Tulipán, restaurante muy famoso en Madrid. No tuve que pagar nada. Anita era muy simpática y estaba con su novio. Los dos no hablan inglés así que tuve que hablar en español toda la tarde. La cena era riquísima. Comí sopa de verduras, filete de pescado con patatas y huevo y después comí un helado enorme.

Anita llevaba una falda gris de seda y una blusa blanca. Era muy guapa. Llevaba gafas de sol todo el tiempo. Hablaba de sus planes para el futuro: va a casarse y quizás irá a los Estados Unidos a jugar allí.

Después de cenar, Anita me dio dos entradas para un gran concurso de tenis así que podré ver a Anita en Londres el mes que viene. ¡Qué suerte!

Writing Test 6

Blackpool

23 de marzo

Estimado Señor:

He visto su anuncio en el periódico y me gustaría trabajar en su hotel. Quiero trabajar en España porque aprendo español y quiero conocer las costumbres de España. Podría trabajar en el bar lavando los vasos porque he hecho este trabajo ya en Inglaterra durante un período de experiencia de trabajo. También he trabajado en una tienda vendiendo ropa. Llevo cuatro años aprendiendo español y francés y hablo las dos lenguas casi perfectamente. También me gusta encontrar a nueva gente y me gustó muchísimo mi trabajo en un hotel.

¿Puedo trabajar seis semanas durante julio y agosto? ¿Cuánto ganaré? ¿Tendré que pagar mis comidas y mi alojamiento?

Le saluda atentamente

Alex Young

Writing Test 7

Acabo de comprar la revista y estoy seguro que es la mejor revista que haya leído. Me interesan los artículos sobre la moda y el deporte. También los artículos sobre los problemas de los jóvenes en España son interesantes.

Me gusta viajar porque quiero conocer los otros países del mundo y quiero hacer amigos en todas partes. Viajaría con mi hermano y mi hermana porque aparte de ser miembros de mi familia son mis mejores amigos.

Los dos sitios que me interesan más son Nueva York porque he visto la ciudad tantas veces en la televisión y Honolulú porque me han dicho que el clima allí es perfecto. Me gustaría hacer el viaje durante las vacaciones de verano porque quiero volver antes de que empiecen mis clases en setiembre.

Yo creo que es mejor que me den el premio porque nunca he ido al extranjero. Mis padres son muy pobres y si no gano quizás nunca podré ir al extranjero.

Writing Test 8

Londres

12 de marzo

Querida María:

Gracias por la carta que me mandaste. Estoy muy decepcionada. ¿Por qué no vienes aquí para aprender inglés? Yo creo que tus planes son una pérdida de dinero. Hay cursos similares en Inglaterra y probablemente son mejores. ¿Por qué no vienes a quedarte conmigo y con mi familia? Es la mejor manera de aprender inglés. Si vienes, podemos ir a conciertos y visitar los sitios interesantes de Londres. Hay otra razón: Peter, el chico a quien encontraste el año pasado quiere verte.

¿Qué dicen tus padres sobre tu visita a los Estados Unidos? Quiero saber también ¿qué piensas de mis sugerencias?

Un abrazo

Margaret

Writing Test 9

Londres

18 de junio

Estimado Señor:

Acabo de pasar una semana en su hotel en la habitación número trece. Llegué el dos de junio y me marché el nueve de junio. Dejé algo de valor en mi habitación. Era un reloj de oro que me regaló mi padre. ¿Puede Vd. buscarlo? Si lo encuentra, haga el favor de mandarlo a mi dirección.

Acabo de descubrir que mi traje nuevo ha sido estropeado. No me lo puse nunca durante mi estancia así que los daños ocurrieron en mi habitación. Haga el favor de hablar con la chica que limpiaba mi habitación. Quiero que Vd. haga algo para solucionar este problema.

Le saluda atentamente

D. Ferguson

Writing Test 10

Mi novio y yo estábamos pasando las vacaciones a orillas del mar y un día decidimos comer un helado ya que hacía buen tiempo. Nos sentamos en un muro al lado del puerto. Detrás de nosotros un pescador pescaba con una caña de pescar. Al terminar los helados decidimos volver al hotel y nos marchamos en bicicleta. Desafortunadamente habíamos dejado un bolso en el muro y había un aparato fotográfico dentro. No notamos lo que habíamos hecho hasta el momento cuando llegamos a nuestro hotel. Afortunadamente el pescador había visto lo que había pasado y vino a nuestro hotel con la bolsa.

Writing Test 11

Belfast

12 de mayo

Querida Marta:

¿Cómo estás? Espero que todo vaya bien. El viaje de regreso era muy interesante. Al salir de tu casa, tomé un taxi. Cuando estuve a cinco kilómetros del aeropuerto el taxi tuvo un pinchazo pero afortunadamente el taxista lo reparó en cinco minutos.

Después de llegar al aeropuerto fui a la oficina de Iberia y me dijeron que había un retraso de cinco horas porque había niebla en el aeropuerto de Londres. ¡Cinco horas! ¡Qué barbaridad!

Afortunadamente tenía una novela conmigo y me senté en un banco. Escuché música en mi estéreo personal y comí mis bocadillos. Un español vino a hablar conmigo y luego me invitó a tomar algo con él. Fui al café con él y bebí una limonada. Hablamos en español todo el tiempo y aprendí mucho. Finalmente Iberia dijo que el vuelo iba a salir y dije adiós tristemente a mi amigo nuevo y fui a bordo. El vuelo fue sin incidente y la comida durante el vuelo era excelente. Al llegar a Belfast, estaba lloviendo a cántaros como siempre. Me sentía bastante cansada y tenía hambre. Mis padres estaban allí y no fui directament a casa. Fuimos a comer una hamburguesa antes de volver a casa.

Un abrazo

Catherine

Writing Test 12

Descripción de mi casa

Nuestra casa es bastante grande y tiene dos pisos y un total de ocho habitaciones. En la planta baja hay una cocina, un comedor y una sala de estar. En el primer piso hay cuatro dormitorios y un cuarto de baño.

Los muebles en la casa son todos nuevos. En los dormitorios hay una cama individual en cada dormitorio salvo en un dormitorio donde hay una cama doble. En la cocina hay una nevera, un lavaplatos y una máquina de lavar.

Hay un pequeño jardín y hay muchas tiendas en la localidad. Hay también un cine y un teatro muy cerca. Se puede tomar un autobús de enfrente de la casa al centro de la ciudad.

Writing Test 13

Preston

5 de mayo

Muy señor mío:

Le escribo porque quiero pasar unos días en su albergue durante el verano. He visitado España muchas veces pero me hospedé en hoteles y campings solamente.

Llego el dos de junio y me marcho el nueve de junio. Quiero pasar tiempo en España porque aprendo español y tengo amigos en la ciudad.

¿Puede Vd. mandarme detalles sobre el albergue y los sitios de interés en la región?

¿Puede decirme cómo puedo encontrar el albergue? Está en el centro de la ciudad?

Llegaré en coche. ¿Dónde puedo aparcar?

Le saluda atentamente

J. Harris

Chapter 13
Complete GCSE paper

13.1 Introduction

In this chapter, you have the complete GCSE paper of *WJEC (1994)*. Probably the best time to attempt it is about a week before your Spanish exams start. The recording for the listening tests are on the cassette accompanying this book. Also the transcript of the recordings and suggested answers for all parts of the paper are given.

- Try to do the papers under examination conditions.
- Try to adhere to the times allowed for each paper.
- Ask your teacher to mark your written work.

13.2 The examination paper

Listening: Basic Level

Recording 37

1 Here are some announcements which you might hear in Spain.
   (a)   Why is the airport closed? (1)
   (b)   When will the camp supermarket be closed? (1)
   (c)   When will the train from Sevilla arrive? (1)
   (d)   Why might fans of JUVER, the Murcia basketball team, be disappointed? (1)
   (e)   Why must you remember 7 o'clock? (1)

Recording 38

2 On a touring holiday in Spain, you have been given the number of a small hotel in Rosas. You 'phone for information.
   (a)   Firstly, you enquire whether they have any vacancies. What sort of rooms are available? (2)
   (b)   You then ask the price per day of a double room. What is the cost? (1)
   (c)   You ask whether there are washing facilities in the rooms. What is the reply? (2)
   (d)   The receptionist then asks you a question. What does he ask you? (1)
   (e)   You then ask him to reserve two double rooms. What *two* things should you tell him? (2)

Recording 39

3 Listen to these Spanish teenagers talking about their free time and make notes under the following headings.
   (i)   Amount of free time.

(ii) How long he/she spends watching T.V.
(iii) How often he/she goes to the cinema.
(iv) When he/she plays sport.
   (a) Rafael   (4)
   (b) Marisa   (4)

Recording 40

4 You are alone at your pen-friend Francisco's house in Spain as his parents are at work and he has gone to the dentist. There is a 'phone call which you answer. You jot down some details so that you can pass on the message when your pen-friend returns.
   (a) Who has called?   (1)
   (b) Why can he not come as expected?   (2)
   (c) When will he come?   (1)

Recording 41

5 On the radio in Spain you hear a brief weather forecast for the following day.
   (a) What is the forecast for the morning?   (2)
   (b) How will the weather change later in the day?   (2)

Recording 42

6 While staying in an hotel in Spain you need to buy aspirin for your mother who has a severe headache. This is in five sections.

Section 1
   (a) You ask at reception where the chemist's is. Where is the nearest chemist's? (1)

Section 2
   (b) You then ask how to get there. What must you do when you get to the traffic lights? (1)
   (c) How far away is it?   (1)

Section 3
   (d) The receptionist then gives you some advice. When must you be careful?   (1)
   (e) What is the reason for the problem today?   (1)

Section 4
   (f) What suggestion does the receptionist then make?   (1)

Section 5
   (g) What does he finally remind you about?   (2)
   (h) When does it start?   (1)

Transcript: Basic Level

Recording 37: transcript

1 (a) El aeropuerto de Barajas está cerrado a causa de la niebla.
   (b) Señoras y señores El Camping 'Las Olas' les recuerda que el supermercado no se abrirá mañana por la mañana porque es fiesta.
   (c) El tren expreso procedente de Sevilla llegará al andén número cuatro en quince minutos.
   (d) BALONCESTO. EL JUVER de Murcia perdió anoche el primer puesto en la segunda división de la liga, al perder contra el Real Madrid.
   (e) Señores pasajeros hemos llegado a la isla de Benidorm. Por favor no olviden vds. que el último barco para volver a Benidorm sale a las siete.

Recording 38: transcript

2 (a) Sí, claro, nos quedan varias habitaciones dobles e individuales.
   (b) ... una habitación doble cuesta 2500 pts.
   (c) Todas las habitaciones dobles tienen baño y ducha.
   (d) ¿Cuánto tiempo vas a estar en Rosas?
   (e) Con mucho gusto – una cosa – ¿quiere vd. decirme la fecha y la hora de su llegada?

Recording 39: transcript

3 Rafael

Tiempo libre … pues tengo poco, muy poco porque en junio tengo exámenes importantes así que tengo mucho trabajo. Durante las vacaciones me gusta mucho ver la tele y cuando tengo tiempo paso la mayor parte de la tarde viendo televisión. Nunca voy al cine porque nunca dan películas que me interesan. Mi pasatiempo preferido es jugar al baloncesto. Juego al baloncesto todos los fines de semana.

Marisa

Tengo deberes todas las noches así que no tengo tiempo libre durante la semana – pero no estudio los sábados y domingos – los dejo libres para divertirme. No me gustan mucho los programas de T.V. así que sólo la veo durante 2 o 3 horas por semana. Voy al cine todos los sábados con mi novio. Algunas veces vamos a una discoteca. No me interesa el deporte excepto nadar y voy a la playa cada día durante las vacaciones de verano.

Recording 40: transcript

4 Hola, soy el tío de Francisco, el tío Juan de Málaga. No puedo venir mañana porque tengo que visitar a mi madre. Está en el hospital.

¿Quieres decirle a Francisco que vendré pasado mañana – es decir – no vendré mañana sino el sábado?

Bueno gracias y espero que lo estés pasando bien aquí en España – adiós.

Recording 41: transcript

5 Mañana hará sol por la mañana con temperaturas altas hasta 40 grados pero por la tarde habrá vientos fuertes y existe la posibilidad de tormentas en la costa.

Recording 42: transcript

6 Section 1

Pues hay varias aquí en San Sebastian, la más cercana está enfrente del museo.

Section 2

Sigue todo recto hasta el semáforo después toma la segunda calle a la derecha. Está a unos 20 minutos a pie.

Section 3

Oye – cuidado al cruzar la calle – es mejor usar los pasos de peatones. Habrá mucho tráfico hoy a causa del partido de fútbol entre Real Sociedad y Bilbao.

Section 4

A propósito, si te interesa el fútbol podrás ver el partido en directo en la tele aquí en el salón del hotel.

Section 5

Y no te olvides que es viernes y hay una discoteca esta noche en Bugatti – empieza a las nueve.

Listening: Higher Level

Recording 43

1 On holiday in Spain you feel unwell and visit a doctor. Listen to what he says as he examines you.

    (a)   What possible cause of your illness does he suggest?   (1)

    (b)   What does he say which will spoil your holiday?   (2)

    (c)   He prescribes pills, when must you take them?   (1)

    (d)   When does he want to see you again?   (1)

Recording 44

2 While staying in Calpe on the Costa Blanca you hear an item about the tourist resort of Benidorm and its plans for young people under the title of *'Benijoven'*.

    (a)   What is *'Benijoven'*?   (2)

(b) What does the campaign consist of? (2)
(c) Why has the association felt the need to introduce this plan? (2)

Recording 45

3 On Spanish radio you hear some teenagers who talk about their lives, ambitions, fears and beliefs. This is in three sections.

Section 1
(a) What is Pasajes? (1)
(b) What career does Marisol want to follow? (1)
(c) What is her attitude towards her future? Tick the correct box. (1)

    (i) confident ☐   **(ii)** pessimistic ☐

    (iii) unconcerned ☐   **(iv)** optimistic ☐

Section 2
(d) How old is José? (1)
(e) Why does he want to go to Africa? (2)
(f) Which of these words best describes his attitude to life? Tick the correct box. (1)

    (i) ambitious ☐   **(ii)** caring ☐

    (iii) greedy ☐   **(iv)** bored ☐

Section 3
(g) Briefly state Mari-Carmen's likes and dislikes. (2)
(h) Why does she not want to stay in Pamplona? (1)
(i) How would you describe her attitude to life? Tick the correct box. (1)

    (i) responsible ☐   **(ii)** fun-loving ☐

    (iii) studious ☐   **(iv)** dedicated ☐

Recording 46

4 While on holiday in Spain you hear a report of a robbery in Altea.
(a) When did the robbery take place? (2)
(b) Why must the robbers be considered dangerous? (1)
(c) How did they escape? (1)
(d) Give *three* reasons why the police can be optimistic about identifying them (3)

Recording 47

5 On Spanish T.V. you hear a review of a film to be shown later that day.
(a) Briefly state the theme of the film. (3)
(b) Why would it be worth watching? (2)

Recording 48

6 On Spanish radio you hear an item about camping in Spain.
(a) How many campsites are there in Spain? (1)
(b) What is the best time to go camping? (1)
(c) What information does the tourist guide offer? (3)
(d) What are the *two* advantages of this type of holiday? (2)

Transcript: Higher Level

Recording 43: transcript

1 Bueno … me dices que tienes dolor de cabeza y de estómago. Es posible que hayas comido fruta sin lavar … ¿Sí? … Es muy importante lavar la fruta antes de comer sobre todo los melocotónes … a ver … sí, tienes fiebre … tendrás que guardar cama hasta que no tengas fiebre … Te voy a dar una receta de unas pastillas. Hay que tomar 2 pastillas 3 veces al día después de comer … Ven a verme otra vez el lunes que viene … adiós.

Recording 44: transcript

2 La Asociación de Bares y Discotecas de Benidorm va a introducir un plan de turismo bajo el nombre BENIJOVEN para promocionar las noches de la ciudad entre la juventud de varias ciudades como Alicante, Valencia, Murcia, etc. La campaña BENIJOVEN consiste en ofrecer a los jóvenes unos paquetes de fin de semana que incluyan además de gastos de viaje y alojamiento a precios más bajos, la posibilidad de visitar gratis determinados pubs y discotecas. La intención de la asociación es atraer a la gente joven a los bares y discotecas de sus miembros, sobre todo durante el invierno cuando no hay tanto turismo y cuando algunos establecimientos tienen problemas económicos y otros se cierran.

Recording 45: transcript

3 **Section 1**
Bueno … me llamo Marisol … tengo 18 años y soy estudiante. Vivo en Pasajes, un barrio industrial de San Sebastián. Espero ser enfermera pero lo que más me preocupa es el paro. Mis 2 hermanas no han podido encontrar trabajo y tengo miedo de que aún si apruebo mis exámenes tampoco podré encontrarlo.

Section 2
Me llamo José López Sánchez. Cumpliré 17 años el mes que viene. Soy de Salamanca. Soy estudiante también. El año que viene quiero estudiar C.O.U., es decir, Curso de Orientación Universitaria, y quiero estudiar Medicina. Pero en el futuro lo más importante para mí es trabajar de médico en Africa porque mucha gente allí sufre enfermedades porque son muy pobres. Creo que los países ricos tienen la responsabilidad de ayudar a los países más pobres del tercer mundo.

Section 3
Hola. Soy Mari-Carmen. Soy de Pamplona, tengo 15 años. Vivo con mi hermana y mis padres. Me gusta mucho la música 'pop' y bailar. Colecciono discos y cassettes. No me gusta mi colegio, me dan demasiados deberes. Cuando sea mayor quiero salir de Pamplona. Quisiera vivir en Barcelona o en el extranjero. Creo que aquí in España la gente joven no tiene bastante libertad. A los adultos sólo les interesa el trabajo y siempre me están diciendo que hay que estudiar para aprobar los exámenes.

Recording 46: transcript

4 Dos ladrones armados robaron en una relojería en Altea en la madrugada del domingo pasado y se llevaron artículos valorados en un millón de pesetas. Según el propietario, que vive sobre su tienda, entraron tras haber forzardo la puerta principal. Los dos tenían fusiles.

En la policía ha encontrado un coche, robado el sábado, en el que se escaparon los 2 ladrones, en la autopista cerca de Calpe. Habían dejado los fusiles en el coche.

El propietario de la relojería ha podido dar un buena descripción de los ladrones que no llevaban ni máscaras ni guantes. Tienen sobre 40 años, uno es muy alto con el pelo corto y el otro tiene pelo largo y barba. Hablaban con acento madrileño.

Recording 47: transcript

5 Esta noche. La Patrulla Perdida. A las 9.05h en la dos.

Veinte soldados británicos se pierden en las montañas de Africa después de la muerte de su jefe. Es una región muy peligrosa y van cayendo uno tras otro sin poder hacer nada para evitarlo hasta que por fin su sargento les conduce a un río.

La parte final es una de las más emocionantes en la historia del cine y ha habido muchas imitaciones. Además la música de Max Steiner aumenta la tensión de cada instante.

Recording 48: transcript

6 En España contamos con más de 900 campings. Aunque muchos permanecen abiertos durante todo el año, la mejor época para alojarse en ellos es durante los soleados meses de verano.

La Secretaría general de Turismo publica cada año una guía donde se registran los campings de nuestro país con sus respectivas localizaciones, tarifas, características y servicios.

Recuerden vds. que hacer camping les permite mantener un contacto más directo con la vida del campo y aprovecharse del aire puro.

Speaking: Basic Level

Set 1 Role-play 1

Setting: On holiday in Spain you wish to go to the CORTE INGLES to buy presents for your family. You ask a Spanish boy/girl how to get to the CORTE INGLES. Your teacher will play the part of the boy/girl and you begin.

1 Say excuse me and ask how to get to the CORTE INGLES.
2 Ask how far it is.
3 Ask whether there is a bus.
4 Find out when the buses leave.
5 Thank him/her and ask where the bus stops.

Set 1 Role-play 2

Setting: You are talking to a Spanish boy/girl and he/she asks you about your school. Your teacher will play the part of the boy/girl and begin.

1 Say your lessons start at 9.00 a.m.
2 Tell him/her you have five lessons each day.
3 Say you have six weeks holiday in the summer.
4 Say you bring sandwiches.
5 Say yes, but that you have a lot of homework.

Set 2 Role-play 1

Setting: On holiday in Málaga you go to the market to buy fruit. Your teacher will play the part of the fruiterer and begin.

1 Ask for a kilo of peaches.
2 Find out whether he/she has any bananas.
3 Ask how much they cost.
4 Ask for a carrier bag.
5 Find out how much it comes to altogether.

Set 2 Role-play 2

Setting: You want to go to Barcelona by train and so in a Travel Agency you ask for information about the price of return tickets and the times of the trains. Your teacher plays the part of the clerk and begins.

1 Say you want to go to Barcelona for a few days.
2 Find out the cost of a return ticket.
3 Ask the times of trains in the morning.
4 Find out how long the journey takes.
5 Ask for two tickets, one for yourself and one for your friend.

Speaking: Higher Level

Set 1 Role-play 1

Setting: On the beach in Spain you are talking to a Spanish boy/girl of your age. Your teacher will play the part of the boy/girl and begin.

1 Say you speak Spanish a little and, of course, English.
2 Use words to express surprise and say that you believe that Spanish and Italian are very similar.
3 Say you find Spanish easy to write, but hard to speak.
4 Answer the question. (The examiner asks '¿Por qué estudias español?')
5 Ask how long he/she has been learning English.
6 Ask which he/she prefers, English or Italian and why.

Set 1 Role-play 2

Setting: While staying with your Spanish pen-friend, you talk to his father/mother about the weather in Spain and Wales. Your teacher plays the part of the father/mother and you begin.

1 Say it's very hot today and ask if it's normally so hot.
2 Ask what the weather is like in winter.
3 Say possibly in the large cities in England, but that we don't have fog often in Wales.
4 Say sometimes; in the north it is colder than the south.
5 Say that eight years ago it snowed heavily in your town.
6 Answer the question and give a reason. (The examiner asks '¿Qué estación del año prefieres?')

Set 2 Role-play 1

Setting: On a camping holiday in Spain you have met a Spanish boy/girl who is staying in a nearby hotel. Your teacher plays the part of the boy/girl and you begin.

1 Ask why his/her family stay in an hotel.
2 Say that when you are on holiday your father does the cooking.
3 Say that you like to go to restaurants to try local dishes.
4 Say that last year you spent a fortnight in Rosas.
5 Say you are not sure, if it is too hot you will go to France.
6 Answer the question and give a reason. (The examiner asks '¿Qué país prefieres, España o Francia?')

Set 2 Role-play 2

Setting: On holiday in Spain with your parents, you return to your car and see that a window is broken. Your mother's purse has disappeared and so you go to the police station to report a theft. Your teacher will play the part of the policeman/policewoman and will begin.

1 Say good-day and that you have come to report a robbery.
2 Say that your mother's purse has been stolen.
3 Answer both questions. (The examiner says 'Pues quiere Vd. decirme dónde ocurrió el robo y a qué hora?')
4 Say it's small, black and made of leather.
5 Give your name and address in Spain.
6 Say you will be staying until next week.

Reading: Basic Level

1 You are likely to see the following signs in Spain. Look at them carefully and place a tick in the box next to the appropriate sign.

(a) You arrive at a railway station in Spain and want to buy a ticket. Which sign would you look for?

| SALA DE ESPERA | | SALIDA | |
| EXPEDICION DE BILLETES | | ANDENES | |

(1)

(b) You want to return to your apartment on the 10th floor. Which sign would you look for?

| RECEPCION | | COMEDOR | |
| SERVICIOS | | ASCENSOR | |

(1)

(c) In a HIPERMERCADO you want to buy some eggs. Which sign would you look for?

| DEPORTES | | ALIMENTACION | |
| PESCADO | | MODA JOVEN | |

(1)

2 You are on holiday in Spain travelling by car with your parents. Your father sees the following signs and notices and asks you about them.

(a) What would you see if you visited this exhibition? (1)

(b) Why must you stop in 20 metres? (1)

(c) How much would your father have to pay for a shirt? (1)

(d) **(i)** Would you have to pay if you parked here at 3 p.m. on Saturday? (1)

 (ii) When is there free parking all day? (1)

3

PANADERIA

PALMA

Toda clase de panes
Bocadillos para celebraciones
y banquetes

C/. Cuba, no. 8 - Telf.: 62 60 97
LAS TORRES DE COTILLAS

Carnicería Verónica

*Les desea
felices fiestas*

C/. Sol, 1 - Telf.: 62 72 78
LAS TORRES DE COTILLAS (MURCIA)

DROGUERIA
Y ARTICULOS DE FERRETERIA

ALEGRIA

C/. Cruz, 4 - Telf.: 62 68 46
LAS TORRES DE COTILLAS

FRUTERIA

LEO

*Especialidad en todo tipo
de frutas*

C/. Narciso Yepes, s/n. - Telf.: 62 62 89
LAS TORRES DE COTILLAS

Above are advertisements by 4 shops in the village of Las Torres de Cotillas.

(a) Which shop would you look for if you needed to buy fruit? (1)

(b) Which shop would you visit to buy bread? (1)

(c) Name the shop which wishes its customers 'happy holidays'. (1)

4 Here is an advertisement for young people seeking pen-friends.

Amigos

Busco amistad. Tengo 13 años y espero recibir muchas cartas de chicos y chicas hasta 15 años para intercambiar opiniones. Gemma Andrés. Calle Espinosa, 19. 13700 Tomelloso (Cuidad Real).

Tengo 9 años. Me gustaría cartearme con chicos/as hasta 16 años. María del Carmen Fernandes Ameneiras, Calle Penas de Giritin, 19–21. 15405 El Ferrol (La Coruña).

(a) Why is Gemma Andrés intersted in getting pen-friends? (1)

(b) With whom does María del Carmen want to exchange letters? (2)

5

¿QUÉ INCLUIMOS EN EL PRECIO?

- Estancia en el hotel Sol o Melía de su elección en habitación doble de viernes a domingo (inclusive).
- Espléndido buffet de desayuno.
- Y créaselo, NIÑOS GRATIS!! Hasta 12 años (maximo 2 niños en las habitación con 2 adultos).

✳

¡Qué! ¿Se va animando?

PARA QUE SE DECIDA

¡VEA EL PRECIO!

3.500 Pts.

Por persona y día en una habitación doble con desayuno buffet incluido.

NIÑOS GRATIS

(I. V. A. no incluido)

You have picked up the above brochure advertising hotels in Spain.

(a)   To which days does the 3,500 pesetas offer apply?   (1)
(b)   Under certain conditions children are free. What are these conditions?   (2)
(c)   3,500 pesetas is not the total cost. Why not?   (1)

6   Your uncle who already has a small flat in Spain is thinking of buying a larger one on the coast. He has seen the following advertisement and asks you to explain some of the information it contains.

URBANANIZACION

LA DORADA

LOS ALCAZARES

EN EL MAR MENOR

En los Alcázares con 7 Km. de playa y agradable ambiente nocturno y marinero.

VIVIENDAS UNIFAMILIARES DE 1, 2 Y 3 DORMITORIOS.

Zonas ajardinadas y deportivas, parque infantil, piscinas, supermercados, restaurantes ...

Le llevamos gratis a conocer LA DORADA este fin de semana.

Para más información llame a

VYCEGA sa (91) 542 70 82.

POSIBILIDAD DE TOMAR SU VIVIENDA COMO PARTE DEL PAGO

(a)   To what does the 7 kilometres refer?   (1)
(b)   Name *two* features which are advertised in addition to the flats (**viviendas**) themselves. (2)
(c)   What offer is made for this weekend?   (2)
(d)   What possibility is suggested at the foot of the advertisement?   (2)

7

MENU TURISTICO

Del 8 al 14 Abril

825pts

IVA Inc.

De 12,30 a 16,00h.

▼

Sopa de Tomate
Entremeses de Cheff
Huevos a la Flamenca
Macarrones con Tomate

•••

Conejo a la Cazadora
Merluza Romana
Raviolis de Cheff
Suprema de Pollo

•••

Manzana asada
Fruta del tiempo
Helado variado
Mus de chocolate

•••

Pan, Vino o refresco

You have seen this menu in the window of a restaurant in Spain. Suggest to your friend who does not understand Spanish

(a) *one* dish you could have as a starter, (1)
(b) *one* dish you could choose as main course, (1)
(c) *one* dish you could have as dessert, (1)
(d) *one* thing you could have to drink. (1)

8

DISTINTAS FORMAS DE VIAJAR EN BARCO

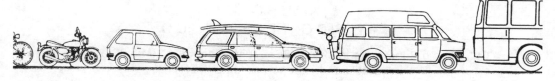

En barco se puede viajar en bicicleta, en moto, en coche más grande, en furgoneta, en camión o en autocar. En barco se puede viajar estupendamente con todo lo que uno quiera. Y mientras, dormir, comer, beber, jugar, charlar, pensar o soñar.

En el barco hay espacio para todo. Trasmediterránea cuenta con servicios regulares diarios de ida y vuelta para los trayectos Península-Baleares, Península-Ceuta y/o Península-Melilla. Así como servicios regulares interinsulares para Baleares y Canarias.

También existe un servicio regular de ida y vuelta para viajar de la Península a Canarias. Consulte en su agencia de viajes o en las delegaciones de Trasmediterránea.

TRASMEDITERRANEA
Viaje por el Espacio. Viaje en Barco.

(a) To what form of transport does the above advertisement refer? (1)
(b) Name *three* things in the advertisement which you are able to do while travelling (3)
(c) Say *one* thing about the service to the Canary Islands (1)
(d) How can you find out about this service? (1)

ALIMENTOS DEL DÍA, AL DÍA, A PRECIOS MUY FRESCOS.
A nuestro Supermercado llegan cada día la carne, el pescado, la fruta,
y la verdura. Así mantenemos toda su calidad, todo su sabor.

SUPERMERCADO

Hasta ahí vamos a llegar

Disfrute de la calidad de nuestro Supermercado sin tener que cargar con la compra. Nosotros se la llevaremos hasta la puerta de su casa. Ampliamos nuestra zona de reparto desde el 1 de julio al 31 de agosto.
Llegando a las siguientes poblaciones:

Rutade envío de martes, miércoles y jueves

Lo Pagan	*Los alcázares*
Santiago de la Ribera	*Los Urrutias*
Los Narejos	

Rutas de envío de martes, jueves y viernes

Los Nietos	*Cabo de Palos*
Mar de Cristal	*La Manga*
Playa Honda	

Ruta de envío de miércoles y viernes

S Pedro del Pinatar	*Cabo Roig*
El Mojón	*La Zenia*
Torre de la Horadada	*Punta Prima*
Dehesa de Campoamor	*Los Balcones*
La Regia	*Torrevieja*

Ruta de envío del Sábado

Mazarrón

MURCIA
PEDIDO TELEFÓNICO

Telf. directo Supermercado 29 04 65 – Telfs. Centralita 29 95 00 – 29 80 50
O utilizando nuestro sistema IBERTEX
Ruta de Acceso ∗ 215060450 #

NOTA: Para recibir sus compras en los días señalados
hágalas, como máximo, antes de las 3 de la tarde.
• *El reparto lo hacemos en modernos camiones frigoríficos*

9 **(a)** Why is the supermarket confident that its food will be fresh? (1)
  (b) What particular service does it offer? (2)
  (c) If you were living in La Manga, name *one* day when you could benefit from this service. (1)
  (d) What according to the note at the bottom, should you do to make sure you benefit from this service on the day that you want? (2)

Reading: Higher Level

1 Here is an article about Felipe de Borbon, son of the King of Spain, written shortly before the last Olympic games.

FELIPE DE BORBON

PREOLIMPICO

El príncipe Felipe, que acaba de cumplir 23 años, es un amante de los deportes náuticos y, siempre que puede, practica y se entrena en deportes de vela. Como recompensa a su esfuerzo, va a participar en los Juegos Olímpicos de Barcelona, en la clase solinq, en un equipo integrado también por Fernando León y Alfredo Vázquez. Su experiencia y cualidades físicas le van a permitir seguir a su padre, el rey don Juan Carlos, quien participó en 1972 en la Olimpiada de Munich, y a su hermana, la infanta Cristina, que asistió a los Juegos de Seúl.

(a) What type of sport interests Felipe?	(1)
(b) What is his reward for dedication to this sport?	(1)
(c) Why can it be said that he comes from a sporting family?	(2)

2 Here is an article about the Spanish golfer Jose Maria Olazabal ('Chema').

JOSE MARIA OLAZABAL

TERCERO DEL MUNDO

Para muchos es el rival y la amenaza de Severiano Ballesteros, cuando lo cierto es que son amigos tanto fuera como dentro del campo. Este año, Chema se ha situado en el tercer puesto en el podio de las grandes figuras, y ni siquiera una mujer — palabras del campeón — podría quitarle esta idea de la cabeza: ser el número uno, el mejor del mundo. Para esta temporada, de momento tiene puestas las ilusiones en Inglaterra: ha dicho que quiere ganar el Open británico.

(a) Read the four statements about the relationship between José María Olazabal and Severiano Ballesteros and place a tick in the box beside the statement which is most accurate according to the article.

(i) They are rivals on the golf course. ☐

(ii) They are rivals except on the golf course. ☐

(iii) They are friends on and off the golf course. ☐

(iv) They are friends only off the golf course. ☐

(1)

(b) What is his overall ambition? (1)

(c) What is his ambition for *this* season? (1)

3

Veinte mil duros para un día en la Sevilla de la Expo

Sevilla. M. J. F.

El coste de la estancia durante un día en la Sevilla de la Exposición Universal para una familia media forastera formada por un matrimonio con dos hijos y que decida alojarse en un hotel de tres estrellas se aproximará a las cien mil pesetas, según los cálculos que ya se realizan en el sector turístico sevillano. El presupuesto de esta familia prototípica para ese día de visita en la Sevilla del 92 sería el siguiente:

– Alojamiento en un hotel de tres estrellas a razón de dos habitaciones dobles por un precio unitario de 20.000 pesetas. Total, 40.000 pesetas una noche.

– Desayuno en el hotel para toda la familia: 3.800.

– Cuatro entradas de un día para visitar la Expo, a razón de cuatro mil pesetas por cabeza. Total, 16.000 pesetas.

– Desplazamiento a la Expo en taxi o tarifa del aparcamiento en caso de ir con vehículo propio: 1.000 pesetas.

– Almuerzo en el recinto de la Exposición Universal a razón de 3.500 pesetas el cubierto. 14.000 pesetas.

– Cena en la misma isla de la Cartuja al mismo precio por cubierto: 14.000 pesetas.

– Telecabina, torre panorámica y «souvenir» baratito: Mínimo, 10.000 pesetas.

No se contabilizan gastos diversos y más que probables, como consumiciones en los bares y kioscos y otros.

100,000 PESETAS

According to the article this was the cost for a typical family of 2 adults and 2 children to stay for 1 day at the World Fair in Sevilla. For what would they pay the following amounts?

(a)   40,000   (2)
(b)   3,800   (1)
(c)   16,000   (1)
(d)   1,000   (1)
(e)   14,000 (*Two* answers are required.)   (2)

4   Here you see a review of a film to be shown on television.

VIVA RECOMIENDA

Rita Hayworth y Tyrone Power, un gran amor con final trágico.

LA2   SANGRE Y ARENA*   22.10**

1941. Drama. Color.
Con Tyrone Power y Rita Hayworth.
Dir.: R. Mamoulian.

Después de muchos años de lucha, un hombre ha conseguido triunfar como torero. Su vida es ahora feliz, al lado de una adorable mujer. Todo esto puede venirse abajo con la intromisión de una mujer de vida tempestuosa y habituada a lograr, a cualquier precio, todo cuanto se propone. Ésta es la segunda versión de la novela del español Blasco Ibáñez. (120 min.)

(a)   In what field has the hero triumphed?   (1)
(b)   What else has contributed to his happiness in life?   (1)
(c)   Why might this film appeal particularly to Spanish audiences?   (1)

5 Look at this article about Blue Flag Beaches.

PLAYAS BANDERA AZUL

PAVILLON BLEU D'EUROPE   BANDEIRA AZUL DA EUROPA   BLAUE EUROPA-FLAGGE   EUROPEAN BLUE FLAG   BANDERA AZUL DE EUROPA   BLAA EUROPAVIMPEL   BANDIERA BLU DELL EUROPA   ΜΠΛΕ ΣΗΜΑΙΑ ΤΗΣ ΕΥΡΩΠΗΣ   BLAUWE VLAG VAN EUROPA

¿Qué espera de usted una Playa Bandera Azul?

«Muchos millones de ciudadanos europeos viajan cada año para pasar sus vacaciones en las playas de otros países. No han esperado a 1992 para percibir toda Europa como su país. La Campaña Bandera Azul, con su objetivo de conseguir playas limpias y seguras en todas partes y para todo el mundo, es un signo real de solidaridad y una contribución práctica a la Europa de los ciudadanos.»

(Carlo Ripa di Meana, Italia. Miembro de la Comisión de las Comunidades Europeas, responsable del Medio Ambiente.)

LIMPIEZA DE ARENAS   SERVICIOS SANITARIOS
RECOGIDA DE BASURA   DUCHAS Y AGUA POTABLE
AGUAS LIMPIAS PARA BAÑARSE   PRIMEROS AUXILIOS DE LA CRUZ ROJA.

(a) According to Carlo Ripa di Meana how do millions of European citizens spend their holidays? (2)

(b) What exactly is the aim of the Blue Flag campaign? (2)

(c) Some of the features expected of a beach which qualifies for the Blue Flag are listed in the article. Write down *four* of these features *in English*. (4)

6 Here is an article about the death of John Lennon.

1980
JOHN
LENNON
MUERE ASESINADO

"¡Mister Lennon!". Ni siquiera tuvo tiempo de contestar. Mark David Chapman disparó contra el "beatle" un revólver calibre 38. Todo el cargador. Eran las diez de la noche de un martes ocho de diciembre. Y acababan de matar a John Lennon. Mark Chapman no intentó escapar. Dejó caer el arma y, según algunos, murmuró "he matado a un 'beatle'". Al lado, abrazada al cuerpo de su marido, Yoko Ono se repetía desconsolada "no puede ser, no puede ser", mientras la gente y la policía llegaban a la calle 72, a la puerta de los apartamentos "Dakota", donde residía el cantante.

La noticia recorrió el mundo como un latigazo. Incluso la agencia soviética "Tass" informó a los países del Este del acontecimiento.

El cuerpo acribillado de John Lennon fue conducido al hospital Roosevelt, donde aún llegó con vida. Pero tudos los intentos del doctor Stephen Lynn fueron inútiles: las heridas en pecho y espalda eran mortales. Lennon falleció antes de la medianoche.

Chapman se convirtió en el centro de atención. El criminal, un desequilibrado, había rondado toda la semana el domicilio de la estrella de la canción. Dicho martes, cuando la pareja salía de paseo, el asesino abordó al cantante pidiéndole un autógrafo. No se lo dio. La negativa, quizá, le costó la vida.

Mientras en Nueva York alguien cubría con pétalos de rosa la sangre sobre el pavimento, Londres quedaba conmocionado. La esperanza secreta de volver a escuchar a los "Beatles" reunidos ya no podría cumplirse.

Chapman fue condenado. Pero, como podrían decirle millones de personas, nadie lo condenó por habernos arrancado parte de nuestro pasado.

(a) When was John Lennon shot? (2)
(b) How did his killer react? (2)
(c) What information does the article give to illustrate the world-wide interest in the tragedy?(1)
(d) What possible motive is suggested? (1)
(e) What secret hopes were dashed as a result of his death? (1)

Writing: Basic Level

1 On a self-catering holiday in Spain it is your friend's turn to do the shopping. He/she does not speak Spanish so you write out a list. Write *five* items of food or drink that you might need and give the quantity you want or the container it comes in, e.g. a kilo of potatoes or a bottle of red wine. Try to give a different quantity and item *each* time. (8)

Quantity/Container	Item
(i)	
(ii)	
(iii)	
(iv)	
(v)	

2 Your Spanish pen-friend has written to accept your invitation to spend the month of August with you. He/she has asked you about what you do, where you go, the weather etc. Write a letter in Spanish *of between 50–70 words* to give him/her information. Include *at least six* of the following points. (12)

(i) Tell him/her what you do with your friends, e.g. go swimming.
(ii) Say what you do as a family, e.g. visit grandparents.
(iii) Tell him/her *one* thing you like doing in your spare time, e.g. reading, walking.
(iv) Tell him/her what sports you play.
(v) Ask what he/she likes to do on holiday.
(vi) Ask what he/she likes to eat.
(vii) Say what the weather is like in August.
(viii) Begin and end the letter appropriately.

Writing: Higher Level

1 *Either,*

(a) Your friend Blodwen has received a postcard from her Spanish pen-friend, but as she has only just started learning Spanish she asks you to help her with a letter.

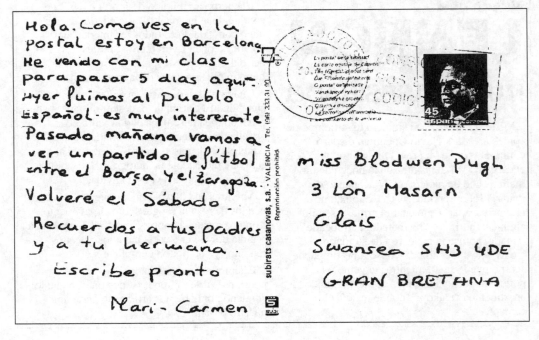

Write a letter, *in Spanish*, of *approximately 100–120 words* including *at least eight* of the following points. (80)

(i) Thank her for her card which you received a few days ago.
(ii) Explain that you have not replied sooner as you have had exams.
(iii) Say that you have not heard of the 'Pueblo Español' and ask what it is.
(iv) Tell her that in May you went on a school visit to Stratford.
(v) Say that you went by bus but returned the same day.
(vi) Ask who won the football match.
(vii) Tell her that your father has changed his job and that you will soon be moving to Bristol.
(viii) Say that you will give more details and your new address in your next letter.
(ix) Begin and end the letter appropriately.

Or,

(b) You are planning a touring holiday in Spain with your elder brother and a friend. You have been given the address of a Car Hire Company. Write a letter *in Spanish*, of *approximately 100–120 words*, requesting information. Include *at least eight* of the following points. (80)

(i) Say that you want to hire a car for two weeks.
(ii) Ask whether it is possible to have the car at Alicante airport.
(iii) Say that you expect to arrive on July 1st at 8.30 a.m.
(iv) Enquire about the cost of a small car per day and per week.
(v) Ask if V.A.T. and insurance are included in the price.
(vi) Find out what documents you need to bring.
(vii) Ask whether you must pay cash or if you can use a credit card.
(viii) Enquire about the cost of petrol in Spain.
(ix) Begin and end the letter appropriately.

2 *Either,*

(a) Imagine that the following incident happened to you in Spain. Write an account, *in Spanish* in *not less than 100 and not more than 120 words* as you would include it in a letter to a Spanish friend. You do not need to begin and end the letter, merely relate the incident. (80)

After a three week holiday you left Valencia for Santander at 7.30 a.m. – Near Zaragoza you saw a car which had hit a tree at the side of the road – the driver was injured so your father drove to a village to call the police – you and your mother stayed to help him. The police and ambulance arrived and you resumed your journey – but you had lost over two hours. Your father drove fast but in Pamplona you got lost. When you finally arrived in Santander the ferry had gone. You stayed the night in an hotel and finally arrived home a day late.

Or,

(b) You have recently returned from a holiday in the U.S.A. with your parents during which you spent the first week on the coast and the second week in a big city. Write a letter, *in Spanish*, to your pen-friend of *100–120 words* to tell him/her about your holiday. Include the following information. (80)

(i) Describe your journey to the U.S.A.
(ii) Describe the accommodation, e.g. hotel, in which you stayed.
(iii) Briefly say how you spent the first week.
(iv) Say what you did in the big city.
(v) Describe the highlight of your holiday.
(vi) Say where you and your family hope to go next year and why.

13.3 Suggested answers

Listening: Basic Level

1 (a) Fog/mist.
(b) Tomorrow morning.
(c) In 15 minutes.
(d) Lost first place.
(e) Last boat leaves.

2 (a) Doubles and singles.
  (b) 2500.
  (c) Double rooms have a bath and a shower.
  (d) How long will you stay?
  (e) Date and time of arrival.

3 (a) **(i)** Not much.
    (ii) Most of the afternoon/evening.
    (iii) Never.
    (iv) Every weekend.
  (b) **(i)** Weekends.
    (ii) 2 or 3 hours per week.
    (iii) Every Saturday.
    (iv) Swims every day in summer.

4 (a) Uncle.
  (b) Has to visit mother in hospital.
  (c) Day after tomorrow.

5 (a) Sunny and hot.
  (b) Windy and stormy.

6 (a) Opposite museum.
  (b) Take second right.
  (c) 20 minutes on foot.
  (d) When crossing the street.
  (e) A lot of traffic because of the match.
  (f) See the game on TV in the hotel.
  (g) Disco tonight.
  (h) 9.

Listening: Higher Level

1 (a) Unwashed fruit.
  (b) You must stay in bed.
  (c) Three times a day.
  (d) Next Monday.

2 (a) Scheme to publicize Benidorm night-life to young people.
  (b) Cheap accommodation/cheap travel/free entry to pubs and discos.
  (c) Little tourism/ financial problems for some bars/some bars have to close.

3 (a) Industrial part of San Sebastián
  (b) Nurse.
  (c) **(ii)** Pessimistic.
  (d) 16.
  (e) As a doctor/ to help the poor, sick people.
  (f) **(ii)** Caring.
  (g) Pop-music and dancing; school and homework.
  (h) Not enough freedom.
  (i) **(ii)** Fun-loving.

4 (a) Early hours of last Sunday.
  (b) Armed.
  (c) In a stolen car.
  (d) They got a good description; not wearing masks or gloves; they spoke with a Madrid accent.

5 (a) 20 British soldiers are lost in the African mountains after the death of their leader. They are in a dangerous situation till a sergeant leads them to a river.
  (b) Exciting climax and good music.

6 (a) More than 900.
  (b) Summer.
  (c) List of campsites, location of campsites, prices and facilities.
  (d) Close to nature and clean air.

Speaking: Basic Level

Set 1 Role-play 1
1 Perdone. ¿Cómo se va al Corte Inglés?

2 ¿Está a qué distancia?

3 ¿Hay un autobús?

4 ¿Cuándo sale el autobús?

5 Gracias. ¿Dónde para el autobús?

Set 1 Role-play 2
1 Mi clase empieza a las nueve de la mañana.

2 Tengo cinco clases cada día.

3 Tengo seis semanas de vacaciones en el verano.

4 Llevo bocadillos.

5 Sí pero tengo muchos deberes.

Set 2 Role-play 1
1 Un kilo de melocotones, por favor.

2 ¿Tiene plátanos?

3 ¿Cuánto cuestan?

4 ¿Tiene una bolsa?

5 ¿Cuánto cuesta en total?

Set 2 Role-play 2
1 Quiero pasar unos días en Barcelona.

2 ¿Cuánto cuesta un billete de ida y vuelta?

3 ¿Puede decirme las horas de los trenes por la mañana?

4 ¿Cuánto tiempo dura el viaje?

5 Dos billetes, por favor. Uno para mi y uno para mi amigo/a.

Speaking: Higher Level

Set 1 Role-play 1
1 Hablo español un poco y inglés, claro.

2 ¡No me digas! Creo que el español y el italiano son similares.

3 Encuentro el español fácil de escribir pero difícil de hablar.

4 Quiero trabajar en España más tarde.

5 ¿Desde hace cuánto tiempo estudias inglés?

6 ¿Cuál prefieres, el inglés o el italiano? ¿Por qué?

Set 1 Role-play 2
1 Hace mucho calor hoy. ¿Hace tanto calor normalmente?

2 ¿Cómo es el tiempo en el invierno?

3 Posiblemente en las ciudades grandes de Inglaterra pero no tenemos niebla a menudo en España.

4 A veces; en el norte hace más calor que en el sur.

5 Hace ocho años nevó muchísimo en mi pueblo.

6 Prefiero el verano porque hace buen tiempo.

Set 2 Role-play 1
1 ¿Por qué tu familia se hospeda en un hotel?

2 Cuando estamos de vacaciones, cocina mi padre.

3 Nos gusta ir a restaurantes a probar platos locales.

4 El año pasado pasamos dos semanas en Rosas.

5 No estoy seguro/a. Si hace demasiado calor iré a Francia.

6 Prefiero España porque la cocina es mejor.

Set 2 Role-play 2

1 Buenos días. Quiero denunciar un robo.

2 Se ha robado la bolsa de mi madre.

3 En la plaza mayor a las diez y media.

4 Es pequeña, negra y es de cuero.

5 Estamos en el Hotel Sol en la plaza mayor.

6 Estaremos aquí hasta la semana que viene.

Reading: Basic Level

1 (a) Expedición de billetes.
  (b) Ascensor.
  (c) Alimentación.
2 (a) Furniture.
  (b) Customs.
  (c) 1990.
  (d) (i) No.
      (ii) Sundays or holidays.

3 (a) Leo.
  (b) Palma.
  (c) Carnicería Verónica.

4 (a) To exchange opinions.
  (b) Boys or girls up to the age of 16.

5 (a) Friday to Sunday.
  (b) When under 12 and a maximum of two children in a room with two adults.
  (c) VAT is not included.

6 (a) Length of beach.
  (b) Gardens, sports areas.
  (c) You will be taken there free.
  (d) Your house or flat may be taken in part exchange.

7 (a) Soup.
  (b) Rabbit.
  (c) Cooked apple.
  (d) Wine.

8 (a) Ship.
  (b) Sleep, eat, drink.
  (c) Regular service.
  (d) See travel agent.

9 (a) Fresh food daily.
  (b) Delivery to your home.
  (c) Tuesday.
  (d) Shop before 3pm.

Reading: Higher Level

1 (a) Water sports.
  (b) He took part in the Olympics.
  (c) His father competed in the Olympics and his sister was at Seoul.

2 (a) (iii).
  (b) To be world champion.
  (c) To win the British Open.

3 (a) 2 double rooms in a 3-star hotel.
  (b) Breakfast.
  (c) 4 tickets to the World Fair.

    (d)   Taxi to the Fair.

    (e)   Lunch and evening meal.

4 (a)   Bullfighting.

    (b)   An adorable wife.

    (c)   Based on a novel by a Spaniard.

5 (a)   On the beaches of other countries.

    (b)   To ensure clean and safe beaches everywhere for everyone.

    (c)   Removal of litter, clean water, toilets and showers.

6 (a)   10pm Tuesday December 8th 1980.

    (b)   He did not try to escape, he dropped his gun and said 'I've killed a Beatle'.

    (c)   The Soviet Press informed Eastern countries.

    (d)   John Lennon refused him his autograph.

    (e)   The hope of seeing the Beatles re-united.

Writing: Basic Level

1 un litro   vino
   una botella   leche
   un kilo   patatas
   un medio kilo   zanahorias
   una docena   huevos

2

Londres

el tres de mayo

Querido Pablo:

Gracias por tu carta. ¿Qué hago? Pues voy a la piscina, voy al cine y escucho música con mis amigos. Con mi familia, doy paseos y visito a mis abuelos. A mí me gusta leer. Leo novelas. También juego al tenis. ¿Qué te gusta hacer durante tus vacaciones? ¿Qué te gusta comer? En agosto hace buen tiempo aquí.

Un abrazo

Peter

Writing: Higher Level

1 (a)

Swansea

el tres de mayo

Querida Mari-Carmen:

Gracias por tu carta que recibí hace unos días. No he podido contestar antes porque he tenido exámenes. El examen de español era fácil pero el examen de matemáticas era imposible.

    No sé qué es 'el pueblo español'. ¿Qué es? ¿Es un barrio de Barcelona? En mayo fuimos a Stratford con mi colegio. ¡Qué bien! Fuimos en autocar pero volvimos el mismo día.

    Y ¿el partido de fútbol? ¿Quién ganó?

    Otra cosa. Mi padre ha cambiado de trabajo y pronto nos mudamos a Bristol. Te daré más detalles y mi dirección nueva en mi próxima carta.

Escribe pronto

Un abrazo

Blodwen

1 (b)

Swansea

el tres de mayo

Muy señor mío:

Voy a pasar dos semanas de vacaciones en España y quiero alquilar un coche durante las dos semanas. ¿Es posible tener el coche en el aeropuerto de Alicante? Vamos a llegar el primero de julio a las ocho y media de la mañana. ¿Cuánto cuesta un pequeño coche al día y a la semana? ¿Puede decirme si el IVA y el seguro están incluidos en el precio? También ¿puede decirme qué documentos tengo que llevar conmigo? ¿Tengo que pagar al contado o puedo pagar con tarjeta de crédito?

¿Cuánto cuesta la gasolina en España?

Le saluda atentamente

Matthew Jackson

2 (a)

Después de pasar tres semanas en Valencia, me marché a Santander a las siete y media de la mañana. Cerca de Zaragoza, vi un coche que había chocado con un árbol al lado de la carretera. El conductor estaba herido así que mi padre fue en coche a una aldea a llamar la policía. Mi madre y yo nos quedamos para ayudarle. La policía y la ambulancia llegaron y nos marchamos otra vez pero habíamos perdido más de dos horas. Mi padre condujo muy de prisa pero en Pamplona nos perdimos. Al llegar por fin a Santander el barco había salido. Nos hospedamos en un hotel y por fin llegamos a casa con un día de retraso.

2 (b)

El viaje a América era fenomenal! El avión era tan cómodo! Vi una buena película durante el vuelo. Nos hospedamos en un hotel de lujo. Había una piscina y aire acondicionado. Durante la primera semana, ¡lo pasé bomba! Fui al cine, visité los monumentos históricos y comí muchos mariscos. También encontré a nuevos amigos y salí con ellos. Después de pasar una semana allí fuimos a Nueva York. Di un paseo por la ciudad, fui a un concierto y visité un restaurante famoso. El mejor momento de las vacaciones era cuando salí con un(a) americano(a) muy guapo(a). El año que viene esperamos volver a los Estados Unidos porque quiero ver mi novio(a).

Index

Index

accidents and emergencies 68, 112, 114, 151, 181, 207

accommodation
see also buildings; hotels; house and home
listening tests 78–9, 83, 90
reading tests 135, 156
vocabulary 67
writing tests 166, 186

adjectives
comparative and superlative 18–19
definition 13
demonstrative 23–4, 40, 48
possessive 24–5, 40, 48
revision 16–17
tests 38–9, 46–7

adverbs 13, 17–19, 39, 47

advertisements 133, 135–8, 140–1, 199–202

age, vocabulary 54

animals 56, 91

announcements 190, 191

answers
exam paper 207–12
grammar revision tests 46–52
listening tests 83–5, 97–9
reading tests 144–7, 159–61
role-plays 105–6, 115–17
writing tests 174–6, 186–9

attitudes, listening tests 193, 194

bank, vocabulary 69

body, vocabulary 68, 154

buildings, vocabulary 56–7

cafés *see* food; restaurants

camping 67, 72, 78, 193

cardinal numbers 19–20

cars 61, 141

cinema 60–1, 110, 204

cities *see* towns and cities

cleaning, reading tests 68–9, 137, 143

clothes 60, 65, 113, 137, 168

colours 54, 168

commands 29

comparatives 18–19

conditional tense 37, 45, 52

conjunctions, definition 13

conocer 27, 41, 49

continuous, present 31–2

conversations 107–8, 117–19

countries, vocabulary 62

countryside 57–8, 77, 82, 112, 136

daily routine 56–7, 59–60, 77, 108, 168–9, 172

deber 27, 42, 49

definite article 13, 14, 38, 46

demonstratives 23–4, 40, 48

descriptions 54–5, 58, 105, 106

diaries, writing tests 164–5

differentiation, examinations 3

directions 58–9, 76, 191, 195

emotions, vocabulary 55

entertainment
listening tests 77, 193, 194
reading tests 134–5, 140, 152
role-plays 114
vocabulary 60–1
writing tests 166–7

estar 26–7, 32, 41, 49

examination technique
listening tests 71, 87
reading tests 124, 149
speaking tests 100–1, 107, 110
writing tests 162, 180

examinations
assessment 3
complete paper 190–212
listening tests 70–5, 86–99
reading tests 123–47
speaking tests 100–8, 109–22
syllabus analysis 2, 3–9, 29, 53, 177–8
writing tests 162–89

examining groups
addresses 12
syllabuses 3–9
writing tests 177–8

exclamations 63

expressions, survival kit 179

families 54, 107, 113, 117–18, 165
see also house and home

food
listening tests 76, 78
reading tests 126, 143, 201

role-plays 101–2, 104, 112
vocabulary 64–5, 66
form-filling 125, 164, 169–70
functions, syllabus requirements 53
future plans 67, 92, 119, 155, 171, 193
future tense 36–7, 44–5, 52

gender 13, 15–16
grammar 13–45
greetings 63–4, 150, 166

haber 32–3, 35–6
health
    listening tests 91, 92, 192
    role-plays 102, 105, 112, 114
    vocabulary 68
hobbies and interests
    conversation 108, 118–19
    listening tests 77, 92, 190–1
    reading test 125
    vocabulary 60–1
holidays
    conversations 108, 119
    listening tests 75, 192–3
    reading tests 156, 157–8, 205
    role-plays 102, 113, 196
    vocabulary 62–3, 67
    writing tests 172–3, 183–4, 184, 207
hotels
    listening tests 190
    reading tests 134, 138, 200
    vocabulary 67
    writing tests 181–2, 184–5
house and home
    conversations 107–8, 118
    reading tests 158, 200
    role-plays 105, 112, 113
    vocabulary 56–7
    writing tests 165, 186

imperfect tense 35, 44, 51–2, 179
indefinite article 13, 14, 38, 46
interrogatives 26, 41, 49
invitations, writing tests 166
ir a + infinitive 36, 45, 52
irregular verbs
    conditionals 37
    future tense 36
    imperfects 35
    past participles 33
    present tense 31
    preterites 34

jobs and professions
    applications 183, 188
    listening tests 77, 89, 90, 91

role-plays 113
vocabulary 55–6, 67
writing tests 183

languages 14, 62
letters
    formal 166, 173, 180–2, 186, 207
    informal 125, 135–6, 142–3, 158, 165–6, 171–3,
        186, 206–7
    writing tests 164, 165–6
listening tests 70–85, 86–99, 190–5
lists, writing tests 162–3, 168, 206
lost property, vocabulary 69

marital status, vocabulary 54
meeting people 63–4, 89, 91, 113, 114, 195
mental processes, vocabulary 55
messages, writing tests 163
money, vocabulary 69
months, vocabulary 53–4

narrator examinations 120–2
nationalities 14, 16, 54
negatives 13, 21, 40, 47–8
notions 53
nouns 13, 15–16
numbers 19–20, 39, 47

object, definition 13
object pronouns 21–2
ordinal numbers 20

past participles 31–2
perfect tense 32–3, 43, 51
personal *a* 23, 40, 48
personal details
    listening tests 75–6, 92
    reading tests 138, 141–2, 199
    vocabulary 54
    writing tests 165, 169–70
personality traits 55, 93, 97
pluperfect tense 35–6, 44, 52
plurals, nouns 15–16
possessives 24–5, 40–1
post office, vocabulary 69, 153
postcards, writing tests 163–4
prepositional pronouns 23
prepositions 13, 23, 28, 42, 50
present continuous 31–2
present participle 31–2
present tense 29–31, 42–3, 50–1
preterite tense 33–4, 43–4, 51, 120, 179
preteritos graves 34
pronouns
    definition 13
    demonstrative 24, 40, 48

possessive 25, 40, 48
relative 25–6, 41, 49
revision 21–3

questions 26

radical-changing verbs 29–30, 34
reading tests 123–47, 148–61, 196–202, 203–6
relative pronouns 25–6, 41, 49
repairs 68–9, 87, 93
restaurants 66, 76, 78, 101, 103, 126, 201
revision, organization 10–11, 13
road signs 128–31, 197–8
robbery 69, 193, 194, 196
role-plays 100–1, 109–17, 195, 195–6

saber 27, 41, 49
school
    conversations 108, 119
    listening tests 76, 90
    reading tests 136, 151–2
    role-plays 103, 195
    vocabulary 59–60
    writing tests 165, 182
seasons, vocabulary 53–4
ser 26–7, 41, 49
shopping
    listening tests 72–3, 74
    lists 206
    reading tests 124, 126–7, 132–3, 139, 199, 202
    role-plays 103, 195
    signs 198
    vocabulary 64–6
    writing tests 172
signs 124, 128–31, 133, 196–8
simple past *see* preterite tense
size, vocabulary 54
skills, Higher Level 86–7, 148–9

speaking tests 100–8, 109–22, 195–6
sport 61, 92, 102, 133, 134, 203
subject, definition 13
subject pronouns 21
subjunctive 29
superlatives 18–19
surnames 16
survival kit, expressions 179

telephone calls 63–4, 91, 112, 115, 137, 191
tener 27, 42, 49–50
tener que 27, 42, 49
time expressions 20, 39, 47, 53
topic areas
    conversations 107–8, 117
    examinations 3–9, 53–69
    role-plays 100, 109
tourist information 103, 106
towns and cities 58, 73–4, 104, 108, 118, 165
transcripts 79–83, 93–7, 191–2, 194–5
transport
    listening tests 73–4, 76, 77–8
    narrator exam 120–1, 122
    reading tests 128–31, 133–4, 141, 157, 196–7, 201
    role-plays 102, 103, 104, 111, 195
    vocabulary 61–2
    writing tests 186, 207

verbs 13, 28–37
vocabulary
    listening tests 71
    reading tests 123
    revision 10
    topic areas 53–69

weather 66–7, 77, 111, 191, 196
writing tests 162–76, 177–89, 206–7

EDUCATIONAL

GCSE Spanish Cassette

If you have purchased a copy of our Study Guide for GCSE Spanish and would like to buy the accompanying cassette, please complete the order form below and return it to:

Letts Educational Ltd
Aldine House
Aldine Place
London W12 8AW
Telephone 0181 743 7514

Forenames (Mr/Ms) _____

Surname _____

Address _____

_____

_____

_____

Postcode _____

Please send me the following:

	Quantity	Price (incl VAT)	Total
GCSE Spanish C90 cassette	_____	£4.00	_____
Add postage – UK and ROI 75p for each cassette			_____

I enclose a cheque/postal order for £ _____
(made payable to Letts Educational Ltd)

Or charge to Access/Visa card No. ☐☐☐☐☐☐☐☐☐☐☐☐☐☐☐☐☐☐

Expiry date _____

Signature _____